The Gentleman of Renaissance France

The Gentleman of Renaissance France

By W. L. WILEY

GREENWOOD PRESS, PUBLISHERS
WESTPORT, CONNECTICUT

Originally published in 1954
by Harvard University Press, Cambridge

Reprinted with the permission
of Harvard University Press

First Greenwood Reprinting 1971

Library of Congress Catalogue Card Number 75-152622

SBN 8371-6169-X

Printed in the United States of America

To the memory of

ABEL LEFRANC

PREFACE

This study of the life of a gentleman in Renaissance France was first conceived soon after World War II. The idea of it was mentioned in 1946 to a few friends and scholars. Though they will accept no credit for it, their enthusiasm for the project in its embryo, and their helpful criticism along the way, have done much to bring that post-war germ to fruition. *The Gentleman of Renaissance France*, therefore, is a considerably better book than it would have been without their assistance.

I am indebted to Robert B. House, Chancellor of the University of North Carolina at Chapel Hill, and to William M. Dey, Kenan Professor and Chairman (emeritus) of the Department of Romance Languages at North Carolina, for making it possible for me to spend the greater part of the academic year of 1948–1949 in France. Two grants from the Carnegie Foundation, in 1949 and 1951, as well as a Traveling Fellowship from the Folger Shakespeare Library in 1951, also aided in the research that had to be done in Paris, Tours, and elsewhere on French soil. I am grateful to many of the staff of the Bibliothèque Nationale for facilitating my work there — in particular, to Mlle Madeleine Chabrier, the head of the photographic and microfilming service, and to M. Guignard, the curator of the reserve collection. Acknowledgement should be made to the French Government for allowing me to work freely in many of the royal châteaux that are now national shrines. A debt is owed to several of my colleagues in the Department of Romance Languages at North Carolina for their generous giving of their specialized knowledge on many points in the book. Also, my gratitude is due James S. Patty and Mrs. Betty Selman for typing and checking the manuscript.

All passages taken from writers of the Renaissance for use in the main body of the text have been translated. The translations are my own; the original French has not been included in the notes unless the passage is very short or the author difficult to find in any standard edition. Every effort has been made to give exact bibliographical references for those who might wish to consult original sources.

It is my privilege to dedicate this book to the spirit of that great gentleman and scholar of the Renaissance, Abel Lefranc. He graciously gave me permission to do so just one month before he died in November, 1952, in his ninetieth year.

Chapel Hill, North Carolina W. L. W.
May 22, 1953

CONTENTS

LIST OF ILLUSTRATIONS

Figures 3, 4, 6, 7, 8, 9, and 17, are reproduced from Dessins Francais du XVIeme Siecle, *with an Introduction by Louis Dimier, published by Alpina, Paris, 1941.*

The Gentleman of Renaissance France

Introduction

THE RENAISSANCE GENTLEMAN OF FRANCE, the *gentilhomme* of the sixteenth century, existed in a segment of time that can be pretty well marked. The golden age of his life on this earth was not much more than fifty years, and it fitted rather naturally into the political and social history of his nation. In a general way, he first began to show a personality of his own with the buddings of the Renaissance in France early in the first half of the sixteenth century, and he died both in body and spirit during the Wars of Religion of the second half. In order to get a complete picture of the forces that created him and destroyed him, it may be necessary to break these temporal limits and occasionally to look both backward and forward. However, the Renaissance gentleman really came into being in the few years leading up to the coronation of Francis I in 1515, and he expired in the civil strife that broke out in the 1560's during the reign of Charles IX.

The French *gentilhomme* was affected strongly by many phases of the Italian Renaissance that had preceded the French. He adopted a number of the refinements and courtesies of the Italian gentlemen who lived in such cultivated places as Florence or Venice. The Italian manuals of correct conduct, too, had a great influence on French manners of the sixteenth century, though the French gentleman was not quite like his model, the Italian *gentiluomo*: he may have lacked some of the elegances of his Italian counterpart, but he probably had a keener sense of honor.

The Renaissance gentleman was different, also, from the feudal baron of an earlier era, a man of more power but less refinement; and he was different from the painted and ornately coiffured dandies, the *mignons*, who bedecked the court of

Henry III. He was almost completely lost in the turbulence of reorganization that marked the regime of Henry IV, nor was his equivalent to be found at Versailles in the seventeenth century, where the courtiers of Louis XIV were primarily decorative and were not allowed the privilege of much individuality. The gentleman of the Renaissance, on the other hand, was a person in his own right, and was not entirely dominated by the monarch. He came in between the vigorous but uncultivated feudal nobility, and the later nobility of social foppery.

Many of the attributes of the Renaissance gentleman were possessed by all those who felt the spirit of the age. However, a man was not a gentleman at this time through his own volition or simply because he had certain qualities inside him. France in the sixteenth century was not a democracy as we understand the word, nor was it a very easy place in which to change one's compartment in society. The Renaissance was a period, nevertheless, of great zest and enlarging of interests in all directions, of a renewed confidence in the enjoyment of life on this earth, of added and varied concepts of manners and culture. All of these diversified and interlocking influences went into the makeup of the gentleman of Renaissance France.

The broad cultural and literary movements, the major sweep of economic and political history, the discovery of new lands, or the explosions of new wars — none of these will be the object of this story. They have already received authoritative treatment by a variety of students of the Renaissance, and their results will be borrowed freely for a plateau on which to erect an edifice for the gentleman. He was inevitably a part of all activities that went on around him. Therefore, it can be expected that a portion of him will be in history, for there certainly were some men of the century who deserve to be called gentlemen. Also, he will be in part a theoretical ideal, visible only in the literary and artistic efforts of his age.

The term *Renaissance* will be used in these pages in its more or less usual sense. That is to say, the Renaissance in France simply means here, the sixteenth century. There are many who feel today that *Renaissance*, with its suggestions of rejuvenation and resurrection, is too strong a word for the changes that took place in Western Europe after Petrarch, who has been called the first modern man. In any case, the sixteenth century in France was different from those centuries that had gone before. Among other things, the perfection of movable type for printing and the growing use of artillery, the study of languages and literatures as well as theology, a more accurate knowledge of classical antiquity and of Italy, the influx of precious metals from the New World, and a strengthening of the royal power: all these brought about an alteration in the conditions of man's living. The native Gallic spirit, the *esprit gaulois* of the French nation, revealed itself just as easily in the Renaissance as it did in earlier centuries. The word *Renaissance*, then, should require no special interpretation or modification. As the historian Louis Batiffol suggests in his *Century of the Renaissance*,* there is no reason to modify a vocable which expresses what everybody understands.

Renaissance will be accepted, possibly, without any more argument. *Gentilhomme* will require some defining, even though the prerequisites for gentility in the Renaissance were the same in some respects as those of today.

* On page 106 of the tenth French edition, *Le Siècle de la Renaissance* (Paris: Hachette, n. d.)

I

Defining the Gentleman

IN THE SONG OF ROLAND, THE GREAT FRENCH EPIC of the eleventh century, the author states in the three hundred seventy-seventh verse that the Franks are very much "gentil home," and the statement is made with pride. The appearance of the Latin *gentilem hominem*, a "man of race *or* family" and by extension a "man of good family," thus occurred very early in the French language. *Gentilz hom* is frequently found in Old French, and the Italian equivalent *gentiluomo*, the Spanish *gentilhombre*, the English *gentleman* were not long in coming into the speech of these nations. By the twentieth century, it was to be expected that certain transfers and extensions of meaning would be given to the term. In American parlance, the use of "gentle" in the sense of "well-born" is classified in our dictionaries as archaic; and "gentleman," with the connotation of "one entitled to bear arms," is chiefly historical. We have sought today to substitute for absolute measurements of gentility vaguer qualities like fine feelings, general culture, and social position. In England, too, *gentleman* has become less automatically restrictive in its meaning. Not only does it refer to a man of heraldic status, but it is used more broadly to indicate a person of some distinction without precise definition of rank. *Gentilhomme* has undergone the same alterations in French. In fact, the present-day French idiom, *vivre en gentilhomme*, "live like a gentleman," means usually to take life easy and do nothing at all. At almost an exact mid-point between the *Roland's* "gentil home" and their leisurely contemporary descendants, we have the *gentilhomme* of the Renaissance.

The gentleman of the sixteenth century was, first of all, a noble. His progenitor was the medieval knight, the chevalier of the Middle Ages who had many of the qualities if not the external social graces of the gentleman. Much of the lustiness of the age of chivalry passed into the Renaissance, including a love for tourneys and outdoor competitions. However, the nobility of the sixteenth century had more varied responsibilities to the nation than did the earlier knight, who was primarily a master in his own limited domain and interested in the art of war. Many of the prerogatives of the knight were taken away from him with the progress of the centralized power of the monarch. In the Middle Ages, according to established custom, a knight could bestow the rights and privileges of chivalry on any companion of arms. This process normally lifted the recipient of such rites to noble rank. Later, with the increasing power of the Crown, the king reserved for himself the ceremonial granting of chivalry. Royal edicts from the thirteenth century on supported this policy, and by the sixteenth century those who assumed nobility were punished and subjected to a monetary penalty. The great fortified castles of the preceding centuries, with their strong defenses and symbolic suggestions of the noble's independence in his own domain, were no longer constructed. A new strength of the state and change in military tactics made them obsolete except as visual proof of lofty ancestry. Any new château built in the sixteenth century might put on the marks of medieval warlike exterior — like towers, crenelations, or drawbridges — only with the king's permission. Such reminiscences of the past were greatly admired for social reasons, inasmuch as they were visible evidences of antiquity of family.[1]

Chivalry as an institution, then, did not fit into the Renaissance. It was a strange paradox that Francis I, the chivalric king himself, gave the final blow to chivalry as a political and governmental structure. His remodeling of the royal residences to make them more pleasantly livable was symptomatic of the new age. In 1528 he tore down the great tower of the palace of the Louvre, from which spot, says the architectural historian Viollet-le-Duc, emanated all the feudal estates of France. The destruction of this great tower caused comment at the time that it happened. The Bourgeois de Paris, that very observing chronicler of daily life in the sixteenth century, says that the demolition of the tower was begun early in 1528 by command of the King in order to make the Louvre more pleasant to live in. The Bourgeois thought it was a pity for the tower to be destroyed, since it was "very beautiful, lofty, and strong," eleven feet thick at the top and twenty-three at the base. Along with the reparations of the Louvre, the Château Madrid was begun in the Bois de Boulogne and the embellishment of the château of Fontainebleau undertaken, all for the King's pleasure, in the opinion of the Bourgeois de Paris. In any case, the ancient residences of the ancient nobility were no longer what they once were, seats of the noble's own power.[2]

The King, nevertheless, had great consideration for the noble as an individual and admired his prowess and accomplishments as a person. He respected family position and was thoroughly familiar with the traditions of the ancient nobility of his realm. With his remarkable memory, "this so genteel King" could chat with the gentlemen of his court on matters of genealogy even as he was at ease with the scholars in the fields of philosophy and literature. The original idea of a chevalier, a knight in armor and in the field, appealed strongly to Francis I. He cared not too much for the weakened extension of it into the level of social position, but felt rather that it was a title to be won. The same thing, which Francis I objected to in France, happened to the Italian *cavaliere*, originally a knight on horseback, but in the sixteenth century a synonym for gentleman.[3]

The story of Francis I and the Chevalier Bayard at the battle of Marignano in 1515 has been often told. Among sixteenth-century chroniclers it was repeated many times: the story of the King's receiving the Order of Chivalry from a man who, though of modest rank, was the greatest fighting captain of his day. Bayard, who had had a horse shot out from under him in the fighting around Milan, had been most valiant and the King knew it well. Therefore, "the King wished to do him [Bayard] great honor, for he received the Order of Chivalry from his hand; he was indeed right, for he could not have received it from a better man." The episode is told by the Loyal Serviteur, one of the two early chroniclers of the life of Bayard, admiringly but with surprising brevity. The *Mémoires* of Martin and Guillaume du Bellay give a very few words to the ceremony in their general description of the battle, which contains the names of the principal participants, including the Chevalier Bayard, "to whom the King did the honor of wishing to receive from his hands the Order of Chivalry, the very day that the battle took place." Brantôme, the most versatile and gossipy commentator of the century, also mentions the fact that the King was made a knight by Bayard after the "battle with the Swiss," and he thinks it was a fine thing, infinitely better than the present-day practice of young noblemen receiving the Order of Chivalry before rather than after battles. As a result of such a practice, there are more knights in France than there used to be squires, "so great is the abuse of chivalry." Francis I, says Brantôme, did not wish simply to be a knight of the Order but in reality to be a fighting knight as a result of his accomplishments on the field. He did not want the honor until he had won it in battle, although he was a king. Vieilleville in his *Mémoires* boasts that he was made a knight by the King in 1536, a "knight of the sword." However, he suggests that now (i.e., later in the century) there are more knights than good swordsmen. Pierre de L'Estoile states in his *Mémoires-Journaux* that by 1579 the old Order of Chivalry had become commonplace and full of "lowly persons and pseudo-gentlemen." In any case, despite the gossipings of the writers of memoirs during the century, a knight was a gentleman, and especially so in the time of Francis I, who liked to be known as the "chivalric king" and swore on his "word of a gentleman." [4]

A nobleman whose family had fought for the defense of France in the Middle Ages — the medieval term would more likely have been sweet France — was therefore automatically a gentleman, a gentleman by birthright, in the sixteenth century. His was the ancient nobility, the nobility of the sword, and he was officially a gentleman. His position was simply one of priority and continuity and had nothing to do with his own personal qualities. He occupied a place that put him in the top military, governmental, and social brackets, and he held it until death, unless he disgraced himself in some way before the King.

The sixteenth century, in its blossoming, brought many changes in the life of the French nobleman. The old provinces of the North of France — such as the Ile-de-France, Champagne, Touraine, Orléanais, and Picardy — became closely attached to the Crown, and the high nobility that had ruled them previously lost its directive powers over them. The nobles retained more of their privileges in the area to the South, in Provence, though the King's interdiction removed from them their feudal rights to levy taxes, to raise private armies, and to wage private wars. However, the development and expansion of the nation made more and more royal appointments available, and the nobleman became the servant of his King in many capacities. He was the administrator of royal justice and he held the high offices of the Crown, like those of *chancelier*, *connétable*, *grand maître*, *grand chambellan*, *amiral*, and *maréchal*. The *chancelier* was the supreme arbiter in the administration of royal justice. He could be almost a prime minister, as was the famous *chancelier* Michel de l'Hospital. The *connétable*, whose office was abandoned after 1627, was the king's top military administrator, though seldom a commander in the field. The *maréchaux* were under the *connétable*, and there were three marshals in the time of Francis I. The *amiral* was the administrator of maritime affairs, which were almost non-existent; but he might have land duties, as did Bonnivet and Coligny, with armies. The *grand maître* was in complete charge of the King's Household. He had the keys to the King's reception rooms and introduced ambassadors and other dignitaries. The *grand chambellan* was in command of the King's bedchamber, and of the many gentlemen attached thereto. In addition to these highest offices, there was a multitude of others of military, administrative, or judicial nature that had great appeal to the ancient nobility. The office of grand master to the royal stables, for example, was very lofty. Beneath the grand master were twenty-five masters, all gentlemen.[5]

The members of the ancient nobility were on the whole, then, more than willing in the sixteenth century to have a share in the affairs of the Crown. However, the passage from a medieval society to a more nationalized state brought some shifts in class structure along with an increase in population. The nobility ceased to be the exclusive military caste because of the hiring of mercenaries and a broader basis of enlistments, though the noblemen did provide the leadership for the King's armies and make up the officer corps. A commoner could under certain conditions in the Renaissance be ennobled, and thus he became an *anobli*. By the purchasing of a piece of property attached to a noble fief and rendering homage to the King, or by fulfilling certain political offices recognized as being important to the Crown, a man of the middle classes could become a noble. But it was necessary that his condition and services be recognized by royal letters of designation, since the King alone could bestow nobility. In the time of Francis I, these ennoblings were limited to a few hundreds, while in the reign of Louis XIV they reached several thousands.

It is important to remember that an *anobli* was not a gentleman, in the official and legalistic sense of the word. The acquisition of noble status was only the commencement of gentility. In a treatise of 1586, wherein methods of obtaining nobility are considered, a distinction is made between ennobling and gentility, as can be seen from the following excerpt: "In regard to nobility, which is the beginning of gentility, it is acquired: first, by those who fulfill great offices for the Prince, and by this means acquire nobility for themselves and their posterity; and, by the process of a good marriage and by living in a noble manner, the heirs of these may be called gentlemen; thirdly, when a servant of the Prince has lived honorably and is made a knight, he is ennobled and his posterity; indeed, there is not so much to be done in creating a knight as in making a gentleman." [6] The author of the treatise goes on to give further details concerning the acquisition of nobility, but none of the methods described will make a man a gentleman.

The *anobli*, in order to retain his newly-acquired rank, had to live after the fashion of a noble. This meant that he must act like a noble, with a noble's privileges and prerogatives, be exempt from the *taille* (a tax that became permanent during the Hundred Years War), possess lands, be admittted to the assemblies of the nobility, wear a sword, serve in the army, and indulge in no unworthy practice like manual or commercial labor. If he and his descendants did this for three generations according to witnesses, his position was secure and he was safe from royal investigations into assumed nobility. He should, certainly, be very careful to appear personally when there was a royal call for military service, and it was most advisable to marry his eldest son to the daughter of a family whose ancestry was less debatable than his own. Yet the bourgeois with sufficient wealth to acquire a fief and its château, a collection of hunting dogs, a pigeon house and some pigeons to occupy it, was well on the way to founding a noble dynasty.

Another circumstance that assisted the *anobli* on his way up the ladder of society was the breaking down of the hierarchy of seigniories of the Middle Ages. The first class of seigniories included the *comtés*, *duchés*, *marquisats*, *principautés*, and the particularly lofty *pairies*. The second order embraced originally the *baronnies*, *vicomtés*, *vidamies*, and *châtellenies*. There was a confusion of these rankings in the sixteenth century, when they ceased to involve the exercise of sovereign power over feudal terrain, and became no more than honorific titles. The kings were most generous in passing out new labels of rank to their favorites, and the vanities of courtiers were satisfied without sacrifice of any royal authority. The title of prince, for example, was quite empty and was frequently taken over by the socially ambitious. With the lines of demarcation in the upper classes becoming blurred, a commoner could purchase property and improve his status in life simply by living in the manner of the nobility.

Only the descendants of the *anobli* were recognized as gentlemen, and this recognition was scarcely accorded before the third generation. It was never fully granted by the old nobles to the newcomers whose nobility, though legal, was considered inferior. There were, however, several more or less official shadings in the word *gentilhomme*. A *gentilhomme de nom* or a *gentilhomme de race* was a man of ancient and noble ancestry. He was also called a *gentilhomme d'armes*, since he and his family would have borne arms in defense of his country. A point that gave the ancient nobility great pride was the fact that even the King himself could not create a *gentilhomme de nom* or a *gentilhomme d'armes*. A *gentilhomme de quatre lignes* was a man who belonged to distinguished and ancient houses on both sides of his family. For the establishment of nobility by decree, only the paternal family tree was examined. A *simple gentilhomme* — the adjective was not always present — might come down from the new nobility and he might serve as an official at the court of his king; but in royal ceremonies and functions he would be preceded by the scions of the ancient families. Etienne Pasquier, the great jurist and critic of the century, said that "gentlemen who rest the claim of their nobility on arms" can legitimately look down on any urban or judicial nobility, and they should be given added honors for the hardships they have endured. Sémainville in his *Code de la noblesse* indicates distinctions in the use of *gentilhomme*: "In the reign of Louis XII, it was sufficient for a man born in the Third Estate, in order to be called a *gentilhomme*, to make a profession of arms or to have acquired a noble fief. A man descended from a noble race and the first noble of a line were both called *gentilshommes*, with this difference: the noble by birth was called *gentilhomme de nom et d'armes*, and the first noble was called simply *gentilhomme*." This statement would make an *anobli* immediately a simple gentleman, in the time of Louis XII, but it is unlikely that such a man had much standing in established circles.[7]

The attitude of the nobility toward its own position and toward the general concept of gentility was reflected in its reports to the King at the meetings of the Estates-General, which met four times in the sixteenth century, in 1560, 1576,

1588, and 1593. The reports of the three orders (the Nobility, the Clergy, and the Third Estate) were presented to the King at the end of the sessions, and suggestions included therein were judged by the King's Council. From the report of the nobles in 1576 comes the request that in order to tell "the true gentlemen" from the false, all coats-of-arms should be registered and only those be accredited "who have been noble for four generations." In the report of the nobles in 1560 is found the demand that those who are not noble be forbidden to construct warrens, pigeon houses, dovecotes, mills, or wine-presses in any place in the land. During the same year the nobles request the King to allow no one in his ordonnance companies who is not a gentleman, and this demand meets with royal approval. It is from the report of the nobles in 1576 that the suggestion comes for commoners not to be allowed to have clothes similar to those of gentlemen, and this would prohibit the wearing of velvet hoods by the wives of wealthy bourgeois.

At the sessions of 1576 all three orders seem to have agreed that it is not good for the commoner to rise above his normal social status, and that ennobling is bad for the country. The report of the Clergy asks that the King, Henry III, henceforth grant no ennoblings for money and that he declare such ennoblings created since the death of Henry II null and void. The Third Estate is of the same opinion, and states that, since nobility ought to come from virtue and dignity, as traditionally it has done, it is a shame that commoners have bought their way in. The King was evidently influenced by these combined opinions of the three orders, for he issued an edict in 1579 in which he stated that members of the lower classes, even though they bought noble fiefs, would not be thus ennobled and put in the rank and position of nobles.[8] However, as has been seen, ennobling was a frequent occurrence in the sixteenth century, despite such edicts as the above. Like so many other royal edicts, particularly those concerning duelling, this one was not carried out to the letter; but even the King recognized that the creation of a gentleman depended upon something more than a regal decree.

The privileges of the ancient nobility, which produced the accepted gentlemen, were clearly stated in the reports of the three ranks of society in the sixteenth century: the rights to administer justice, to hunting, to be reared as pages near the King, to fulfill the offices of the royal household, to military service, to govern the provinces, to fill the places of ambassadors, to sit in the King's councils, to have certain ecclesiastical benefits, to be exempt from taxes and imposts. This was a sizable list of favors and responsibilities, which made the noble important in his relations both to the King and the people. And, in the opinion of Chérin, the King's gentlemen had to remember that they, full of sentiments of elevation and generosity, had been put above the people by divine and royal edict only to make the people happy! [9]

There were a number of illegitimate sons of nobles in the sixteenth century, and they were regarded with tolerance. A bastard son who had been recognized and legitimized enjoyed the rights and privileges of his family to a degree just slightly lower than those of his father. He was expected to distinguish himself in service to his King in order to inherit. The bastard, therefore, was frequently a good soldier, like that fine fighter, the Bâtard de Savoie. In the report of the nobles of 1560, it is requested of the King that bastards and sons of bastards be required to have on their coat of arms a bar descending diagonally from left to right (the bar sinister) to indicate their origin.[10] Otherwise, there might be quarrels and debates. A bastard thus experienced some difficulties and restrictions; he did not necessarily lose his caste, but it was hard for him to be a gentleman.

Such is the rather complex official and technical definition of the gentleman of Renaissance France.

II

The Legacy from the Past

NOTHING COULD HAVE BEEN MUCH MORE SOLID than the inherited position of a gentleman in the best years of the sixteenth century. He had responsibilities that were well defined and he had rights and privileges that were not seriously questioned. The legality of his gentility could be confirmed by consultation of the records, and the sartorial splendor of his exterior marked him as a gentleman for everyone to see. However, none of these trappings gave any indications whether underneath he was a man of honor or a deceptive fop. The inner qualities of character that stimulated his thoughts and actions, the principles and beliefs that motivated his conduct, were not readily visible to the naked eye. Many of the sublimated concepts that went into the formation of the gentleman's personal code had their roots deep in the past.

The philosophical and literary ideas of Greece and Rome received a renewed welcome in France during the Renaissance. Italy had taken the initiative earlier in rediscovering the ancients and passed this enthusiasm on to France. No longer was there fear of mixing pagan and Christian ideals, and classical figures ceased to be coated with allegory to make them palatable for popular consumption. This new process has been called "taking the direct road to antiquity," and the ancients were welcomed into Gaul with open arms, including that most "dangerously alluring pagan," [1] Ovid. The Renaissance was certainly more pagan than Christian, with its emphasis on the full development of life on this earth rather than on a stoic acceptance of bodily ills in anticipation of a serenity of spirit after death. Many of the virtues and graces of character to be sought in a gentleman stemmed from classical antiquity, especially from Plato and Aristotle. Plato, in the interpretation given him by the Church fathers and the Italians, comes nearer to being an amalgam of Christian and Greek ideals.

Plato's *Dialogues* were frequently translated in France during the sixteenth century. A number of them, like the *Ion*, *Timaeus*, and *Symposium*, formed the basis for Platonistic mysticism, literary criticism, and literary obscurity of the period. The Platonic academies of the preceding century in Florence had already set the fashion for the study of Plato in genteel circles. But it is from Plato's *Republic*, which contains some statements on literature (chiefly derogatory), that come his most significant opinions on man and his connection with the state. Justice, which is a combination of virtue and wisdom, should be a guiding principle. However, the citizens in the state are not all equal: those who command are made of gold, the auxiliaries of silver, and the husbandmen and craftsmen of brass and iron. There may be some mixture of the metals as the years pass, but the gold will rise and the brass fall. There should be no effort to change classes — traders becoming warriors and warriors becoming legislators — for this will result in the ruin of the state. Warriors should have some education, nevertheless, in order to civilize and humanize them. Education brings a harmonizing of passion and reason, and assists in the creation of courage, wisdom, temperance, and justice. Riches decrease virtue, because men become lovers of trade and money instead of glory.[2]

For Plato, a soldier who is guilty of cowardice is reduced to the rank of husbandman or artisan, but the hero in battle will receive honors from his countrymen and the favors of his beloved. He will also be given better foods, and will have precedence in ceremonials. Civic courage, in fact, comes chiefly from the soldier and he is a very important man to the state, though the best governor of the state is the philosopher, who might well be called a scholar-gentleman, since he "has taste for every sort of knowledge." It is he who is gentle, sociable, harmonious, a lover of learning, possessed of a good memory, and gifted with a sense of proportion. The people will never have taste or judgment, and therefore the philosopher is debased by them. Democracy results when a large impoverished group of the people conquer their opponents, and magistrates are elected by lot. All principles of order and good taste are thereby violated.

Temperance and moderation are of prime importance to the state. Intemperance is everywhere, but "the simple and moderate desires which follow reason, and are under the guidance of mind and true opinion, are to be found only in a few, and those the best born and best educated." The temperate man is under the dominion of reason and goes to sleep "after having first indulged his appetites neither too much nor too little." The man who is tyrannized by appetites is a slave to lust and desire, while the pleasures of the philosopher are balanced and ordered, bringing harmony to the soul. The governors of the perfect state are, ideally, a combination of the "best philosophers" and the "bravest warriors." [3] The gentleman of the Renaissance borrowed from them both, though he was more concerned with war than with philosophy.

Aristotle, many of whose writings came into sixteenth century France by way of Italy, stressed even more strongly than did Plato the desirability of moderation and temperance in man's actions.[4] The primary Aristotelian doctrines dealing with the idea of gentility are in his *Nicomachean Ethics*, a work well-known during the Renaissance. At variance in many respects from the Christian ethical ideal, the *Ethics* of Aristotle has been called, nevertheless, "a touchstone for that modern idea of a gentleman." It was very influential in England as well as in France. For Aristotle in the *Ethics*, virtue is superior to honor, though men of refinement like to be honored on the ground of virtue. Virtue also enters into the composition of happiness. As for the question of happiness, "there are certain external advantages, the lack of which sullies supreme felicity, such as good birth, satisfactory children, and personal beauty." Human virtue consists in the excellence of the soul, and the soul consists of two parts, one irrational and one capable of reason.[5]

In the discussion of intellectual and moral virtues, Aristotle takes up the question of moderation and the golden mean.

Wisdom, understanding, and prudence are intellectual virtues, while liberality and temperance are moral. Moral or ethical virtue is the product of habit, and nature gives us the capacity to receive virtues. Training in childhood is important since "we become just by doing just acts, temperate by doing temperate acts, brave by doing brave acts." In all actions the perfect mean is to be sought. Strength is destroyed by too much or too little exercise, health by too much or too little food. Courage is the mean of cowardice and rashness, and temperance is in between profligacy and insensibility. Truthfulness is the mean of boastfulness and self-depreciation, while friendliness is a midpoint between flattery and peevishness. However, there are certain definite vices — like malice, shamelessness, envy, adultery, theft, and murder — for which there is no mean. As for modesty, "though modesty is not a virtue, it is praised and so is the modest man." In further application of the mean, Aristotle says "handsomeness involves size: small people may be neat and well-made, but not handsome."

Courage is shown in dangers where a man can defend himself with valor or die nobly, and a courageous man endures "for the sake of what is noble." Cowards are degraded by situations that bring out the best in brave men, and therefore "brave men are held in honor." Citizen soldiers fight to the death more often than mercenaries because the citizen feels that it is a disgrace to run away, an opinion later held by Machiavelli.[6]

The *Ethics* devotes several pages to an ancestor of the Renaissance gentleman, the Great-Souled Man. The Great-Souled Man is generous without hope of return, is haughty toward men of position and fortune, but courteous toward men of moderate station, because it is ill-bred to show strength against the weak. He will be concerned with undertakings of distinction, and he cares more for the truth than for what people think. He is no gossip, nor does he bear a grudge. He never speaks evil even of his enemies, except when he intends to give offense! He likes to own beautiful and sometimes useless things to show his independence. He will have a slow gait and a deep voice. He is one who claims much and is worthy of it.

He will be desirous of honor, "for honor is clearly the greatest of external goods," and "honor is the prize of virtue." The Great-Souled Man is a good man and has "moral nobility." Aristotle admits that men of wealth and power have also been honored, "but in reality only the good man ought to be honored, although he that has both virtue and fortune is esteemed still more worthy of honor, whereas those who possess the goods of fortune without virtue are not justified in claiming high worth, and cannot correctly be styled great-souled, since true worth and greatness of soul cannot exist without complete virtue." It is to be noted that for Aristotle, honor is a completely external reward, and has nothing to do with the internal qualities of a man. *Honneur* in the Renaissance will have additional connotations.

Aristotle spends some time on justice, which he considers "the perfect virtue," in that it is concerned with the good of others. Friendship is esteemed because it "involves virtue." It is a bond of society and morally noble. Certain types of pleasure are legitimate, but the life of the intellect is the happiest, and "in order to be good a man must have been properly educated and trained." [7]

With due allowance for some semantic inexactitude in the transfer of Plato and Aristotle into Renaissance French, these two great philosophers were very much in the background of the concept of gentility in the sixteenth century. They were supported by the *Characters* of Theophrastus, who had sat at the feet of both Plato and Aristotle, and headed the Peripatetic School after Aristotle's death. Theophrastus lectured in the Garden at Athens to several hundred pupils, and out of his contacts evolved a book on manners, his *Characters*, which remained popular well into the eighteenth century. Twenty-eight of Theophrastus' thirty characters were known in the sixteenth century,[8] and they assisted in the formation of society's code of politeness. Theophrastus, in general, gives examples of traits that are to be avoided — such as boorishness, dissembling, flattery, gossiping, and surliness. He is opposed to the man who makes bad jokes, is too loud, or who spits out something across the dinner table at the butler. He has contempt for the man who is ill-kempt, spits and hiccoughs, blows his nose at the table, or who goes to bed with his shoes on. He disapproves of the man of petty pride who loves display: such a man's lackey is a blackamoor, he is overly-dressed in the market place, he keeps a pet monkey and imports foreign objects, he has his own wrestling-place and ball-court. As for the man who is willfully disreputable, "he will keep inns and brothels, he will farm the taxes; crier, cook, dicing-house man, there is no trade so low but he'll follow it." Such methods of gaining a livelihood were under condemnation in the Renaissance, and a man could not live in a noble fashion and practice them. The substance of Theophrastus' *Characters*, then, also helped to form the manners of the gentleman and at times made deeper impressions on his personality.[9]

The legacy of classical ideas on gentility, the contributions of Plato, Aristotle, Theophrastus, Plutarch, Cicero, and others, found a most complete reincarnation in the Italian writers of the sixteenth century. The Italians at this time were much interested in what constituted gentility, and the two most famous treatises on the subject were Baldassare Castiglione's *Il Cortegiano* and Giovanni della Casa's *Galateo*. The *Cortegiano* or *Courtier* is abundantly filled with Platonism, and the *Galateo* has been described as "a mosaic of Greek and Latin borrowings." Both books, popular in their own country, were not long in being translated into French, and they were thus available in two languages to the man of culture.[10]

The purpose of the *Courtier*, as is stated in the letter of dedication to Messer Alfonso Ariosto, is to enable a gentleman to gain favor and consideration at court. The setting of the book is in the North Italian town of Urbino, which had become under Duke Federico de Montefeltro (1422–1482) and his son, Guidobaldo, a center of culture. There was an excellent library and a number of "most noble and valorous gentlemen" around Guidobaldo, and the day was full of fine exercises of both the body and the mind. In the evening a distinguished group sat in a circle around the Duchess Elisabetta — the Duke retired early because of his gout — and discussed various philosophical and literary topics. On the occasion described by Castiglione, they decided to analyse the qualities of the Good Courtier, "in order to reject many silly fellows, who through presumption and ineptitude hope to acquire the name." In the very beginning, there is offered the opinion that the courtier should be born noble, and be of "genteel family," since it is less bad for a man not born a gentleman to fail in courtly acts than a man of good family. The proponent of this idea, the Count of Canossa,[11] goes on to say that in any situation involving valor in arms or other manly operations, the most illustrious men are noble, since men wellborn have a natural grace of mind and body. An objection is brought forward to the effect that loftiness of birth is not necessary to the courtier, since many noblemen have been full of vices. Canossa contends, however, that being wellborn gives a courtier a flying start, because the world is prone to think well of him immediately.

A courtier should know the use of weapons, be distinguished in feats of arms, and have on him no stain of cowardice. He should avoid boasting and praising his own deeds, though he may mention them with proper modesty. He should be a good horseman, adept at hunting, swimming, tennis, and vaulting; and be brave in individual combat. On the other hand, tumbling and climbing a rope are not suitable for a gentleman. He should have comeliness and grace, but not be pretty. He should not be too large or too small, but it is better that he be of moderate size, for men too large are clumsy. Both slovenliness and over-preciseness are to be avoided. Simplicity is to be sought, in all activities. Everything that the courtier does should appear easy and done without thought or effort.[12]

The courtier should speak and write well, but should avoid the affectation of foreign tongues, like Spanish or French. He should have a well-modulated voice, and may use the few foreign words that are accepted by custom. His grace comes from moderation in all things, just as feminine beauty comes from the moderate use of cosmetics. The courtier might well know something of Latin and Greek, and he should be able to write both prose and poetry; but he should not reveal his literary efforts unless they are good.

Frenchmen are more interested in arms than in letters. However, there are great expectations for improvement in the French attitude if there is a change of dynasty in France. Letters and glory go hand in hand, and anyone who fights a war for money and not for glory is not a gentleman, but a most vile merchant. It is admitted, incidentally, that the Italians have been lacking in fighting ability. Men of war should be learned, since arms and letters go together. Music does not soften men of war, and painting is also worthy of a gentleman's attention, since it makes him a better judge of feminine beauty.

There is a discussion as to whether old men should be courtiers. It is concluded that old men at the court are more wordy, young men more blustery. But gentleness and quiet are laudable in a young man, even if, as a courtier, he is gifted in conversation. He should be modest before possible promotions, and not seem to seek them. Progress at court should be made by merit and not by favor. Merit and modesty are not always rewarded, unfortunately, and this makes for arrogance, though some modest and courteous gentlemen are to be discovered in France and also in Spain.

The courtier should be sober in his dress except at parties. His raiment should reflect his personality even before he speaks. Clothes may not make the man, but general appearances have their effect, even as does the choice of friends. Friends should be carefully chosen and then given full loyalty. Reputation is important since it is built up by the outside world. It is not wise to seek to be ingratiating by using gross and filthy words, nor should the courtier be a glutton, a drunkard, or be dirty of person. He can be amusing, with clever jests and conceits, without being a buffoon. Vile gestures and low words to create laughter are beneath the estate of a gentleman. References to physical infirmities are not funny — which is a deviation from the medieval inclination to make the infirm the butt of ridicule. There is a long discussion over the position of women, with the conclusion that it is the courtier's duty to defend them and never put in doubt their honor.

The next evening the discussion deals with the question of the lady at court. It is agreed that she should have qualities of gentleness, sweetness, and circumspection not demanded of the courtier. Both should have virtues of the mind, but the lady is not expected to play tennis, wrestle, ride horseback, or practice arms. She should dance modestly and avoid such mouth-distorting musical instruments as the flute or trumpet. Some of the group affirm that woman is fundamentally less perfect than man,* but it is readily agreed that no court is complete without women, though they may be weaker than men. There are many opinions concerning the basis of continence and chastity, and procedures in courtship. Some believe that men learn the art of love naturally, but that it must be taught to women, and that Ovid is a valuable source for this instruction. A woman should not accept a man's protestations of love too quickly; the ideal situation exists when the courtly lady is the beloved of the ideal courtier.

After another day, the final discourses on the qualities of the courtier are begun, and they are tinged with a great deal of Plato's doctrines. To the elements of temperance, courage, health, skill at music and sports, should be added in the courtier the solid quality of judgment, since his prince will need from time to time his advice. Princes should be good with God's goodness because they are the stewards over the people; it is better for the people not to be too wealthy or too poor. It is doubtful that a man can learn virtue, but moderation is important, and a courtier should be careful of the advice that he gives his prince. The courtier should seek, if possible, to increase the virtue of the prince he serves, as Aristotle did for Alexander. There are three kings-to-be who have particularly notable virtues — Francis I, Charles V, and Henry VIII.

One of the distinguished members of the company, Pietro Bembo, speaks on love, which he says is a coveting of beauty by the senses, by reason, and by understanding. Older courtiers

* The matter of the *Querelle des Femmes* is treated more fully in Chapter Eleven.

have more of the last two. Beauty is good and consequently the true love of it is most good and holy. There is an argument against this theory on the basis that beauty sometimes leads to pride, spitefulness, and cruelty. Bembo then launches into a long defense of beauty as the equivalent of goodness, using the solar system, temples, gentle animals, and finally man as examples. Sensual love is not to be condemned, especially in younger courtiers, but the ideal is reached when man is freed from the vexations and suspicions of bodily beauty and carries the concept of his lady in his heart.* The *Courtier* ends with the proposition that men are capable of greater purification than women. The point is not completely resolved, since day is dawning and the session is adjourned.

The *Galateo* is concerned more with manners than with ethical and moral problems, and is based on the assumption that a gentleman wants to be pleasant and agreeable wherever he is. It is a compendium of courtesies that would still be taken for granted by a cultivated man anywhere. Courtesy in its best form, or *courtoisie*, first flowered in Medieval France and particularly in Provence. Many of the formalities of courteous behavior advocated in the *Galateo*, however, would have been considered effeminate in the Middle Ages. The work is, therefore, a modern code of good manners, which has received no major alterations from the sixteenth century to our own day.

The device of exposition used by the author is that of an old man's giving advice to a youth. The adviser says he will not talk of higher precepts, but of what many will consider trifles — methods by which a man may show himself "pleasant, courteous, and gentle . . . which comes very near to virtue." The nobler virtues are not often in demand, he says, but manners come into play every day. Courtesy is, in essence, a desire to please others, though not as a juggler or cheap entertainer. Yet by avoiding the unpleasant in word or deed, the mechanism of society is given a coating of oil and rolls more smoothly, and the gentleman makes progress, even in business affairs! Therefore, don't mention in conversation

* This question of beauty if taken up further in Chapter Eleven.

things that are unpalatable or malodorous, don't obey the needs of nature in front of other men, nor wash your hands afterward in front of genteel company. Don't proffer unsavory objects for your companions to smell. Don't grind your teeth, or whistle, or file upon iron, and avoid singing if you have an untuneful voice. Don't cough, sneeze, or yawn offensively, and remember well that yawning indicates boredom with the company. Don't open your handkerchief after you have blown your nose,* and refrain from sniffing your friend's meat or giving him a cup out of which you have already drunk. It is bad to gulp your food, to cover your napkin with grease, or to wipe your face with the napkin. The servants that minister to the table should be neat and clean, too. Talking so near your companion that you breathe in his face is not recommended.

Don't slouch in your chair or go to sleep, and make a lot of noise in a social group. Have your clothes well-fitted and neat. Be careful of your speech, avoid filthy words and double meanings as unbecoming to a gentleman, but be agreeable in conversation. This is accomplished not by talking boastfully about yourself, your wife and children. Don't scorn or scoff at those who stutter, limp, or are misshapen. Be sure that your jesting is in proper spirit. Distortions and contortions are for jugglers, and not for gentlemen. Let your tones be well-modulated, and don't imitate the language of launderers and hucksters. Listen politely to the conversation of others, and don't try to fill in the details of another man's story. Walk with the gait of a gentleman, and not like a lackey. Again, manners at the table are brought up — spitting, belching, and such things are not the mark of a gentleman. In fact, there are many places where a gentleman does not expectorate at all! Avoid intoxication, and seek moderation and appropriateness in all things. A motto to remember is, "It is not enough for a man to do things that be good: but he must also have a care that he do them with good grace." [13]

* Handkerchiefs became popular with men only in the sixteenth century; they were first used in Venice. The medieval knight would have considered such an article an effeminate affectation.

The gentleman of Renaissance France had at his disposal a pretty large collection of ancient and modern treatises, in several foreign languages, on how to be a gentleman. Most of them, for his greater ease, had been translated into French, and he was therefore able without too great difficulty to learn that certain qualities throughout a number of centuries had been considered inherent in gentility. Among these desired qualities would be moderation and modesty; and, very basically, justice and valor. Even a manual of apparently trivial externals, like the *Galateo*, summed up for him a code of polite behavior that he tacitly obeyed. As for the *Courtier*, it probably had the greatest influence of any contemporary document on Europe's developing ideal of the genteel.[14]

One of the problems in transferring the writings from foreign lands — from Greece, Ancient Rome, Italy, or Spain — into French is the accurate translating of certain key words. This is especially true in dealing with terms that designate the many attributes of gentility, where a given word may have a different shading of implication in going from one language to another. The Latin, *virtus*, with the original meaning of "manliness," or "courage," is a case in point. As it came into modern tongues, it gave the English *virtue* and the French *vertu*, which have, from the sixteenth century down to the present time, referred to moral standards of worth and bravery. For the Italians, on the other hand, *virtù* and *virtuoso* in the Renaissance suggested capability, virtuosity, versatility, and the general faculty of getting along. All these variants in connotation are to be borne in mind in examining the qualities which the French themselves considered necessary to the make-up of a gentleman.

III

French Concepts of Gentility

THE FRENCH FOUND IT EASIER TO MEASURE a gentleman by his inherited position and his family background than by trying to decide what qualities he should have inside him. It was not a debatable issue in the Renaissance that a gentleman had to be a noble, that he was to carry on the tradition of the medieval knight — a proud external and visible legacy in that chivalry, though now outmoded, had evolved its most complete ritual in France; and that the best jobs connected with the operation of his nation were his. He had the obligation of living in a manner becoming to a noble, and of doing the expected things at the expected times, as summed up in the traditional phrase, *noblesse oblige*. However, none of this put much of a demand on him as an individual personality, or showed any of the ideological attributes that several centuries of critics said a gentleman should have. In other words, a nobleman could be technically and officially a gentleman without, necessarily, having many of the inner qualities of gentility. The French made some comments on this complex situation during the sixteenth century, and earlier.

A recurrent note was sounded even in the writings of medieval France: it said, in effect, that "gentle is as gentle does," and that rank is not the measure of gentility. The thirteenth century allegorical poem, the *Romance of the Rose*, which had so much influence upon the manners of succeeding centuries, makes the point very clearly. In the idyllic first part of the poem, Amors (Love) is advising the young lover how he can best be of service to the god. Amors says the lover must begin by avoiding low actions, for "a vile action is the mark of a vile person, and for this reason it is not right that I hold him in esteem." Amors calls attention to Keu the seneschal (a title that would mark a man as being theoretically a gentleman), who was a person of ill repute because of his crudities, while Count Gauvains was worthy of position and esteem because of his natural courtesy. It is not the artificiality of external rank that makes either man genteel. Amors continues his counsel to the young lover, telling him to dress neatly, keep his teeth white, and to avoid all dirty words and deeds, since "a man is not to be regarded as genteel who talks of matters low and vile." [1]

A great deal of the literature of the Middle Ages in France is derogatory of the nobility. The lyric form, the *pastourelle*, regularly shows the noble attempting seduction of a girl of the lower classes. In the dramatized *pastourelle* of the end of the thirteenth century, *The Play of Robin and Marion*, the noble seeks to effect his will with the shepherd-lass, Marion — and unsuccessfully. When the shepherd, Robin, objects to the noble's pursuit of his sweetheart, the noble gives Robin a sound thrashing. It is true that Robin is cowardly as well as boastful, but the noble, with his superiority of weapons and fine clothes, is not portrayed as admirable. The whole thing is done with gaiety of spirit, in keeping with the tone of the French comic theater of the Middle Ages, which satirized all classes. But it is interesting to note that the soldiers and nobles came in for their share of this satire.

With the growing middle class of the fourteenth and fifteenth centuries there continued to germinate the idea that every man is as good as every other man at birth, a belief not destined to receive full fruition until many centuries later. There were some minor uprisings at this time against the entrenched upper classes, and many verses were written suggesting that the people were just as good and as brave as the barons. The essence of many of these lines was that a man should be measured by his own good or bad actions, and not be put by the chance of ancestry into a higher or lower niche in society than he deserves. Such is the spirit of: "No man who acts nobly is common; but any nobleman is vile who conducts his life ignobly; no man is unworthy if he does not make himself so." [2] This is slightly reminiscent of Dante's statements in the *Convivio*, where he identifies nobility with virtue in the soul and not with wealth or position; and in the *Paradiso*, where he says that nobility of the blood is a little thing unless it is constantly renewed by the accomplishments of lofty deeds.[3]

An even stronger attack on the nobility was made in the story of the fox, *Renard the Deceiver*, a continuation in the middle fourteenth century of the famous beast epic, the *Romance of Renard*. Here the idea is expressed that it would be a splendid thing if every "gentleman" died off and reproduced himself no more, even as it would be for the wolves and heavy horses of battle to become extinct. Then the world as a whole would live in peace![4] The popular writing, as opposed to the courtly, of the Middle French period was pretty hard on the upper classes.

The sixteenth century saw the word *gentilhomme* come into more and more general use as a descriptive term. The writers of both prose and poetry, the critics, the chroniclers and historians, and others all make free application of it. It was supported by such related expressions as *homme de bien*, and *honnête homme*, though *honnête homme* with the connotation of "gentleman" belongs more properly to the seventeenth century. Extensions like *gentilfemme* and *honnête dame* are also found, as well as the generic *gentillesse* and *honnêteté*. *Seigneur* and *chevalier* tended to become more restrictive and were usually applied to specific persons. All these words indicated, in the standard language of the Renaissance, qualities or persons belonging to the upper stratum of society. *Gentilhomme*, along with the kindred terms associated with it, acquired with its growing popularity in the century many shadings in meaning.

The poets in the first part of the century, men like Clément Marot or Melin de Saint-Gelais, were likely to use *gentilhomme* to designate simply a courtier or favorite at court. This was a very natural procedure, since such poets were closely associated with the King's household. However, in some of the prose of the early century, usage is somewhat different. The Bourgeois de Paris in his *Journal* describes several "gentlemen" who were quite ordinary fellows. The Bourgeois, who mentions every conceivable type of catastrophe in his chronicle, says that in the year 1523 there was much robbing and thievery going on in France. In this connection, a "gentleman of Auvergne" was decapitated in the city of Paris, along with his son, because they were leaders of a band of robbers. And in 1529, according to the Bourgeois, "four gentlemen of Poictou" lost their heads in Paris, after spending some eighteen months in prison, because they were "thieves, plunderers, and ravishers of women and girls." None of these gentlemen, obviously, was endowed with much gentility. Nor was a certain "gentleman named de la Morlière" who took carnal advantage of the wife of a "gentleman" of the district of Brie. The second "gentleman" killed the first "gentleman" as well as his own wife, and was in turn decapitated in the city of Paris in July 1574. Even the prince of Renaissance poets, Ronsard, who can be most lofty in his concept of gentility, speaks not too admiringly of "simple gentlemen" or "braggart gentlemen." Montaigne, the writer of essays, also uses the term without any honorable implications when he describes his wanderings over the land of France during a momentary truce in the Wars of Religion. His journey was interrupted by his arrest at the hands of "fifteen or twenty masked gentlemen," who rifled his baggage and held him and his companions prisoners for ransom. He was finally released, says Montaigne, because of the frankness of his speech and the openness of his countenance.[5]

In military circles, where "gentleman" usually had high indications of honor and virtue, sometimes casual references are found to such things as the services of "the least important gentleman in the army." When the Chevalier Bayard died, for example, he was mourned for by his friends and his enemies, by persons high and low, including "even the poor gentlemen of his company." A very slightly admirable gentleman appears in the story of an uprising around Bordeaux in 1549 protesting the *gabelle*, or salt tax. The Maréchal de Saint-André was despatched to the area with sufficient forces to suppress the disturbance. The cohorts of Saint-André conducted themselves in general, according to reports, with consideration for the populace. Lodgings were paid for promptly, and any soldier found guilty of looting was punished immediately. However, an important lady of the city, Madame Valvyn (whose husband was an official in the law court of the province) brought complaints against the soldiers who were quartered at the house of her nieces and their widowed mother. Apparently these soldiers were very rough types and the nieces were very beautiful. Particular complaint was made against "a young gentleman" who wanted to break down the door to the bedroom of the beautiful nieces, who were thus compelled to jump out the window on to a pile of brush. Further investigation brought forth the evidence that the young gentleman in question was the bastard de Bueil, a low specimen with no consideration for virtuous young ladies, whom he would like to reduce to the same level as his own maternal ancestry. It turned out, for added complication, that the father and commanding officer of the bastard de Bueil was the same person, the Count de Sancerre. The Count had previously recognized his offspring, and therefore the son was technically and legally a gentleman. In any case, when the father heard of the insolent behaviour of his son, the young man received such a paternal upbraiding that he might well have wished to be dead.[6]

A somewhat sour note, in support of the unlofty use of "gentleman" by the French, was sounded in Italy by Machiavelli, whose writings on statecraft were beginning their influence on the sixteenth century: "I say that they are gentlemen who live at leisure and abundantly off their possessions, without bothering about the cultivation of land, or any other useful activity." Machiavelli considers such gentlemen "pernicious" to the welfare of any state or province.[7]

But these derogatory overtones of reference were scarcely the standard of measurement for *gentilhomme* in the Renaissance. For most of the writers of the century, the term implied qualities beyond the automatic position conferred by the luck of birth. Even with its more moderate suggestions, it had implications of graciousness and politeness; and in its loftier connotations, *gentilhomme* could fit the king himself. Many monarchs might well, in fact, be lacking in some of the ideal attributes of gentility.

Most of the commentators in the century thought that "gentleman" was a dignified word, and the gentleman a privileged person. For illustration, tourneys should be made up ideally of competitions between "gentlemen," and after gallant engagements on the mock field of battle the "young gentlemen" should escort courteously to Mass the ladies who had graced the spectacle with their presence. Bayard, who was admired by all the chroniclers, was called a "gracious and courtly gentleman," and noted as much for his sense of honor as for his ability in arms. The King's court was made up of gentlemen, an all-inclusive term which might be further broken up into "princes, dukes, counts, and gentlemen," some twelve hundred of whom were present at Francis I's entrance into Paris after his coronation at Saint-Denis. The King sent his gentlemen on all sorts of expeditions, private and official, and he was constantly surrounded by his "nobles and gentlemen." These "gentlemen following the Court" were granted many special privileges, forbidden to the ordinary citizens, such as the carrying of swords, daggers, and other weapons. The gentleman was also allowed more ornamentation in his attire than the bourgeois, which situation led later in the century to the desire on the part of the bourgeois, as he acquired greater quantities of gold, to imitate the elegance of dress of the gentleman.[8]

Other writers talk of the gentleman and his military associations. The seigneur de Fleurange, the childhood companion of Francis I at the château of Amboise and later a sharer of the King's captivity in Spain, speaks in his *Mémoires* of the young gentlemen who played at being soldier with the future King, the future King "of genteel heart." For Fleurange the noblest exercise that could occupy a prince or a gentleman was that of war, if the reason for the conflict was good. Since the belief in the pursuit of war as a necessary attribute of gentility was a standard concept of the Renaissance, gentlemen were constantly engaged in warlike games and improvements of military skills. War and the gentleman, in fact, went together.* Brantôme felt that one of the values of tourneys was

* See Chapter Nine.

that they showed foreigners that France had so many gentlemen brave and skillful in the use of arms. The great captain and fighter in Italy, Blaise de Monluc, gave support to the feeling that the mark of a gentleman was a career in arms, but Monluc was not of the opinion that such a career came easy. As for himself, says Monluc, although he is a gentleman and the son of a gentleman, he has had to work hard at the profession of war, even as the poorest soldier of the realm. A distinction is made by Monluc, however, between a gentleman and a common soldier, who is on a much lower social and military level.[9]

This military foundation for the edifice of gentility was largely accepted through the whole of the sixteenth century, although an amusing argument against it is offered in one of the stories of Marguerite de Navarre's *Heptaméron*. Marguerite, the sister of Francis I, could mix in her writings the earthy and the ethereal; the *Heptaméron*, modeled after the *Decameron* of Boccaccio, has little of the latter quality. The twentieth tale from the *Heptaméron*, then, relates the incident of a lady who refused a gentleman his desires because of her sense of honor and virtue. He later finds her lying in a secluded grassy plot with a stableboy. The company to whom the story is told is somewhat surprised, not by the matter of any moral issues, but at the lady's preference of a driver of mules to a gentleman. The realist of the group, a certain Hircan, says to one of the ladies present that the choice is not too surprising: "Alas, my lady, if you knew the difference that there is between a gentleman who has borne the harness of war and followed the profession thereof all his life, and a farm-boy who is well-nourished and not fatigued by travel, you would excuse this poor widow." Ronsard, the favorite poet of Henry II, has a few words to say about the cultural condition of the young gentlemen who have spent too much time under arms. In his advice to those who would like to improve the poetic quality of the French tongue, he suggests that they might well borrow good words from the various dialects, "without leaning too much on the speech of the Court, which is sometimes very bad, through being the language of young ladies and young gentlemen, who make more of a profession of fighting well than of talking well."[10]

Honnête homme was at times employed during the century as a synonym for *gentilhomme*. *Honnête dame* is also to be found during the Renaissance, in which case the adjective not only implied gentility, but also womanly virtue and chastity. Both adjectives are combined occasionally to make *honnête gentilhomme*, as in the brief story concerning Louis XII: this monarch, though he had great respect for the ladies around his court, did not want the "honnêtes gentilshommes in his service" to be without mistresses. *Gentilfemme* is rarer in occurrence, though Montaigne speaks of the *gentils-femmes* who were permitted to depart from a beseiged city with anything they could carry on their backs — and they took their husbands.[11]

An illustration of the complexity of the terminology of gentility and its application to a variety of social classes is seen in the story of the young prince who was amorous of the girl far beneath him in social position. She rejected his advances with the statement that she had a heart not less "honest" than that of the finest princess in Christendom, and that she esteemed "honesty" more than anything in the world. She hid, therefore, when the prince came to her house, though she was advised not to be afraid of so "honest" and "virtuous" a prince. The prince insisted that he was considerate of her "honor," which she said she held too dear to diminish, but that she was not insensitive of the "honor" the prince would do her! Unfortunately, in view of the fact that her social condition would not make it possible for her to be the wife or mistress of the prince and since she esteemed her "honor" dearer than life, she would not be able to grant the prince the desired favors. The prince considered this a very "honest" reply and mentioned the "honesty" of the girl to one of the gentlemen of his chamber. The gentleman, intrigued, sought to win the girl's caresses with the assistance of money, some five hundred crowns.* These she refused, since she preferred "honest pov-

* The crown and half-crown (*écu* and *demi-écu*) were the only gold coins minted in France in the time of Francis I. The *écu* contained around

erty" to tarnished riches. The gentleman was furious at such an attitude and did not consider that his own "honor" had been enhanced by a rebuff from a girl of the lower classes. Nevertheless, with the approval of the prince, she married one of his "servitors" and lived in a respected position the rest of her life. The gentleman, obviously, in this little tale was not the hero. Nor was he very heroic later in the century in the time of Catherine de' Medici, when he was banished from the company of Catherine's group of "honest maidens" because he did not talk to them properly and courteously. However, each day after dinner the Court went into the Queen's quarters and there a gentleman was allowed to chat with Catherine's "troup of human goddesses." [12]

Gentilhomme goes down the top rungs of the social ladder in the legend of the reception of provincial noblemen at the court of Francis I. The first day they were received as "little kings," then as "princes," and on the third day they were no more than "gentlemen." Higher levels of application are to be seen in the vision of the countryside decorated with "gentlemen's houses," and in the proverb which said there was nothing more impressive or formidable than a "French gentleman" when he was angry. Bayard was an "accomplished gentleman," and the weapons in a duel should always be becoming to an "honorable gentleman." In affairs of honor a man should conduct himself as a "genteel and worthy man," and he should have with him "gentlemen companions." [13]

The episode of the two schoolmasters on the road to Orléans demonstrates the differences between the ordinary professions and the life of a gentleman. One of the masters was about fifty paces in front of the other, and both were followed by a group headed by the Count de La Rochefoucaut. The first master was asked who the gentleman was behind him — meaning the Count. The reply was, assuming that it was a question of the second master: "He is not a gentleman; he is a grammarian and I am a logician." The two pedants, with their grammar and logic, were then forgotten, since it was not important for

3¼ grams of pure gold, and would be worth today $3.67. The franc, a silver coin, was introduced in 1576 by Henry III.

a youth — and the story is part of an essay on the training of the youth — to imitate a grammarian or logician, but rather a gentleman.[14]

Many of those who wrote about gentility and the gentleman in Renaissance France thought that to be a gentleman was about the highest calling a man could have. All the terms involving the nobility and the genteel classes are used, in the minds of these writers, with the loftiest of connotations. In spite of the derelictions of any specific gentleman the ideal of what he ought to be was for these men never forgotten, and thus they helped to keep intact the long chain of measurements of gentility that had begun centuries before. And, viewed in this sense, a noble or a gentleman had a greater responsibility to society than just the passive inheritance of a title or the wearing of a pretty suit at a royal party.

In the year 1535, the learned and versatile doctor of Lyon, Symphorien Champier, brought out a small but meaty volume on the origins of the nobility and the reasons for its foundation. After having given in detail the technical and legal methods by which a man may become a noble, Champier looks at some of the basic properties of nobility and gentility. The "first gentlemen," he says, came into being through their "virtuous works" and "acts of valor." Also, "if it is from virtue that the nobility derives, by virtue must it be maintained." After a noble has taken oaths and sworn his allegiance to his prince, he should make assurances of his feelings of respect for his own honor, and "besides, swear and promise that he will protect the honor of women, girls, and orphans," and help them if they are impoverished. He will "avoid all lying and slander, public taverns, brothels, and forbidden gaming houses." And, gentlemen who have inherited titles and property must remember that they have done so "through the valor of their forefathers," and if they as descendants show themselves to be unworthy they can be "called vile." All nobles are not equal in their gentility, since those "most ancient lineages which have not been corrupted or stained by crime" are superior. Some say everybody is noble that descended from

Adam and Eve, but that is a silly belief which would include all criminals. To say to a man, "I am as fine a gentleman as you," is ridiculous, unless your line is as ancient and as unsullied as his. The King, though he can grant "political" nobility, can not give the background of a fine and honorable family, which is based upon "natural" and "spiritual" nobility. The situation is ideal when natural, spiritual, and political nobility are all combined to produce the finest of gentlemen.[15]

With such requirements as these demanded as prerequisite for gentility, the title of gentleman was good enough for anybody, even for a king. Francis I thought so much of it that he made oaths on his "faith of a gentleman." In the opinion of some, to be called a gentleman "is the finest title that a prince can have after that of his principality." Other peoples as well as the French have had this interpretation of "gentleman," and "that is why a gentleman, when he is really a gentleman, is much to be esteemed; that means, indeed, a gentleman by blood, by valor and merit, by repute and by ability in arms." Such a gentleman would have been able to occupy any place in society. He would have been easily at home in Rabelais's idealized *Abbaye de Thélème*, with the "genteel companions," who were wellborn and free. He would also have shared Bayard's disgust with the Spaniard, Dom Alonce, who was given as a captive the free run of a château. Alonce, against his word, tried to escape — which was not "the action of an honorable gentleman."[16]

Many critics thought that in battle the gentleman should be at his noblest. He was expected to fight harder than anybody else, and thus animate the people and win the respect of his King. Monluc, as a commander in the field, tells his captains that, in order to show their valor and be honored, they will have to take risks with their soldiers. Though wounded himself, Monluc urges the nobility to stay with him in the midst of the fight, for it is they who can bring victory: "Oh *gentilshommes*, my friends, the brunt of the combat is on the nobility: we must hope that victory may come to us through ourselves, who are gentlemen; let us move forward, I will show you the road, and I will make you know that a good horse never becomes a nag. Follow me boldly and, without hesitation, strike, for we would not be able to choose a death in which there is more honor." And then the gentlemen of France march ahead shoulder to shoulder. Many are killed by enemy fire, and Monluc is wounded again, in his rash ignoring of danger. Nevertheless, the old marshal maintains that he and his officers should give leadership to their troops, since fifty gentlemen in battle are the equivalent of two hundred soldiers. This is the case, says Monluc, because "we, the *gentilshommes*, still have the spirit of honor that our fathers won for us when they gained the splendid title of noble." Such a background would prevent a nobleman of France from allying himself with the Spanish or Huguenots, a nobleman who has loved honor too much to allow one spot of villainy to stain his family name.[17]

The poet, in some very revealing verses on the inherent demands on a nobleman, has François, Duc de Guise, addressing his soldiers before the fighting around the city of Metz. The duties of the men in the ranks are outlined clearly and they are told to fight bravely and stand firm. As for the nobility and the princes of the blood, it is considered unnecessary to urge them on to deeds of valor: "And you, Princes of the blood, whose noble ancestry gave you in the cradle a haughty disdain for death, it is not you who must be encouraged like the rabble weak of heart in the outburst of battle; your innate courage teaches you better than I the ways of war." In other words, a gentleman had to be brave before the enemy or it was a disgrace to him and his family. The matter of noble lineage comes up again in some lines dedicated to the Duc d'Epernon: "The eagle is descended from the eagle, and the noble lion engenders the lion; thus you, a valorous son, are born of a valorous father, and will become powerful and glorious in the service of your King." Breeding was therefore indispensable to the creation of a gentleman, and with his background of good birth, he was expected inevitably to be a military leader. Yet it was an empty thing to do brave deeds in battle just for display, and honor was not gained by actions done for show. Many of the bravest exploits of a gentleman are not likely to be seen in the tumult. On the other hand, if a cowardly man is honored for exploits that he did not do, he cannot really be a gentleman, because valor is an attribute of a gentleman and thus no coward can be one.[18]

Of all terms denoting desirable qualities in a gentleman of the Renaissance, *honneur* is probably the most difficult to define. It was both active and passive in its suggestions. A gentleman possessed an honor to be defended if necessary — a different meaning of the word from that of the ancients, who thought of honor as a more external quality — and he could be the recipient of honors, in the Aristotelian sense. *Honneur*, when applied to women, involved moral purity, and was not restricted to ladies of the nobility. For Rabelais, it was that instinct in wellborn and cultured persons that encouraged them to do noble rather than ignoble deeds. As for Ronsard, he loves a man who is upright, and not a servant of vice, who scorns the avarice of the Court, who would rather die than be corrupt, and who loves honor more than a mandate of the King. François de La Noue, that doughty old warrior who lost his left arm in battle and rigged up an iron mechanism to replace it, seeks to give some of the proper concepts of *honneur*, and to distinguish between "false honor" and "true honor." * For him as for everyone else, it was a complicated problem to find a good definition of honor.[19]

Vertu was a noble attribute, and different from *gloire*. *Vertu* dwelt inside the gentleman, while *gloire* was the result of man's approbation and was, consequently, variable. "Virtue" was regarded philosophically as being superior to "nobility," [20] because "nobility" by the luck of birth might fall on an inferior and vicious man — a point of view not popular with the nobility. In any case, virtue, which involved physical courage and a sense of justice, was needed to make an ideal gentleman.

A summing up of the qualities that might well belong to the genteel ideal was made by Ronsard in a discourse on the moral and intellectual virtues pronounced before the *Académie du Palais*, in the presence of Henry III. In the words of Ronsard: "The moral virtues are habits learned and acquired through

* See Chapter Ten.

long application and usage, deeply imprinted in the irrational part of the soul, to correct and keep in obedient subjugation the passions of the appetite and of the senses; these virtues are: fortitude, patience, constancy, good faith, truth, justice, liberality, and magnanimity — and their relations. These moral virtues rest on a midpoint between two vices, that is, they are in between the too much and the too little." [21] Ronsard goes on to give examples of the mean, the substance of which is based on Aristotle: fortitude is in between rashness and cowardice, temperance is in between debauchery and stupid asceticism, liberality is in between prodigality and avarice, etc. The passions, says Ronsard, are seated in the lower part of the soul. As for the other phases of man's structure, the liver is like a "merchant," while the heart is like the "nobility." The reason sits above to guide and direct. The moral virtues definitely are superior to the intellectual, and thus a man of action is to be preferred to a man of contemplation. Too much contemplation leads to the life of a hermit and makes a man like a sword which has never left its scabbard.

In most cases, the gentleman of the Renaissance left it to the poets and philosophers to decide what qualities he should have inside and outside. He was very busy, for his own part, fighting wars, hunting stags, governing provinces, and following the court of his King.

IV

Brilliance of the Court

THERE WAS NEVER ANY DOUBT that "the great King Francis I" was both King and the first gentleman of the land. He looked and acted the part of a leader, and would have been dominant in his group of gentlemen without the support of any regal position. He simply was the head man, a fact readily admitted and easily verified. His doting mother, Louise de Savoie, thought so too, even when she worried about stones striking him in the head as he played boyhood games, or about his fighting in Italy as a lieutenant general when he was barely twenty-two, or about an injury to his little finger incurred in jousting before the royal residence in Paris, the Hôtel des Tournelles. For Louise he was always "my Caesar" and in her mind the "perpetual dictator." And one month after the episode in the lists of Les Tournelles that resulted in the wound "between the first joints of the little finger," on January 1, 1515, "my Caesar" became King of France.[1] He was destined to fill this office with considerable success for more than thirty years. With him the word *cour*, which had previously been used generally to designate a lawcourt, came to mean the collection of handsome ladies and gentlemen that surrounded the King, who was called even before the end of the century "the great King Francis I."

The reigns of Charles VIII and Louis XII had been just a trifle dull. Charles VIII died at the château of Amboise in 1498, according to the story told by Commynes and repeated by Brantôme,[2] from having bumped his head against the top of a door of a gallery, where he had gone to watch a game of *jeu de paume*.* It was a strange accident, since Charles was

* A game something like handball: however, by the sixteenth century a racket was used instead of the palm of the hand. See Chapter Eight.

"quite small"; and it was an ignoble place to die in — which he did around nine o'clock on the evening of April 7, lying there on a pallet — since the passage had come to be used pretty much as a common urinal. The regime of Louis XII, who followed Charles VIII immediately, was marked among other things by the great rivalry between his queen, Anne de Bretagne (previously the wife of Charles VIII), and Louise de Savoie, the widow at the age of eighteen of Charles d'Orléans, Comte d'Angoulême. Happily for Louise, at his death, Charles left her a baby boy, François, a new Comte d'Angoulême, who first saw the light of day, his mother said, at two o'clock in the afternoon of September 12, 1494. This child was destined to become the "great King" because Anne de Bretagne was never able to produce a male heir, a queenly deficiency over which Louise never ceased to gloat. She records in her *Journal* that Anne, "queen of France," did give birth at Blois to a son on the day of Saint Agnes, January 21 (the year is not recorded, but it was in the early 1500's), but he had a "deficiency of life" and consequently could not "retard the exaltation of my Caesar." Anne de Bretagne understandably despised Louise de Savoie, and opposed the marriage of her daughter, Claude de France, to François, the dashing young Comte d'Angoulême. The marriage took place, nevertheless, in May 1514, after the death of Anne earlier in the year. She had previously taken the precaution to send her most beautiful furniture from the royal château at Blois back to her ancestral home in Nantes on the lower Breton coast, a conservational measure against the inroads of the new Valois-Angoulême dynasty.

The old king, Louis XII, had not given up hope, though he was "very antique and debilitated," in the opinion of Louise de Savoie. He proceeded to marry Mary of England, the daughter of Henry VII, at ten o'clock in the morning of October 9, 1514 — "and that night they slept together," reports Louise laconically. The ensuing few weeks in the life of Louis XII attracted the attention of several sixteenth-century chroniclers. Rumor had it that the new queen was pregnant, but this turned out not to be true. Most people thought it would have been one of the wonders of the time if it had been true, unless an earlier interest in Mary on the part of the ever alert young Comte d'Angoulême might be bearing some belated fruit. But Louise de Savoie had managed effectively to keep her son distracted from such high-level amatory enthusiasms. Everybody agreed that it had been a splendid wedding. The Loyal Serviteur in his life of Bayard gives a frequently quoted description of the return of the royal couple to Paris and their triumphant entry into the city. Many jousts and tourneys were held which lasted six weeks — these included, incidentally, a clash of arms wherein the Comte d'Angoulême and seven doughty captains defended a fort against all comers, English and French. There were many fine banquets and festivals, which forced a change in the daily routine of Louis XII. He had been accustomed to dining in the evening, but now he dined in the middle of the day; "because of his new wife," he went to bed at twelve o'clock when he had been in the habit of retiring at six. As a result of all this change and added activity, he fell sick at the end of the month of December, and died on January 1, 1515.[3] Fleurange said that Louis had sought to be a "genteel companion" for his young wife, but that the effort involved was too great. And some of the gossips of Paris told the story that the King of England had sent to the King of France a nice little filly to take him to hell or maybe all the way to Paradise.[4] A credit for an assist in this operation might well be given to Louise de Savoie, who had not allowed her son's casual interest in the English princess to block her marriage with the old King.

François, first of the name, Duc de Valois and Comte d'Angoulême, thus came to the throne at the age of twenty and brought to fruition the long range plans of Louise de Savoie, who had indoctrinated him from his earliest youth for the role he was destined to play. He had learned a variety of sports and games at the château of Amboise, and at Blois he had received cultural training in the classics along with his sister, later the erudite Marguerite de Navarre. At twenty he was tall, he was graceful, he was rugged, and he was considered handsome because of the fire in his eyes and the mobility of his countenance. All his portraits show him with too long a nose (he was called familiarly Long-Nose) for perfect balance of features, but the Renaissance felt that a sizable nose was a good thing for a man. According to Benvenuto Cellini, who spent several years at Francis I's court, he was more than six feet tall: the King had ordered from Cellini six silver statues of gods, each one to be exactly the size of His Majesty, "which was just a little less than four *braccia*." * After full allowances are made for Cellini's powers of exaggeration, it seems certain that Francis I was a tall and well-proportioned man.[5] The Loyal Serviteur said of him that when he came to the throne he was "as handsome a prince as there was in the world," and that "never had there been seen a king of France whose nobility was so resplendent." As for the intellectual capacity of the new king, a compliment is paid to that by Castiglione in the *Courtier*. In a general discussion in the first book of the *Courtier*, the remark is made that Frenchmen are not much interested in letters. However, the Lord Magnifico, one of the participants in the discussion, says that he has recently been in France and was greatly impressed by the intelligence of the young Comte d'Angoulême, who is deeply concerned with cultural matters, "contrary to the manner of his country." If he should come to the throne, there are great expectations for the improvement in the intellectual attitude of the land of France.

The *sacre*, or religious phase of the coronation of Francis I, took place in the cathedral of Rheims on January 25, 1515, and "all the noble knights and princes of the blood were there in a very great number." In another contemporary report, it was said that when Francis was crowned, he was surrounded by "all his princes, gentlemen, and officers, of which he had so great a number that it was a thing almost unbelievable." The ceremonies continued on to Saint-Denis, just outside Paris, "where there was a very beautiful and excellent festival, and where there were many princes and seigneurs." The celebra-

* A *braccio* was a measure of some variation in different parts of Italy. It could be around six-tenths of a meter, and thus Francis I would have been over seven feet tall.

tions then moved to Paris, where the new King's entry was "the most triumphant that has ever been seen in France, for there were more than a thousand or twelve hundred princes, dukes, counts, and gentlemen in it."[6] This entry occurred February 15, 1515, and there were jousts and tourneys on the Rue Saint-Antoine before the Hôtel des Tournelles, all of which had earlier been announced by criers throughout the realm. It was all a very successful affair, "and there was killed by a lance in the jousts a gentleman named monsieur de Saint-Aubin; messieurs d'Alençon, de Bourbon, and de Vendôme were the defenders" — thus the Bourgeois de Paris, who was there, describes the incident. It will be noted that in his satisfaction with the general excellence of the jousts, the Bourgeois never gets back to monsieur de Saint-Aubin, who lost his life in the entertainment. The King himself, as might be expected, participated in the jousting, and Francis was a tough competitor, a very "rude lance."

But "the great King Francis I" was not great simply in stature and figure; he also possessed grandeur through his "virtues, valor, fine deeds, and lofty worthiness," even as Alexander and Pompey.[7] Not only was he "the genteel King" but he was also "the father and true restorer of arts and of letters," possibly the most famous epithet that has been applied to him through the centuries. He was the great builder, particularly of Fontainebleau, which was a "desert" before his reconstruction and became one again in the time of Henry III. Such châteaux as Chambord (which is literally covered with Francis' fire-defying emblem, the salamander) and Saint-Germain-en-Laye must also, among others, be remembered as favorite spots for his mobile court. Of Saint-Germain, the great architect and engraver, Androuet Du Cerceau, said that King Francis was so attentive to its construction that you "could scarcely say that any other than he was its architect."[8] His generosity to artists, scholars, and men of letters has been chronicled many times, with such figures as Cellini, Leonardo da Vinci, Primaticcio, and Rosso being prominent Italian recipients of his patronage.

Francis I was much at home and completely at ease in the

company of his gentlemen; he was equally relaxed among the ladies of his court. There is no doubt that he had a vigorous interest in the opposite sex. His two wives, the gentle Claude and, later, Eleonora (the dark sister of his old enemy, Emperor Charles V), and his two official mistresses, Madame de Châteaubriant and the Duchess d'Etampes, were not the limits of his investigations under the guidance of Aphrodite. Some writers, including Brantôme and Mézeray,[9] suggested that he caught syphilis and passed it on to Queen Claude, thus shortening her life. Such accusations have been denied by later historians, but Francis I did have a strange abscess that recurred every four or five years. It was regarded by many as an effort on the part of the King's body to purify itself by a concentration of poisons in one spot. The sober Tavannes in a very quotable passage said that Francis I was "wounded by *les dames* in body and in spirit, and dominated by the little band of Madame d'Etampes. Alexander saw women when there was no business to be looked after; Francis I looks after business when there are no women." [10] Belleforest, writing not many years after the death of Francis I, conceded that he was a graceful and gracious person, the "restorer of fine learning," and the best king of the last two or three hundred years, but felt that his virtues were a trifle obscured "by a certain vice" that shortened the course of his life: he was "given over to women a little more than was necessary" and "in that, set a bad example for his subjects." [11] But even Mézeray called him "the great King," who, "when he appeared on the throne in the flower of his youth, with the bearing and figure of a hero, with a marvelous skill in all the noble exercises of a cavalier, brave, generous, magnificent, courteous, debonnaire, and gracious in speech, he attracted the adoration of the people and the love of the Nobility." [12]

The sixteenth century saw the beginnings of exchanges of ambassadors between states, and the Venetians started early in the century to send representatives to the French Court. From them, as well as from the envoys of other Italian city states, came many rather detached reports on contemporary life in France. Marino Cavalli, the Venetian, in his *Relations* of 1546 gave a picture of the mature Francis I: "The King is now fifty-four years old.* His appearance is completely regal, to such a degree that without ever having seen his face or portrait, you would say immediately on looking at him: that is the King. All his movements are so noble and so majestic that no prince would be able to equal him. . . He is of very solid judgment, of very extensive erudition; there is no subject, no art, on which he can not discourse very pertinently . . . he is learned in matters of hunting, in painting, in literature, in languages, in the different bodily exercises appropriate to a fine courtier."[13]

Despite Cavalli's opinions concerning Francis' robust condition, he died of a fever, says Martin du Bellay,[14] the following year in 1547, just before Easter. Francis was continually on a horse, riding to the hounds, and visiting various châteaux during these final days. Rambouillet, about twenty miles southwest of Paris, was the last one. Tavannes's comment on the King was that "women rather than old age caused his death." [15] Among his last acts were the recommendation of his people and his personal household, which included the gentlemen in his service, to the kindly consideration of the Dauphin, soon the new King, Henry II.

Henry II was not the man his father was, but still he was a good one. He had grown up to young manhood in the varied and vigorous atmosphere of Francis I's court, and upon the death of the Dauphin François in 1536, Henry, then Duc d'Orléans, was in line for the throne. He had been married in order to strengthen political ties in Italy to a daughter of the Medici, the dark-eyed Catherine, when no one thought that she would some day be Queen of France or produce three sons who would each in his turn be King of France.† In these earlier days she simply participated fully in the life that was guided by Francis I, and masked a keen intelligence and gift for intrigue behind beautiful hands and a nicely rounded figure, which included a pretty leg and thigh — "or so I have

* Cavalli makes Francis I two years older than he actually was in 1546.

† Francis II (1559–1560), Charles IX (1560–1574), and Henry III (1574–1589).

heard from the ladies around the Court," says Brantôme. Henry was strong and athletic, though not quite so tall as his father. He had had in his earlier years the hardening of military service, and possessed a muscular quickness and wiriness. Cavalli has left a picture of the Dauphin just before he became King. After the broad statement that Henry might well be the most worthy king that France has had in two hundred years, the Italian adds a few qualifying particulars: the Dauphin at the age of twenty-eight has a "very robust constitution, a disposition that is just a little melancholy; he is very skillful in the use of arms; he is not very clever in conversational exchanges, but he is very exact and very firm in his opinions . . . his intelligence is not of the quickest . . . he is scarcely interested in women, his own wife being sufficient for him; as for feminine conversation, he limits himself to that of Madame la Sénéchale de Normandie,* who is forty-eight years old. He has for her a real tenderness, but no one thinks there is anything lascivious about it — it is rather like mother and son." [16] This is something of an advance notice on the strange triumvirate — Henry II, Catherine de' Medici, and Diane de Poitiers — who were to mold the setting for a brilliant life at Court for the next dozen years. It was apparently an amicable ménage of three that lived together, externally at least, in harmony.

Diane de Poitiers was an alumna of Francis I's training school, and there was some gossip, never really confirmed, about her and Francis. In any case, her influence on Henry II was tremendous, comparable to that of Madame de Pompadour in a later epoch. Diane — who may have acted as model for Jean Goujon's Diana and the Stag, done for Diane's château at Anet, a gift of Henry — received the full vitriolic treatment from Mézeray. He calls her a charmer without charm, forty years old (he is kinder in this estimate than Cavalli), and with the marks of age rather than modesty on her brow. As the fires in her eyes have dimmed, the flames of lubricity have been lit in her heart. Everything around the Court has crescents and bows and arrows on it, "the symbol of this im-

* Diane de Poitiers.

modest Diane." Everybody at Court, even the King and Queen, bows to her dominion. As for Henry II, he would have been faultless if he had had a soul as fine as his body. He was adept at every "noble exercise," as much so as any cavalier in his realm.[17] A contemporary Italian, Giovanni Capello, gives a kinder picture of Henry II in 1554, just past the middle of his reign and in the prime of his middle thirties: "His Majesty is thirty-six years old; his figure is straight and well set-up; his complexion is a little dark; his manners are agreeable. He is courteous and affable, and he deigns to talk to anyone, even those of most humble position." As for the Queen at the age of thirty-six — Catherine de' Medici and Henry were almost the same age — "you would not praise her beauty," though she has strong lips and large eyes. She loves the King very much, says Capello.[18] Catherine was already getting heavy and this tendency toward corpulence was given the loyal support of the Queen's voracious appetite. The delicate little Dauphin, the future Francis II (for less than a year till his death in 1560) and childhood husband of Mary Queen of Scots, lacked vigor at the age of ten and was not much interested in letters, despite the assistance of good tutors. All of which augured ill for the future, and displeased Henry II.

Diane de Poitiers, whose magic spell over the King was never broken while he lived, acquired a château or two here and there, including the most beautiful of them all, Chenonceaux, sitting astride the river Cher. Henry II, who could do such things with very little difficulty, made her a duchess, the Duchesse de Valentinois. Courtiers and court poets sought to be in her good graces because of her intercessionary powers at Court, but it was not a very easy thing to do. Ronsard, the greatest poet of the Renaissance, dedicated verses to her and asked for her favor, which he never got. Diane was just not particularly interested in poets or poetry, though she did like books with pretty bindings.[19] Every royal residence, or function, or banner, or decoration came to be marked with an overlapping device that looked a little like a misprint: it was made from an *H* and a *C* and a *D* all piled one on top of the other.* It symbolized the triumvirate of Henry, Catherine, and Diane, which exercised a subtle and powerful dominion over the land of France for more than a decade. Many thought it was more splendid than the regime of Francis I.[20]

Henry II's love for vigorous exercise cost him his life. He enjoyed the shattering of a lance against the chest of a solid adversary, and was a very active participant in the jousts celebrating the marriage of Elisabeth of France, his daughter, to Philip II of Spain at Paris in June 1559. Lists had been set up from Les Tournelles to the Bastille, and the tourneys had been going on for three days. An added reason for celebration was the marriage of Marguerite de France, the King's sister who had been around the Court for some years, to Philibert-Emmanuel de Savoie, another move to bring peace in Henry's time. In the jousting, the King had already broken several lances, but wanted to crash one more against Montgommery, a captain of the guards. There are many reports of what happened next, and also the fine contemporary engraving to visualize this last ride of Henry II along the barrier.† Montgommery, it seems, thought the King had done enough, and was not at all enthusiastic about breaking another lance. In any case, they rode; the King's visor was not well closed (Mézeray says he left it open in a spirit of bravado), and the splintered butt of Montgommery's lance, after the shaft had snapped off against the target on the left side of Henry's chest, struck the King in the right eye and penetrated his brain. He lived for eleven days but never regained consciousness. Montgommery was in deep despair, the Court was shocked, and jousting was never again very popular in France. Henry II, then, the strong man with a black beard, died in the early days of July 1559, at the age of forty-two. Tavannes said he had all the weaknesses of his father without his father's brains, Mézeray said his court was full of dissolution set by his example, Belleforest said he had no bad habits and loved scholars without being one, and Monluc thought he was the best king France would ever have.[21]

* See Figure 13.

† See Chapter Eight and Figure 23.

With the death of Henry II, Catherine de' Medici assumed command of the situation. She took back Chenonceaux from Diane de Poitiers and managed to consign Diane to oblivion. When the listless little Francis II died in 1560, Charles IX became king at the age of eleven. He was a nice looking lad, but frail, and the usual exercises worthy of the first young gentleman of the realm were too violent for him. He continued to be lacking in strength but became very much interested in hunting, and wrote a little treatise, *La Chasse royale*, on the subject. In the meantime, the reins of government were turned over more and more to Catherine de' Medici, who in her early fifties was still vigorous though plump, ate anything and everything, and was a bit feared by everybody. She maintained a brilliant court, with much pageantry and ceremonial, despite the sad condition of France during the Wars of Religion. Charles IX, exhausted by the affairs of Diana and Venus rather than those of state, died at the age of twenty-four in 1574. He was succeeded by his brother who reigned as Henry III, surrounded by his perfumed and bedecked favorites. He did not create a happy atmosphere for the gentleman whose memories went back to an earlier epoch. Catherine de' Medici, though her son made assertive gestures from time to time, was still at the governmental controls. Henry III was assassinated in 1589, there was a change of dynasty, and the fury of the Wars of Religion somewhat abated. With the end of the Valois, there came to the throne another strong man, Henry IV, the first of the Bourbons — but his reign is beyond the temporal limits of the Renaissance gentleman.

The gentleman's association at Court revolved, in general, around the dominant personalities of Francis I, Henry II, and Catherine de' Medici. It was well for him, also, not to forget the uncrowned queens: Madame de Châteaubriant and her successor, the Duchesse d'Etampes; and the wife (merely coincidental) of Louis de Brézé, the Sénéchale de Normandie, the Duchesse de Valentinois, the lady who was said to be beautiful until the very time of her death — Diane de Poitiers.

The gentleman of the Golden Age of the sixteenth century

had a fine balance of life at the Court and life on his own estates. The high peak of the year would be the months spent in the splendor of the King's radiance, but more than half the time he would be found on his own domains, where he was no longer a feudal lord, but where he filled important duties under royal control. And, from time to time, the King and his ambulating court might swing by his château for a visit, as Francis I did for Jean de Laval, his agent in Normandie, in 1532. There was not yet the primarily decorative nobility of the Court of later centuries — though before the end of the century the embryo of this emasculative process was already formed — and the gentleman had a good deal of independence. Paris was, in spite of its size — around a teeming half million souls — a place chiefly for the merchants, artisans, lawyers, and several thousand poor students. The gentleman was either with the King's armies in the field, or living on his own lands, or fulfilling some duty at Court. And the King, with his inherent powers of a personal administration of justice and application of favor, could make life pleasant or disagreeable for his gentlemen. The blunt Monluc, Maréchal de France and veteran of many campaigns, lamented the fact that the royal ear had become deaf and the royal shoulder cold. Indeed, it was at the Court that the sun shone, and a gentleman yearned for the warmth of its rays. The historian Lavisse has described the process: "The noblemen follow the King's presence even as butterflies seek the light." [22] All the royal offices in the provinces, like those of *sénéchal* or *bailli*, were eagerly sought because they insured a closer proximity to the royal effulgence.

The promising young gentleman was sent by his family, if possible, to become a royal page. He might begin by being attached to the household of some great provincial noble, such as would be found in Bretagne, Provence, or Savoie, which in the earlier part of the century were imperfectly linked to the Crown. The youngster would wear a pretty costume and run errands for his lordly master or sometimes pour wine at his table, and have a quick ear and eye for elements of gossip and intrigue around him. The royal pages were certainly in a position to learn much, but it was no place for a weakling.

They could become noisy and raucous in courtyards and palace halls, and an occasional royal edict had to limit their turbulence. François de La Noue, a rigid disciplinarian in an age that was becoming corrupt, has in the latter part of the century several remarks to make about young gentlemen serving as pages at Court: they see "many beautiful things, like *triomphes*, feastings, and *combats*; * they learn to dress correctly, to address persons according to their quality, and to regulate their gestures." However, they learn also to be "dissolute in their speech," to be "very mocking," and "expert in lying." Fathers should therefore not let their sons be pages in royal service for more than four or five years.[23] La Noue is justifiably critical of the decadent tendencies in the era of Henry III, but his is different from the attitude usually held before 1550.

A young gentleman might be even more favorably placed by being attached to the royal household as a companion and playmate of the infant sons in the royal family. Robert de La Marche, seigneur de Fleurange, went at the age of nine to Amboise, and was the friend and childhood companion of Francis I, who was about two years younger than Fleurange. Fleurange, who died in 1536, remained very loyal to Francis I all his life, and shared the King's captivity in Spain after Francis' defeat and capture at Pavia in 1525. Fleurange, who calls himself the "young adventurer" relates in his memoirs the many games they played as children, in the company of other young gentlemen. They devised all sorts of ball games, set traps to catch stags and other "wild beasts," and built fortified castles which they would both attack and defend. Never did a prince have such a good time as "the said young gentleman," François.[24] Charles de Cossé, Comte de Brissac, spent a great deal of his youth with the children of Francis I at Blois and other châteaux along the Loire. They rode horses, romped with their dogs, and jousted in armor — and studied a little Latin on the side. Charles was particularly the companion of

* *Triomphes* were various sorts of triumphal processions, *combats* refer to jousting and tourneys. For more of La Noue's ideas on the training of a young gentleman, see Chapter Six.

the Dauphin François, who never lived to become king. Arthur de Cossé, one of the two brothers of Charles, illustrates a more difficult side of being a royal playmate: he went with his mother, who was a governess in the King's Household (an excellent position), to share the arduous captivity of the two princes, Francis I's sons, in Spain for two years. They were demanded as hostages by Charles V in exchange for the release of their father. The pathetic imprisonment of the two little royal pawns lasted until 1530. Another well-known gentleman and soldier of the sixteenth century, who found the society of princes no obstacle to his career, was François de Scepeaux, sire de Vieilleville and Comte de Duretal, later marshal of France. He served as a companion to the youthful Duc d'Orléans, later to rule as Henry II. Gaspard de Tavannes, who is so hard on Francis I in his memoirs, was a page at the monarch's court in his early teens. He was later the companion of the King's son, Charles, and helped toughen the young prince, who was supposed to be just a bit effeminate.

As the gentleman grew older, he could aspire to one of the many fine positions at Court open to the right man. Francis I was lavish in his general outlook toward things, and Henry II, though a little less openhanded by nature, carried on the tradition. The highest officers of the Crown, like the *connétable*, *chancelier*, etc., along with their duties, have previously been mentioned. They were the major servants of the King, chosen in theory on the basis of military or administrative qualifications. In addition, there was an incredible number of other titles, much sought after and admired, that were honorific as well as remunerative, and which offered a gentleman a good excuse for being at Court. Francis I, by handing out so many of these distinctions, began the conversion of the nobility to courtiers. One of the splendid offices at Court was that of *grand veneur*, or grand master of the royal hunts, and it was held at one time by the fine soldier, François, Duc de Guise, who was assassinated in 1563. There were several assistant hunt masters, all of genteel origin, who looked after a dozen servants for the dogs, who looked after a few bloodhounds and some sixty or more other hunting dogs. There was also the office of *grand fauconnier*, or grand master of the King's falcons, which was held by such figures as the Connétable de Montmorency and the Maréchal de Brissac. Under the grand falcon-master were a number of well chosen minor falcon-masters to do the heavy work.

In the King's Household in the 1530's there were four first gentlemen in charge of the royal bedroom and over fifty secondary gentlemen of the royal bedroom. There were around twenty maîtres d'hôtel of impeccable families, with dozens of *panetiers* and *échansons* (masters of the pantry and of the royal bottle) of excellent family background under their jurisdiction. At this time, Francis I had for his religious needs over forty distributors of royal alms, among them a cardinal and a few bishops, and half a dozen chaplains. The royal stables were under the control of a quantity of gentlemen. All these offices had attached to them a collection of more lowly underlings to carry out the dirtier tasks. Hovering immediately around the King were some thirty pages, the honored youngsters who graced parties and hopped around in sprightly fashion at the King's bidding. And there was always near him his personal guard of two hundred gentlemen marked by their batons with the falcon's beak. It must be remembered that in addition to the King's Household, other members of the royal family had on occasions separate households, with a framework similar to that of the King. Louise de Savoie and Catherine de' Medici had their own establishments. When the Dauphin became Duc de Bretagne in 1532, he was given a more elaborate personal entourage. The poet Melin de Saint-Gelais, for example, was alms distributor of the Dauphin. Saint-Gelais was well equipped for this job since he was in all probability the bastard son of Octavien de Saint-Gelais, the bishop of Angoulême and a scion of the upper nobility. An ecclesiastical bastard was perfectly qualified for the duties of distributor of alms, but it was scarcely an officc to be filled by a lowly commoner.

These royal offices carried with them good pay as well as plenty of honor. It took a quantity of money to run the King's operations. Francesco Giustiniano said in 1537 that the King's Household required 1,500,000 livres a year to keep it going. This figure included the upkeep of two hundred gentlemen (the King's own guard), one hundred archers, one hundred Swiss, and the stables and the hunting. It did not have in it two hundred guards for châteaux (which cost 200,000 livres extra), the expenses for banquets and tourneys, and Christmas presents. The merchants of Paris, fortunately, were in good financial shape and the King coaxed a few sous out of them from time to time. After the death of Francis I, Catherine de' Medici, who loved all the activities of Francis' court in addition to having her own admiration for ballets and the theater, played a prominent role in seeing that everything was continued. A little past the middle of the century, Henry II was reported to be spending 800,000 crowns on clothes, his stables, and the "upkeep of the queen." This really was the sum expended for the Court with its offices, but did not include the military. Toward the end of his reign, no one ever saw a "more lavish court" than that of Henry II, and it cost more than 2,500,000 francs* to make it run, according to stories told at the time.[25] Expenses were reduced during the regimes of the lackluster sons of Henry II, and everybody had much less fun. This was the tragic period, however, of the Wars of Religion, which destroyed a great portion of France's gentlemen in a Catholic-Protestant conflict that was more political than religious.

The Court was wherever you could find the King. In the time of Francis I this was likely to be almost any place in his realm. He was probably the most ambulatory king France ever had; Henry II was more inclined to restrict his journeys

* The livre and franc were used interchangeably, and represented the same monetary unit for the period, though the livre was a term in more general use early in the century. Cotgrave in his *Dictionarie* (London, 1611) says the livre of Tours is the "most ordinarie French pound," and that it is worth two English shillings. The franc, which became the official monetary unit in Henry III's reign, was a silver coin weighing a little more than fourteen grams and would be worth, at the present price of silver, around thirty cents. The franc was divided into twenty sous. The crown contained from three to six livres.

to a few preferred châteaux. Francis I, on the other hand, was continually on the move, and ambassadors who were attached to his court were necessarily almost constantly in the saddle, a circumstance that made them lament the financial strain of providing more horses than they could afford. As for horses, France produced not many of her own, except some hackneys from Brittany for the ladies. The more spirited steeds came from the Low Countries and Germany. It must have been, therefore, quite a problem in equine logistics to assemble the eight to twelve thousand horses necessary for Francis I's court to get on the march. And this number did not take into consideration the mules and carts needed for the timid and infirm. Cellini, who was never disposed to understatement, said that when he tried to keep up with Francis I's moving train, it was composed of more than twelve thousand horses and in time of peace eighteen thousand men. On the road, they camped in tents and were often uncomfortable.[26] The fine château of Chambord, with its great assemblage of stables, was taxed to capacity and more when the Court descended on it in full force.

Francis I, like many other French monarchs, did not enjoy being cooped up in Paris. The royal residences, Les Tournelles and the old Louvre, were not spacious or comfortable enough for the "chivalric king." In addition, the river Seine, which had become for all practical purposes a common sewer, was an imposition on royal nostrils. The streets of Paris, too, were crowded and muddy and full of the various projects of the merchants who needed money to meet the royal levies. Fontainebleau, some thirty miles south of Paris, with the legend of its spring and its nymph, its frescoes by Primaticcio, Rosso, and Niccolò dell' Abbate, with its forest and vistas, was part of the answer to this problem of odors and elbow room. Saint-Germain-en-Laye, on the hill overlooking Paris, and the Château Madrid, on the outskirts of the city, were pleasant spots for the King and his gentlemen if they wanted to be closer in.[27] Anet, with its forest and Diane de Poitiers, was just about the only château that Henry II needed. But Francis I was likely to put everybody on a horse at a moment's notice and head for the valley of the Loire.* The twelve volumes of Francis' collected ordonnances and acts show, from the variety of places in which these edicts were signed, how much Francis traveled over his kingdom. And he preferred to take every man, woman, and child at Court along, his prime favorites keeping pace with him in a fairly compact group and the rest trailing behind in a lengthy train.

In the very first year of his reign, Francis dragged his court to the big château of Amboise for the marriage festivities of the Duc de Lorraine and Renée de Bourbon — and this meant that Amboise was completely full of "princes, princesses, ladies and young ladies, nobles and gentlemen." The young King felt that things were getting a trifle dull; so he sent several of his best huntsmen, who were expert in the ways of wild beasts, into the forest of Amboise to catch in nets a very wild boar at least four years old — an age which would mark him as being dangerously mature. The huntsmen managed to ensnare the boar and put him in a heavy box. Francis' idea was that he would take his sword and "fight him, man against boar, in front of the ladies." He was dissuaded from this risky operation by the Queen and Louise de Savoie. As a substitute for it, lifelike mannequins were rigged up in the courtyard of the château and the boar was released in the open area while everybody watched his reactions from the galleries above, including the King "with his gentlemen." The boar smashed the mannequins to bits, and then in his fury started running around the courtyard. The four stairways leading up to the galleries had been blocked with heavy coffers. The boar knocked over these obstacles in one of the stairways and charged up into the first gallery, while the feminine occupants thereof cried out in terror. The boar drove straight at the King. Francis I, cool and unperturbed, pushed everybody behind him, and waited for the beast "with as complete an assurance as if he had seen coming toward him a demoiselle." Five or six of the King's gentlemen moved up to help him, but he brushed them aside and drew his "good strong sword," which he always wore.

* The river Loire was at this time a great traffic artery, and not full of sand as it is now.

The boar's attack was determined: at a distance of about two yards, it looked as though his charge might lay open the royal thigh. However, the King sidestepped this thrust and drove his sword all the way through the boar's chest. The beast wavered, tottered back down the stairway, and fell dead in the courtyard while the upper-bracket audience cheered the King. . . This is exactly the way it all happened, according to Nicole Sala, formerly a maître d'hôtel of Louis XII, who saw the whole episode "with his own eyes," and never had he gazed on a more assured countenance than that of the "genteel King Francis." [28]

Life with Francis I and his gentlemen was not likely to be boring, whatever château or locality might be the momentary habitat of the Court. The escapade that took place at the village of Romorantin must have had everybody talking because it is recorded by several chroniclers.[29] The King and his retinue, after having made a little sojourn at Amboise around Christmas, went on north a few miles to spend the *fête des Rois* (or Twelfth Night) of 1521 * at Romorantin. It all started when the news came to Francis that the Comte de Saint-Pol in his house nearby had just chosen a king for the festival: some courtier had already by chance found in the Twelfth Night cake the large bean that made him king for the day, a gay ceremony that is still done in France on the sixth of January. The King, in high good spirits, decided "with the young gentlemen of his court" to challenge the authority of this king that had got his crown so easily. Saint-Pol and a group in his domain accepted the challenge, and laid in a supply of ammunition to defend the temporarily royal castle against the besiegers. The defense material consisted of a "prodigious quantity of snowballs, eggs, and apples," which turned out not to be enough to repel the assault, for the attackers were soon pushing in the doors and the ammunition was all gone. In the excitement, someone snatched a burning chunk of wood from a fireplace upstairs and threw it out a window. It struck the King on the side of the head, wounding

* According to the old style calendar, which did not start the new year until Easter.

him quite seriously. Nevertheless, he would permit no investigations to be made as to who had thrown the almost deadly missile, saying that if he indulged in such tomfoolery, he would have to take his chances on any accident that might arrive. It seems likely that the episode caused the King to have a permanent scar on his cheek, which he covered with a beard — and thus popularized beards at Court. The whole affair worried Louise de Savoie very much: she would have been a "lost woman," she said, if the King had died; but motherly solicitude was not enough to keep Francis I from tearing around with his gentlemen.

Paris was a good place for temporary diversion. Francis would often go riding around the city with an escort of his gentlemen, with a mask and the darkness hiding his royal features. Stories of these escapades got around and the legend of the iron dealer's beautiful wife and the malady she supposedly bequeathed to the King evidently had broad circulation. In any case, a certain Monsieur Cruche put on a number of little plays in the Place Maubert, some with symbolic significance. He had a magic lantern, through which all sorts of things could be seen, among them a *poule* * which was being nourished on a salamander — and the *poule* had something about her "which could kill ten men." The King, whose salamanders were becoming better known all the time, heard of Cruche's little dramatic diversion, and did not really care for what was told him about it. He therefore sent "eight or ten of his principal gentlemen" to the Chasteau tavern, rue de la Juiverie, in Paris for supper; part of their entertainment was Monsieur Cruche with his little playlet of the *poule* and the salamander. The gentlemen were not particularly amused, either, by Monsieur Cruche's dramatic efforts. They were so little amused, in fact, that they gave him a sound thrashing and almost threw him in the Seine — which they would have done except for his priest's tonsure.[30]

Henry II, while still Dauphin, was involved in many bits of roughhousing with the gentlemen around the Court, but never got his picture in a magic lantern. A tragic episode happened

* *Poule*, literally, "chicken"; by extension, "woman (of easy virtue)."

in 1546 at the château of La Roche-Guyon near Paris, involving "the young gentlemen around the person of Monseigneur le Dauphin." It was in connection with another snowball fight, since there was a great deal of snow on the ground at the time. Some of the young men around the Dauphin were the defenders of a "castle," while others attacked it with snowballs. In the melee, the seigneur d'Enghien, François de Bourbon, started out of the house and was struck in the head by a heavy chest that some ill-advised person pushed out the window. From this injury the young gentleman died; and it was a great loss, since he was much beloved, even by his enemies in war.[31]

In the peregrinations of the Court, all was not amusement of a competitive nature, with snowballs and wild boars and fortified castles to be stormed. Along the route of the royal column, the various cities through which it passed staged brilliant receptions to receive the King. The more in advance a city had notice of the arrival of the royal procession, the more elaborate was the reception. These royal entrees were occasions for the exchanges of dazzlement on the part of the King and his ladies and gentlemen, and the city dwellers who received them. The King might on occasions be paying a special visit to a given city in commemoration of a specific event, and not just passing through. This could happen very easily with metropolises like Lyon, Paris, or Rouen. In such a case, the preparations on the part of the urban population for the royal entree were nothing short of super-colossal — and the King had all his gentlemen properly booted and spurred and brightly gleaming as they rode in.

The entree of Francis I into Paris after his coronation in Rheims was, as has already been seen, a very impressive affair. Some idea of the effect of it on the King's gentlemen may be gained from a description of what Charles, Duc de Bourbon, and Connétable de France, wore as he accompanied the King through the various stages of the reception. This account comes from the secretary of the Connétable and is not likely to be an understatement: "It [the entree] was the most triumphant that had ever been seen. At this entree Monsieur de

Bourbon was very richly attired, and so were his horse and his squires, pages, and lackeys; and the said gentleman was still more so at the King's supper in the palace, where he wore a long robe made up from twelve *aunes* * of cloth of gold (which had cost two hundred eighty gold crowns an *aune*, in cash), trimmed with fur of sable martin, and his hat was weighed down with jewels to the value of one hundred thousand crowns." At the jousts that followed Monsieur de Bourbon wore "cloth of gold" and "crimson velours." He must have been a splendorous spectacle; unluckily, he was wounded in the left arm and could not continue the competitions.[32]

The theme of the triumphal arch, a favorite with the Romans and Italians, came to be used very frequently in the royal entrees before 1550. The King and his gentlemen, especially at an entree into Paris, would ride through arch after arch erected for the occasion. Philibert Delorme, the great architect and sculptor of the period, devised a fine arch for Anet and also one for the tomb of Francis I at Saint-Denis — these latter, obviously, were permanent applications in stone of the arch concept. Another popular motif for an entree was that of the triumphal chariot filled with mythological deities like Mercury, Juno, and Minerva, or a chariot occupied by Mars to symbolize the King's victories in the field. The equestrian statue, also a symbol of triumph, was used many times, too, as part of the setting for a royal entree. When Francis I came into Rouen in 1517, where he received ambassadors from Scotland, there had been erected of him (and for him) a simulated bronze statue on a rearing horse. Unfortunately, in the festivities attendant to this reception, a certain seigneur de Gaillarboys, while making his live horse rear and caper, fell off and broke his leg, which had to be amputated because "it got fire in it." The gentleman finally died, an unexpected casualty to a moment of pageantry. There was a tremendous reception in Paris in 1518 for some ambassadors from England. The King marched in a big procession with his royal archers, followed by his Swiss guards, followed by his "two hundred gentlemen each one having on his shoulder his baton with a

* The old measure, *aune*, was around forty-five inches.

falcon's beak." High Mass was said in the cathedral of Notre Dame, there were a number of banquets, jousts were held before the Hôtel des Tournelles, and the Bastille dripped from its crenelated walls handsome hangings in the colors of the King, namely, white, tan, and black. Inside Notre Dame there were other brilliant draperies, which had among them a shining raised salamander that stood out from its background because it was embroidered in thread of gold.[33] It must have been a colorful affair also when Francis I and his gentlemen met Henry VIII of England in 1521 on the Field of the Cloth of Gold. French chroniclers of the event, strangely enough, give an unexpected paucity of details.

When the two little royal hostages, the Dauphin and the Duc d'Orléans, came back in 1530 from over four years of captivity in Spain, the town of Bayonne at the frontier gave them a gladsome reception. Francis I and his gentlemen, as well as Louise de Savoie, were there. An ingenious bridge had been constructed so that no one could tell whether he was on the land or water, in a street or in a château; and the city was hung with artificial skies and tapestries, there were plays and tableaux, nymphs came down out of the heavens, and gentlemen in a variety of dress threw coins to the people. Bordeaux made most elaborate preparations when in 1530 the city entertained Francis I, his new Queen Eleonora (Queen Claude had died in 1524), and his gentlemen. Three theaters were built for the diversion of the Court, and Eleonora was presented with a little ship made entirely of gold. Paris welcomed Francis I on his return from Marseille in 1534 with, among other things, sixteen days of jousts around the Louvre — and a young gentleman named Monsieur de Fontaines was so seriously injured in them that everybody thought he was dead.[34]

Lyon erected two victory columns for Henry II in 1548, and the river Saône as it ran through the city was the scene of a mock combat between galleys of Roman design, commanded by two feminine captains, one dressed in the King's colors of black and white and one in Catherine de' Medici's color of green. Neptune and other sea deities rose out of the waves to take a hand in the proceedings. Not only would artists like Philibert Delorme and Jean Goujon lend their talents to the preparations for these royal entrees, but also scholars and men of letters like Thomas Sebillet, Jean Daurat, and Ronsard lent theirs. Maurice Scève, the Platonist poet, was director of the Lyon entree in 1548.

One of the finest of all entrees was that staged for Henry II and his court by the city of Paris on June 16, 1549 (though Rouen's setting up in 1550 of a whole Brazilian forest on the banks of the Seine, with parrots, monkeys, and three hundred savages is not to be tossed off lightly). The 1549 entree had five arches erected between the gate of Saint-Denis and Notre Dame. Vieilleville, in his *Mémoires*, has given a description of the splendid spectacle: in the regal procession, there were two thousand pages marching with their masters — and "the Parisians, on their side, in order not to seem ungracious to their sovereign prince, accomplished marvels to receive him well; for there was not a square, precinct, or intersection which was not decorated, either with a theater, or with a triumphal arch, or with a pyramid, or with an obelisk . . . gold and azure [cloths] were not used sparingly, and they were decorated, too, with festoons and trophies of war, which were illustrated here and there by the very learned Greek and Latin verses of the royal poet, Daurat, and by the odes and royal songs in French of the divine Ronsard." [35]

The poets as well as the writers of prose had many things in their own compositions to say about these entrees. Ronsard, in a poem called *Avant-entrée du Roi*, foresees the brilliance of this 1549 entree of Henry II into Paris. The gifted Ronsard, prince of poets, imagines in advance a great tourney, with the sound of trumpets, the shining harness of the horses, the crash of the lances, and the murmuring of the ladies — and the falling to earth of any knight who opposes "my great King." Saint-Gelais tells the story of gentlemen dressed as Amazons who presented the ladies of Catherine de' Medici's suite with gold coins as the Queen came into Lyon in 1548. Henri Estienne, with his disposition to decry the decadence of the mores of his age, deals not only with the splendor of the royal entrees, but also stresses their license — bedecked oxen ambling along in the processions, for example, with women on their backs more naked than Lady Godiva.[36] 1549, incidentally, was a very gala period, full of rejoicing and pompous entrees, since Henry II and Catherine de' Medici had had a second son born at Saint-Germain. Paris spent a great deal of time during that year watching the Court come into the city, and preparing for the King and his gentlemen proper tourneys, ballets, and festivals — "all the vain pastimes that an ingenious and opulent idleness can imagine." [37]

The Court, naturally, was not always on the march or making official entrees into the urban centers of the realm. It remained reasonably stationary from time to time and with all its ladies and gentlemen, its poets, artists, musicians, and functionaries, it was a "marvelously large Court." Anne de Bretagne, says Brantôme, was the first monarch to begin dressing up the Court with ladies, and under her they were well and wisely cared for. Anne also had one hundred Breton gentlemen who awaited her commands on the terrace outside her apartments at Blois. However, it was with Francis I that first appeared the brilliant mixture of ladies and gentlemen, destined to be a distinctive feature henceforth of the French Court. Francis is supposed to have made the observation that a Court without women is like a year without spring time, or a spring without roses. The "great King Francis" said, in addition, that the ladies at Court made his gentlemen as valiant as did their swords; therefore, "a Court without ladies is a Court without any Court." [38] The ladies who were there were of good families, were demoiselles of reputation, and shed their radiance over the Court like goddesses from the heavens. Francis demanded both beauty and intelligence from his feminine entourage; qualities that the King's first favorite, Françoise de Châteaubriant — if the crayon portrait of her at the Bibliothèque Nationale and the poetic exchanges she had with Francis I are any indications — had to a superlative degree. The King, who knew the genealogies and family backgrounds of his gentlemen, liked for them to be able to converse with genteel ladies. Out of the larger group of ladies, Francis had a "small band," selected for their beauty, charm, and riding skill, who went with him and his gentlemen on weekend jaunts. Catherine de' Medici belonged to this group and it was she who popularized a lady's riding with a leg thrown over the horn of the saddle. It would be unrealistic to suggest that the conversations between the ladies and gentlemen on these excursions did not reach a certain stage of intimacy. Nevertheless, lines of demarcation in the King's services were rather sharply drawn, and on a different level were the operations of the limited number of prostitutes under royal control.

Catherine de' Medici had an even larger feminine court, which consisted of more than three hundred ladies. They were all beautiful and virtuous, according to reports, and a gentleman could talk to any one of them every day outside the Queen's private rooms, if he did it properly and modestly. But any gentleman who failed to maintain suitable decorum was threatened with banishment. Of this charming aggregation of femininity around the Queen, Brantôme lists by name one hundred ten ladies and seventy-four damsels — all of whom were beautiful, pleasant, and accomplished — and he is apologetic for any omissions he may have made. It was a fine sight to see when all this bevy of beauties got on their hackneys and went riding with the Queen.

Madame de Châteaubriant became the royal favorite early in the reign of Francis I. Jean de Laval, sire de Châteaubriant, and his wife, Françoise, were called to the Court from Brittany soon after the beginning of the year 1517. The reason was that this province needed to be more solidly tied to the Crown through the presence of its gentlemen at the royal center of things. Jean de Laval was a good soldier, a captain of one of the King's ordonnance companies, and his services, unfortunately, were needed in the campaigns in Italy. Françoise de Châteaubriant, beautiful in her middle twenties and pleasantly knowledgeful in Latin and Italian, became the King's preferred before the end of 1517 and remained so until 1526, when Francis I returned from his year of captivity in Spain. During this time she had occupied a ceremonial position just behind the princesses of the royal house of France. However, Louise de Savoie disliked her cordially, and the

King's Mother arranged for a bright-eyed lass named Anne de Pisselieu to be in the party at Bordeaux in 1526 to welcome the King on his return. Anne, while still barely in her teens, had admired the beautiful jewels of Françoise de Châteaubriant, the gifts of the King and some of them inscribed with tender sentiments. Francis I, after an affectionate reunion with his mother at Bordeaux, turned to greet the other members of the welcoming group, and his eye fell on Anne de Pisselieu, now eighteen years of age and ready for conquests. Françoise de Châteaubriant, a tottering antique of thirty-two, had not made the trip — which was a mistake. In the ensuing competition for the King's favors, Françoise lost. She had been robbed of very strong support when the Maréchal de Lautrec, her elder brother who was very influential with the King, died of the pestilence in Naples in 1528. It was at about this time that she left the Court, to live in dignity at her château in Brittany. Anne de Pisselieu was made Duchesse d'Etampes in 1529. She asked to have the royal jewels that had been given to Françoise de Châteaubriant returned to her, Anne, and Francis I sent one of his gentlemen to pick them up. Françoise said she would need a little time to get them together; when they were handed over to the gentleman, they had been melted into ingots of gold and not one tender message on them had escaped the neutralizing heat of the furnace's fires. When the heart of a noble woman is scorned, contemporaries said in connection with this episode, it is capable of doing "amazing things." The clever Diane de Poitiers, though nineteen years the senior of Henry II, never had any problem of keeping sentimental trinkets out of a rival's hands. Her ascendancy over the King was never challenged.

A great era of sumptuosity began with Francis I. He ate and drank copiously himself, and slept splendidly with it all. His banquets were in the manner of Lucullus, and great dinners were given in the field as well as in the palaces. The King was very brilliant in his dress, "which is trimmed and decorated with lace, rich in precious stones and ornamentations; the doublets even are intricately wrought and sewn in gold; his under shirt is very sheer, and shows through the opening in the doublet according to the fashion in France." [39] One of the reasons given by chroniclers for the capture of Francis at Pavia was the King's propensity for sartorial brilliance: he was wearing a jacket in cloth of silver, which made him a shining target for the enemy. The Dauphin, though more somber in dress than his father, put on quite an exhibition in a tourney in 1545 where he was garbed in a motif of white with a silver crescent on his head, "because of Diane de Poitiers." He was riding against the Comte de Laval, who carried out a fashion color note of incarnadine.[40]

It must have been much more pleasant to stay with the ladies at Court than to fight the mud and rain and Charles V's Imperials in Italy. Clément Marot, the poet of "elegant trifling" who was valet de chambre of Francis I, thought so in his forty-sixth epistle where he says "good-by to the Court, and to the ladies . . ." as he follows the King off to the wars of 1537. Saint-Gelais has a poem, *To the Gentlemen of the Court*, wherein the gentlemen are chided for their absence by the damsels who have been left behind. The gentlemen, for their part, certainly could not have enjoyed being away from the Court, because that was where the music and the dancing and the frescoes and the poetry and the ladies were, where Saint-Gelais chanted to his own accompaniment on the lute verses to the happy violets that rested on the bosom of Diane de Poitiers,* and Ronsard read aloud from his own sonnets. It was there that Saint-Gelais dedicated verses to Diane de Poitiers and Henry II's daughter, who was known affectionately as "madame la Bastarde"; and Ronsard, in later memory of all these happy hours, around 1565, wrote a poem to Catherine de' Medici asking her to renew the round of festivities at Fontainebleau.[41]

There had been some big parties at Fontainebleau. One occurred in 1551 when the King entertained with a fine dance there a delegation of Germans: "When the dinner was finished, the ball began as the Queen appeared with her ladies in waiting and other demoiselles, all so richly adorned, orna-

* Diane liked Saint-Gelais and the fine poet, Joachim du Bellay, better than she did Ronsard.

mented, and attired with every grace and beauty that these Germans were astounded at so rare and marvelous a sight, and one not usual in their region. And after the royal dance, in couples, which the King had begun and led, some German dances were played for the visitors. . ." The Prince d'Orange, who had some fancy steps, would have won the prize if he had managed to keep in time with the music. After this activity there was a collation of sweets and jams.[42]

Catherine de' Medici was herself very fond of dancing, and also of spectacular ballets, staged with superlative elaboration. She liked, in addition, comedies and tragedies, but after *Sophonisbe*, "composed by M. de Saint-Gelais * and very well acted by the ladies, damsels, and gentlemen of her court," Catherine no longer favored the presentation of tragedies because she thought they brought bad luck.[43] *Sophonisbe* was performed at Blois late in 1559 or early in 1560. As a bit of relaxation from political problems, a variety of spectacular entertainment was staged at Fontainebleau by the Queen Mother in 1564. There were some "excellent banquets to the accompaniment of delightful music rendered by most life-like mermaids in the canals of the garden, along with other pleasant and agreeable diversions of an amorous and war-like combination." There was a big fight between twelve Greeks and twelve Trojans for the hand of a beautiful lady, followed by a tragi-comedy acted by ladies and gentlemen of the Court. And the next day there was in the garden an enchanted tower, which held imprisoned several delectable demoiselles, guarded by some "infernal Furies" and two huge giants. The King and his brother attacked the giants and conquered them, released the charming maidens from the enchanted tower, and the whole structure went up in smoke.[44] Brantôme describes a number of these ornate displays, including one given at Bayonne by the Queen Mother to show the Spaniards that France was not ruined by the Wars of Religion, but still had a number of brave and skillful gentlemen left.

The era of decadence under Henry III, "by the grace of his Mother, the uncertain king of France," is revealed in the

* Saint-Gelais translated it from Trissino's Italian original.

scathing denunciations of Pierre de L'Estoile, who says that royal ballets and masked balls went on in spite of the suffering of France, and that the King appeared at them "ordinarily dressed as a woman, with his doublet open at the neck revealing a pearl necklace and three linen collarettes, just like the ladies at his court wore at that time." In 1577 Henri III had a banquet at the château of Plessis-lès-Tours, where the service was done by the ladies dressed in green silk as men; and the Queen Mother shortly thereafter staged a big dinner at Chenonceaux, where the "most beautiful and virtuous ladies of the Court" did the serving in almost no clothes.[45] L'Estoile, the stern critic of his age, sees in such things signs of the nation's decline.

In the midst of this brilliance of setting, of complication of structure, of ornateness of exterior that made up the Court, a gentleman had a difficult time picking his way. Many of the outer and visible refinements that made up the art of living around the King had come up from Italy. Much of the luxury of the Orient had entered the Western world through Italy, where the primary clearing house was Florence. It was there that commerce, culture, and luxury went hand in hand. It was Florence that perfected the silk industry, created gold brocades and velours, and showed the way for similar endeavors in the French cities of Lyon, Montpellier, and Avignon. It was from Italy also that many ideas on the gentleman's education, manners, and behavior found their route into France — and these ideas, particularly as they were expressed in such influential treatises as the *Courtier*, were in part concerned with the gentleman at Court.

The Italian gentleman of the Renaissance, who carried to a high peak of perfection the art of making his way in society and who possessed a remarkable sense of elegance in the midst of violence, felt that the Frenchman of the period — that is, at the beginning of the sixteenth century — was rather crude. The latter had not yet learned the art of delicate subtlety, the superb finesse of devious insinuation by which the man of virtuosity got around obstacles, without bumping them full in the face and without getting a stiletto in the back. As for the French and their crudities, the Pope was about to send a Cellini creation of the horn of a unicorn to Francis I as a gift. However, the Holy Father was advised by a man from Milan not to waste such a fine piece of designing on the gross French who were incapable of appreciating the delicate artistry of Benvenuto.[46] In the second book of the *Courtier* there is a discussion of the progress of a man at Court by virtue of his own merit; it is agreed that this is an ideal situation, but not always an actual one, especially at the French Court, where progress is the result of presumption. The Italians were constantly referring to the French of the period as gross. Yet a man like Cellini, despite his difficulties with the Duchesse d'Etampes and others at the French Court, looked back longingly after he left at the generous and cultured patronage of Francis I, who conversed with him in Italian. In any case, there is no doubt that many of the gentleman's concepts of proper activity at Court came from Italian centers like Urbino, Ferrara, or Florence.

Machiavelli, a realist if there ever was one and not too much concerned with the niceties of gentility, is complimentary of the French gentleman's relations with his king, and feels that France would be a very difficult nation to conquer because of the independence of the nobility. There is a fine balance between the Crown, the nobility, and the people, which makes France one of the best ordered kingdoms of the period.[47] Cavalli gives another slant on the situation in France when he states that "some peoples were born to obey," and the French are in this category. The Crown is getting richer and richer, and the nobility more and more subservient. Lippomano, on the other hand — and he is one of the most delightful of the Italian commentators on the French sixteenth century — is of the opinion that the French monarchs are so affable it is not astonishing that they are beloved by their people, and that few Frenchmen want to live outside their own land. The Valois kings have marked the age of virility in France, and with them there has been a colorful life at Court. However, the French gentleman is naturally haughty and full of pride, with something barbarous interwoven; he is bold in the execution of enterprises, insolent in good fortune, careless of other people, ungrateful, and lacking in fidelity. But it is advantageous to be on friendly terms with him.[48]

The gentleman at Court, despite Italian comments to the contrary, in most cases carried out his duties loyally and faithfully. A king like Francis I or Henry II, with every power to sponsor brilliant careers at Court or bring about signal disgraces, inspired great personal loyalties. When the Connétable de Bourbon, having gone over to the armies of Charles V and after having assisted in a French defeat in Italy in the early 1520's, sought to rally the French gentlemen around the standards of the Emperor, he met with no success. He did learn, from his endeavor, "better to know the character of the Frenchman, who is always faithful to his Prince, and always ready to sacrifice for him everything that he holds most dear, his tranquility, his fortune, and his life." Monluc, who spent so much of his life in wars, told his soldiers that they should employ all their ability and intelligence in battle, for the King would certainly find out how they performed — and he would also know if they had not done their best. François de Bourbon (later killed in 1546 by the chest falling on him in the incident at La Roche-Guyon *) thanked Monluc on one occasion for his help in winning a military victory, and promised to speak to the King about it. Monluc, who was not always in royal favor, replied that such an act was the greatest kindness in the world that could be done to a gentleman. Progress at Court depended so often on these incidental recommendations. Monluc regrets, despite his own difficulties, that his two sons did not live to take their place at Court, for he thinks they would have had qualities that would have made them beloved by the King.[49]

Francis I was very alert as to what was going on in his royal circle and was very quick to show his gentlemen his appreciation or disapproval. As a general policy, for example, he had proclaimed to the sound of a trumpet throughout Paris that only his gentlemen were worthy to carry swords or other

* See page 61 of this chapter.

weapons. And then he underwrote the seigneur de Bonnivet's ornate trip to England with twenty-five well-filled coffers, all covered with "crimson velours." On his return after Pavia he gave out a number of rewards: Monsieur de Brion was made an admiral, the Comte de Saint-Pol was made governor of Dauphiné, and a few gentlemen were made marshals of France. The two great orders, the Order of Saint Michael and the Order of the Holy Ghost,* were prime honors given out by the King, though their ranks got pretty full by the end of the century. Francis I was equally ready to issue punishment at any time to a recalcitrant noble, and sometimes he did it personally. His ears were ever keen to any insidious propaganda against the Crown. The story is related at least twice in the century, by Brantôme and in the seventeenth story of Marguerite de Navarre's *Heptaméron*, of the famous swordsman, Comte Guillaume de Saxe, and his veiled threat to kill the King if Francis were ever without the protection of his royal guard. The King heard of the Count's whispering campaign and shortly thereafter arranged a hunt in which the Count was invited to participate. Francis allowed the other gentlemen of the party to ride far ahead while he and Guillaume de Saxe remained alone in the deep woods. He then drew his sword and asked the Count if he knew anyone who would like to challenge the might of that single weapon, it being unaccompanied by anything but the breezes in the trees. The Count understood the reference, but backed down in confusion; shortly thereafter he left the Court.[50]

Many varieties of opinion were offered in the sixteenth century concerning the gentleman in the surroundings of the Court. Saint-Gelais, who was not always serious but who knew the Court thoroughly from personal association with it, says with a sober air in one of his epistles: "The wiser and more worthy a prince is, the more intelligent and noble gentlemen he has around him, and in his palace men of honor rather than a horde of valets are held in esteem." Ronsard, who said he learned to "tickle the ears of kings" by listening to Saint-Gelais but who laments that he has followed the

* See Chapter Nine.

Court a long time and got no reward, praises Henry II, nevertheless, and royalty in general: "He who does honor to kings does honor to God: princes and kings hold the highest place next to the Deity." In passing, Ronsard gives some advice to kings on the operation of a monarchy: it must be operated on the basis of reason and virtue, the upper classes and the people must live together in harmony, and money must be spent wisely; if a prince is unable to govern his own household he need not expect to have the skill to govern a nation. A very sage comment on the association of the king with his gentlemen is given by Etienne Pasquier, the great scholar and chronicler of many phases of life in the sixteenth century. Pasquier says that life at Court and the relation of the king with his gentlemen is very much like a game of chess. The gentlemen are altogether like the knights on a chess board: they can leap about in all kinds of unexpected directions and check the movements of the king. Therefore, "there is nothing a king has so much to fear in his state as the revolt of the nobility." [51]

Other opinions, some light and some disillusioned, were presented during the century concerning the gentleman and his position at Court. One was to the effect that, though it is very delightful to hunt and fish, there is more fortune and honor in following the Court. And, too, royal grandeur must be given its due respect and service, because everybody bows to a king but a horse. On the other hand, Montaigne asks in a more serious tone: "How many gentlemen have rejected and abandoned their solid holdings in life, and are still doing it, to pursue the whim of the favor of kings!" If these gentlemen carried on their lives in the dignity of their own lands and their own provinces, they would scarcely ever come in contact with the Court and its devious processes. For anyone who takes a post at a prince's court, it is "good-bye pleasures; such a man is worried, harried, disturbed, opposed, suspected, made afraid; a dream, a word, a woman may destroy his position of favor, and may also involve the loss of his honor and his life." However, this was not the general feeling in the time of Francis I, when "it was useless to be valiant and accomplish as many fine exploits in war as Caesar, if you were not known at Court or there was no one there to give you a little push." A prince's crown and his court, it is true, do not protect him from such things as the sun and rain, and he is not too different from a "man of moderate fortune" — but he would be different, naturally, from an humble peasant, since France at this time was not a rail-splitter's republic, and the vulgus was held to be of little worth.[52]

The competition among the gentlemen at Court was always very keen and not always carried on in the loftiest spirit of good clean sport. The situation in this respect got much worse as the century progressed, and we find the Third Estate in the reign of Henry III complaining that money is too influential in getting favors from the King, and that there are too many women following their husbands to Court. Monluc would like to see the King "stop up the mouths of the ladies who do so much talking at Court," since they cause infinite trouble with their babbling and gossiping. Throughout the century, the perquisites and prerogatives of rank and office were highly regarded and jealously insisted upon. The Connétable de Bourbon, for example, at the dinner for the King after Francis I's coronation in Rheims, stood rigidly at attention by the King (a constable's privilege) all during the affair, his drawn sword in hand, "without budging from his place." At the coronation of Henry II, there was some confusion in the order of banners. The banner of the Connétable Anne de Montmorency was not given the precedence that his office demanded, and Montmorency was very unpleasant about it.[53]

There are many "rare men" that this century has produced, says Montaigne toward its end — men like the Duc de Guise, who died at Orléans, or the late Marshal Strozzi, or the great jurist and chancellor, Michel de l'Hospital, or the poets, Ronsard and Du Bellay, or the noble Duke of Alba and the Connétable de Montmorency. And yet, despite all these noble lives, "dissimulation is one of the most notable qualities of the century." Ronsard, in a long epistle dedicated to the Cardinal de Lorraine, attributes to the Cardinal all the virtues of gentility, but praises him particularly because he knows how to deal with the "monsters of the Court." The prince of poets in the final years of his life became disgusted with the distortions of Henry III's regime. He wrote a letter around 1577 from his château close to the Loire, La Possonière, to a friend in Paris. In it he says that he has heard Henry III is coming to Blois and Tours; therefore, he is fleeing to Paris because he "hates the Court as though it were death." [54]

Disgust with the latter-day courtiers is expressed by an old warrior who says he has no patience with these men who pretend a friendship one for the other when each would like nothing better than to see the other destroyed. They "assume a welcoming countenance, greeting and embracing one another as though they were the best friends in the world. I have never been able to carry on this sort of business; I have shown on my face what I have felt in my heart." [55] This sounds like a gentleman and soldier of the old school, incorruptible and valiant; his species became rare before the end of the century.

The gentleman of the reigns of Francis I and Henry II, the golden age of the Renaissance gentleman, was, then, a significant part of the Court of his king. He was a person of tremendous energy, vigorous in body, and very individualized in his many activities. He has been called a "fighter," fundamentally, and "a man of action." [56] He may have lacked the qualities of measure and calm, of temperance and restraint in his judgments that Castiglione would like to have in his ideal adviser to a prince. He may have been deficient in the ritualistic scraping and bowing demanded by a monarch like Louis XIV. But he was a man.

V

Manners and Dress

THE GENTLEMAN TOOK ON CERTAIN REFINEMENTS of manners and dress that his medieval ancestor, the knight, would not have bothered about. For example, the gentleman learned to eat with a fork, an instrument that was not a usual part of a table setting in the Middle Ages, and he became more and more familiar with a napkin, an article that in an earlier epoch had been virtually unknown. Plates, some of them coated with the New World's silver, came to be used for individual service instead of the flat piece of bread on which the medieval knight placed his hunk of meat after he had sliced it off the communal chunk in the middle of the table. This bread, on which the meat (or fowl) had rested with its juices, was later in normal practice given to the poor — which must have been a rather tasty gift. The gentleman also became acquainted in the sixteenth century with a handkerchief, whereas his earlier counterpart had simply used the back of his sleeve for nasal necessities. Many of these niceties, naturally, came into France from Italy where personal grooming, particularly in Venice, had long been a matter of importance. There was an opinion among the Italians that the French were rather dirty, just as there was an opinion among the French that the Italians were rather devious. Unless a man can keep himself clean and neat in appearance, said the Italians, he should not seek to mix with genteel company: he should spend his time herding sheep.[1] By the sixteenth century, the French were very much of the same point of view, and agreed that more attention should be given to the individual's appearance and demeanor in a more luxurious décor of living. The creation of more and more silks and velvets, the discovery of more and more gold and silver and precious stones, all make the gentleman's façade more and more shining and made implicit a refurbishing of his manners to match. The bourgeois, too, was constantly progressing in financial solidarity and the ability to obtain these luxuries, and edicts had to be passed from time to time to prevent him from looking too much like a gentleman.

One of the first things welcomed into France from Italy was material made of silk. Everybody wanted silk. From the late fifteenth century, therefore, periodic orders were issued by the Crown to limit the bourgeois' efforts toward ornateness of silken dress. No demoiselle, unless she was a chatelaine — that is, mistress of a château and therefore of the nobility — could have more than two new dresses a year. Only the nobles with an income of two thousand livres a year could wear silk freely. A lesser noble, even though he did have an annual revenue of two thousand livres, could not wear crimson velours, but he was permitted to garb himself in damask and figured satin. During the sixteenth century there were eight major ordonnances before 1580 against the tendency of sartorial splendor spreading itself too far down the social scale. "Whoever is not a gentleman," said the edict of 1543, could not bedeck himself with "jewelled ornaments, plaques, or buttons of gold." The wives of men in legal and judicial service were limited by a royal edict of 1547 in their use of silk and velvet: they could put these materials only in short jackets and the sleeves of their costumes. Obviously, these decrees, even as those against dueling and gambling, were almost impossible to enforce. It was said many times as the century progressed that "simple gentlemen" dressed as though they were dukes or barons, and it became increasingly harder to distinguish the nobles from the commoners by looking at their exterior coverings. The boundaries of class could be crossed more easily if the clothes worn were appropriate to a movement up the ladder of society.* The situation in the sixteenth century was summed up by Claude Haton in his *Mémoires*: "The bourgeois of the cities have sought to dress, men and women,

* The tradition of clothes making the man still lasts in England and on the Continent more completely than in America, where it is more difficult than in Europe to tell a clerk from the president of a corporation by the cut of his jacket.

in the fashion of our gentlemen, the gentlemen in the sumptuous manner of princes, and the people in the villages in the manner of the bourgeois." [2] The French continued to import up to the middle of the century a large amount of silk and cloth of gold from Italy, and the Genoese and Tuscans made a nice profit out of it, because the French "got tired of wearing the same costume too long." One of the reasons given for the financial difficulties of the nobility toward the end of the century was the progressive elaborateness of dress, both masculine and feminine. Nevertheless, in spite of advancing bourgeois purchasing power, there was still the sentiment that it ought not to be permitted to the "wives of lawyers, counselors, treasurers, bourgeois and other ignoble women to wear velvet hats or dresses and jackets of silk." [3] But the desire for fine clothes pretty well permeated the whole of Europe before 1600. Montaigne complains in 1581 of the German city of Augsburg, first, because there are no beautiful women in it, and then because it is hard to differentiate the noblemen from the bourgeois since the whole masculine population is wearing velvet hats and carrying swords.[4]

Francis I, with his great interest in dress, was fascinated by Italian fashions as he saw them in Italy. He gave his imprint to Italian modes, and the gentlemen at his court followed his lead. Every effort was made to appear handsome; if nature had been careless in granting the qualities of good looks, the gentleman sought to compensate for such deficiencies by elaboration of costume. The doublet — which had formerly been nothing much more than a vest — now became embroidered and form-fitting, brilliant in contrasting colors and slashed sleeves. The snugly-clinging tights were of silk and, with the help of proper stockings, showed off a well-developed leg. The stockings were not yet of silk, however. The outer shorts covered the tights to the middle thigh, where they fitted closely and made a slight bag. The shorts and tights were in contrasting colors and gave a gentleman an opportunity to create some rainbow effects. The cloak, thrown with careless artistry over the gentleman's shoulders, was a shining object of heavy and handsome material, trimmed with fur and lined with silk. The hat of the period of Francis I — and it was no bare-headed era — was flat, wide of brim, and bedecked with plumes. Shoes were of velvet with rounded ends and slashed. A great deal of lace, ribbons, stripes, and furbelows came into vogue to add further elegance to the gentleman.[5] The portraits of Francis I and of other courtiers of the period illustrate these details of masculine raiment. The same sort of decorative brilliance was applied to military and jousting costumes, as can be seen from the attire of the guards-captain Montgommery as well as from that of other gentlemen.*

Before the end of the reign of Francis I, masks had become more and more of an accessory to the toilette. The ladies at the Court wore them first, but they became rather popular with the gentlemen as the century progressed. Henry III and his favorites never went out into the city without having their faces covered. Francis I and his gentlemen normally wore masks, if we can believe the Bourgeois de Paris on the matter,† when they had some mischief up their embroidered sleeves, and not just in imitation of the ladies. These small masks, which were called *loups*, were made of black velvet and lined with white satin. They could be folded neatly into half their size, and needed no device of attachment, it has been claimed, since they stayed on the face by the wearer's holding in the mouth a little glass ball, which was tied by a string to the mask. This technique would have an added effect of changing the voice slightly, and thus increase the element of mystery in any intrigue that might be in the making. The ladies of the Court had first begun the putting on of *loups* to protect their delicate complexions from the sun and the dust of Paris. Masks gradually came to be another mark of the costume of the nobility, and they were forbidden in theory to the commoners. The secretive quality of such a facial covering, incidentally, met with hearty disapproval before the end of the century: "It is a cowardly and low attitude to go around disguised and hidden under a mask, not daring to make oneself known for what one is or to show in public one's face." [6]

* See Figures 1 and 16.

† See Chapter Four, note 30.

With Henry II masculine attire became more somber and severe, though silk stockings were popularized by him to such an extent that thousands of men were wearing them in the next twenty years. Colors became more sober, and black was very much in vogue. The doublet was no longer open to show the chemise, but a starched collarette was put around the neck. Shoes took on more the shape of the foot, and pockets appeared in the short trousers before 1560 — which must have been a big help. The portrait of Henry II himself in the Louvre gives a very good idea of the dress of a gentleman during the reign.

More luxury in dress returned with Charles IX and more distortion and effeminacy came in with Henry III. The doublet of Charles IX's era was touched with ermine at the wrists and collar. The codpiece, which was simply a hooked-on outside device in the time of Francis I, began to be decorated with precious stones. Hats became small velvet toques with Charles IX and Henry III, and were embellished with jewels and sometimes with white plumes. In Henry III's twisted age, men wore a lump in the doublet over their stomachs and walked bent forward, all of which must have given them a very potty silhouette. A scathing description of the royal favorites of this age was offered in 1575: "These fine dandies wore their hair rather long, artificially curled and waved, flowing out from under their little velvet bonnets, in the fashion of women in a brothel; and from their starched linen ruffs that stuck out a half foot from their necks their heads seemed like that of John the Baptist on a plate. The rest of their costume was similarly exaggerated." Also, they were covered with violet powder and heavy scents, and pretty thoroughly smelled up the houses and streets they frequented.[7] Fortunately, Henry IV came along in a few years and changed all this foppish exaggeration, which had reached such a point that a courtier needed twenty-five to thirty fancy suits in order to be in the main current of fashion.

Beards became popular at the court of Francis I, so the story ran, because the King had a scar on his face left over from the snowball fight at Romorantin in 1521. Short hair, since Francis had a handsome forehead, with a full beard was the vogue. This fashion was disappearing by the latter part of the century, or rather it was being reversed, as can be seen in the portraits of Henry III and his favorites. The beards came off and the hair got longer. Montaigne speaks of "the effeminate and cowardly custom" of men letting their hair go uncut. On the other hand, he complains of not being able to find a barber in Italy who could give him a good shave. As for the Italians, despite the fine advice in the *Courtier* about a nobleman's being conservatively dressed and modestly well-groomed, the French thought that the gentlemen from Piedmont were "grossly attired" and the plumes on their hats much too high. The Italians were accused, in fact, of using plumes so profusely that their hats took the place of parasols. Ronsard sees decadence in all such lavish tendencies: when the cities are full of play-actors, when the women start covering their faces with paint, and when the merchants assume the right to wear the clothes of a gentleman, then there is no doubt that "the Republic is sick." [8]

As the century drew to its close, the blame for excesses in manners and dress in the land was put squarely on Henry III and his court. Royal edicts prescribing moderation were said to be of little effect if they were not supported by royal example, since the "inclination of the king serves as law," and "the rest of France takes for guidance what is done at the Court." Therefore, the "monstrous stuffing of the doublet" with its distortion of the masculine figure, the "long feminine tresses" on a man's head, the removal of a gentleman's hat and sword in petty obsequiousness to minor princelings, all these fashions sanctioned by the Court but contrary to the attitude of the old nobility indicate a chink in the solid wall of the strength of the nation.[9]

Even as the theoretical ideal of the best part of the Renaissance was that a gentleman's dress should be elegant without being distorted, so it was with his manners. The ideas that a gentleman should be modest and moderate in actions, courteous and civil in conversation, considerate and cognizant of the rights of others — all points previously treated by the ancients and the Italians — were restated many times during the century. Erasmus' little treatise in Latin on the proper manners of a well-born youngster — the *Civilitas puerilis*, published in 1530 and quickly adapted into French [10] — emphasizes the importance of good manners being learned early in life. Modesty and an inconspicuous fitting into the social milieu are keynotes of the great Dutchman's advice, some of which is very specific. His general conclusion is that a young gentleman must have good manners as a social responsibility; others through the acquisition of good manners can improve their position in society. As for the training of children in the attributes of gentility, Montaigne later in the century suggests to Madame d'Estissac, whose son will one day be a gentleman, that gentleness is very important on the part of parents. The Maréchal de Monluc regretted, says Montaigne, that he had been so harsh on his son who had died on the island of Madeira, for the boy was a "genteel youngster" who had known nothing but sternness from his father. As for the question of moderation, it can be an element of all the gentleman's actions, including such things as chess or court tennis. Such games as these can be played with much greater satisfaction when there is only a moderate concern with winning or losing.[11]

The conversation of a gentleman, his choice of words and manner of speech, offered considerable variety. His language might be refined, or it could be rough according to the standards of most modern drawing rooms. The Italians had much to say about a gentleman's conversation. Castiglione felt that it should be full of color, not flowery or boastful, but with natural jests and conceits. Yet there should be no low words or vile gestures just to create laughter, and contrary to the courtier's essential gentility. Giovanni della Casa was of the same opinion, and thought that dirty words with double meanings were not for a gentleman, who should speak in a well-modulated voice and avoid the language of the gutter. There were nice locutions to be employed — like calling a "harlot" a "woman of the world." Stephano Guazzo, in his long manual on the art of conversing, the *Civile conversatione*, which had four editions in French before the end of the sixteenth century, devoted a large part of the second book to the differences between the language of a gentleman and that of a commoner. Erasmus believed that a young gentleman should learn early to converse in a well-placed tone without attempting to go too fast — which would cause stammering. He should not swear, should avoid the use of obscenities and not smile when he heard an obscene word, but rather pretend that he did not hear it. None of these treatises involving the niceties of conversation received full practical application in an age as lusty as the Renaissance.[12]

The tone of conversation at the Court itself was undoubtedly kept on a level of politeness and refinement fitting to the presence of the monarch and his favorites. Francis I inaugurated the custom of chatting informally with his gentlemen and ladies just after the midday meal. It was then that a scholar like Guillaume Budé might get to the King's ear with a plan for teaching Greek in Paris, or a poet might read some verses recently composed, or Benvenuto Cellini might describe progress on a new statue. The ladies and gentlemen promenaded casually at this time in the King's aura, and practiced the art of conversational subtlety. These informal sessions took place in the gardens of Fontainebleau, or whatever château the King happened to be frequenting, if the weather permitted. Henry II sought to imitate his father in these early afternoon relaxations, and was assisted therein by Catherine de' Medici. The Court after dinner (which was in the middle of the day) would sometimes retire to the Queen's apartments and there conversation lasted for around two hours. The gentlemen were privileged to be present but Catherine saw to it that their talk was proper, and that a high degree of politeness was maintained. After the two-hour conversational interlude, Henry II was likely to indulge in some vigorous outdoor exercise unless it was raining. At night, if there was no formal ball or ceremonial, further conversation was in order between the ladies and gentlemen — usually in pairs, though some general discussion might occur. The whole procedure was tinged with preciosity and flavored with the mannered gallantry of the Court.[13]

Though the Court favored delicacy and restraint in its formal conversational interchanges, there is every reason to suppose that on other occasions a gentleman's language was lusty and rugged. It was preferable for him to talk like a soldier rather than like a pedant, though "modesty and silence" were qualities ofttimes "suitable in conversation." [14] The tellers of tales during the century — men like Rabelais, Noël du Fail, Guillaume Bouchet, or Bonaventure des Périers, as well as a woman like Marguerite de Navarre — all indicate that in most social circles it was legitimate for a man to call a spade a spade. Brantôme comments upon the fact that all nations like to use strong epithets and mighty oaths, even if the Spaniards and Italians are the worst.[15]

The question as to what was the proper talk in the presence of women came in for a good deal of discussion in the sixteenth century. In the second book of the *Courtier* there is quite an argument as to whether women like to hear crude words and off-color stories. No absolute conclusion is reached, but there is a strong opinion that it is beneath the "estate of a gentleman" to embarrass a lady by the language he uses. One of the prime difficulties, naturally, in determining the exact nature of the way people talked in the Renaissance is to locate an exact piece of conversation that has been written down. It certainly would not be found in the stilted tragedies of the period. For Abel Lefranc, who devoted a long life to research on the century, a comedy like Odet de Turnèbe's *Les Contents* contains several bits of dialogue which is typical of the talk of the time.[16] Some of it is far from being elegant, but the characters in such a comedy are a mixed collection and not representative of the most genteel social levels. The Renaissance was very productive of tales of every description, and these tales have frequently been considered reservoirs of information on the customs and tastes, conversational and otherwise, of the age. These stories, many of which would fit better into a smoking room than a drawing room, were concerned with every class of society, from the King down to the humblest peasant. In general, they would indicate that almost any word or subject would be acceptable to feminine ears. The same opinion could be derived from the conversation found in the novels and plays of both France and America since the end of the Second World War. The reasoning would probably be inaccurate in both cases, and the gentleman of the sixteenth century must have observed certain proprieties in his conversation with ladies even as would be done by his twentieth-century counterpart today. However, there is much evidence that the ladies of the Renaissance were not shocked by a considerable frankness of speech in their presence. The *Heptaméron*, the collection of tales written by Marguerite de Navarre, the erudite, mystical, and paradoxical sister of Francis I, offers much to support this point of view.

The fifty-second tale of the *Heptaméron*, told by a gentleman to a mixed group of ladies and gentlemen, is supposedly a true story to illustrate the general theme of a trickster being tricked. The tale is about a certain seigneur who thinks he has found in a street a piece of sugared pastry beautifully wrapped in white paper and dropped by a valet who was passing by. The valet returns, apparently looking for the lost object, but the seigneur and a friend hasten into a warm inn with the stolen morsel. It turns out to be a frozen bit of ordure which in melting creates a terrible odor and spoils the seigneur's clothes. Simontault, the gentleman who has told the story, admits that it is not very "clean," but that he has repeated it at the request of the company. Dame Oisille, the lady who has had general direction of the telling of the stories, says that she does not consider the words in the above tale so bad, but that there are others "of such bad odor" that they irritate the soul more than the false pastry might irritate the senses. This statement leads to a very quotable interrogation of Oisille on the words she had in mind:

> I beg you, said Hircan,* what are the words so dirty that they do injury to the heart and soul of a proper lady? — It would be a fine

*These are all persons who tell and discuss the stories in the *Heptaméron*. Most of the discoursers are identifiable as actual persons. Oisille, for example, is Louise de Savoie and Parlamente is Marguerite herself.

thing, said Oisille, if I said to you the words I feel no woman should say! — By that statement, said Saffredent,* I understand clearly what the terms are that women who wish to be considered proper don't normally use; but I should like very much to ask of all the ladies who are here, why it is that, though they do not dare to use these words, they laugh so heartily when the words are used before them? — We do not laugh, said Parlamente,* just at hearing these words spoken; but it is true that every person is inclined to laugh, either when he sees someone stumble or hears him stumble over his words, since it often happens that the tongue gets twisted and says one word for another, a thing that can befall the cleverest speaker. But when you men speak vulgarly out of malice and purposefully, I do not know any gentlewoman who is not horrified, and who not only does not wish to hear the words you say, but would gladly abandon the company of those who say them. — It is indeed true, said Geburon,* I have seen women keep making the sign of the cross when they heard certain words said over and over. — But, said Simontault,* how many times have they put their little masks over their faces in order to laugh their fill while pretending to be angry? — It would certainly be better to act thus, said Parlamente, then to let it be known that they found the conversation agreeable. — Then you praise, said Dagoucin,* hypocrisy in ladies as much as virtue? — Virtue would be a better thing, said Longarine;* but where it is lacking hypocrisy must lend its aid just as shoes cause to be forgotten the smallness of our stature. We must do the best we can to cover up our imperfections.

The discussion continues on the subject of feminine hypocrisy and the concealment of faults. No list of words or ideas, so completely "of bad odor" that they might upset the soul of a lady, is ever given, though the matter of a lady's attitude toward stories is mentioned again at the beginning of the sixty-second tale of the *Heptaméron*: "In the time of King Francis I, there was a lady of royal blood, graced with honor, virtue, and beauty; and she knew how to tell a story cleverly and well, and she could laugh at one too, when anybody told one to her."[17] The lady in question was most likely Marguerite de Navarre herself.

There was a story that circulated around the court of

* See footnote on preceding page.

Henry II concerning a lady's use of the *touret de nez*,* the mask that covered the lower part of the face, to hide her smiles at a gentleman's conversation. The seigneur d'Imbercourt had recently returned from the wars in Italy, and was not acquainted with many of the ladies at Court. He encountered one day riding through the woods from Paris to Saint-Germain the beautiful and important Anne d'Este, Duchesse de Guise, who was accompanied by a very small retinue. Imbercourt rode along with her to Saint-Germain, ignorant of her identity. He made gallant conversation with her, indulged in several pretty speeches filled with amorous insinuations and double meanings. The lady listened to them all, "but not, however, without laughing underneath her small little mask." Imbercourt was greatly embarrassed when later she removed her mask and he learned who she was. To his surprise, the lady was not offended by his remarks, but sent word that she would like to see him again.[18]

In the latter part of the century Montaigne, the sceptic, suggests that underneath the covering of modesty, women know all the words in the language. This happens in some way by instinct and they do not have to be exposed to such mundane writers as Boccaccio or Aretino for their linguistic knowledge, for "there is no word, nor example, nor procedure that they do not know better than our books." Women — and Montaigne is talking about women of the upper social stratum — very early absorb from their nurses a more complete list of the forbidden words of the language than they could get from twenty lackeys. Yet, Montaigne does not suggest that the formalities of genteel conversation should be ignored, even though women are not so easily shocked as their pretense of innocence might suggest.[19]

The conversation of a gentleman of the sixteenth century, with all its complications and variations, was not always carried on in the society of women. The gentleman, particularly if he was in the country on his estates or at war, would not see too much of the opposite sex or participate in such parties

* Cotgrave in his *Dictionarie* defines *touret de nez* as "muffler."

as those that took place at Court. In any event, though he might be with or without the refining influence of women on his talk, a gentleman seldom had his conversation unmixed with food or wine, or both. It was an age of great eating and drinking. A gentleman, detached from the Court and somewhat marooned in the country, lacked variety in relaxations, but eating and drinking ranked high on the list of his indulgences. After his morning ablutions and breakfast he did not wait until dinner at midday to assuage his hunger, but managed to insert a little snack in between. Dinner was a very solid operation, consisting of many courses and washed down with copious quantities of wine. Garlic and wine, in the opinion of a storyteller like Guillaume Bouchet, are natural complements to a gentleman's life — and wine, at least, should take precedence over women. This order of preferential interest would normally apply less to life at the Court than to that of the provinces, where a gentleman's diversions might consist chiefly of "wine, gambling, and women," in that order. On the other hand, if a gentleman is to be a successful captain in time of war, he should avoid gambling and wine, "for there is nothing in the world which dulls a man's mind so much or so completely inclines him to go to sleep as wine." Along with his heavy drinking he will eat too much, and thus be in no condition to give or receive orders. Another vice for the gentleman-soldier is "a desire for women," which, if it can not be deleted altogether, should be indulged in "soberly." It is a bad thing for a warrior to try to substitute a distaff for a sword.[20]

In view of the fact that a gentleman was destined to spend so much of his life with food and drink, it was to be expected that he should receive much advice along the way as to his manners in consuming them. The young gentleman is advised by contemporaries to wash his hands, clean his nails, and look after all bodily demands before the meal begins. He should then present himself at the table with a pleasant and agreeable mien. It is permissible for him to put his hands on the table but not his elbows, a privilege reserved for the old and infirm. If a napkin is used, it may be placed on the left shoulder or arm. The meat knife and the glass will be at the right of the plate, the bread at the left. To begin a meal with wine is the part of a drunkard, and a youngster should drink water or very weak wine or beer. A passion for wine, in fact, blackens the teeth, makes the cheeks droop, and dulls the intelligence. In any case, be sure to wipe the lips before drinking from a communal cup. It is bad to wolf the food in large gulps: it is better to take it in small morsels that can be held on the knife or fork. The fingers should not be licked or wiped on the clothes; a napkin or the table cloth should be used to remove bits of debris. Bones should not be gnawed too ravenously or be thrown under the table. Dogs are not to be petted at meals, but there should be some conversation among those persons seated at the table. It is not good to be so concentrated on food that there is complete oblivion to other social interests.[21]

Temperance in drinking, as in other human activities, was held by many of the theorists to be an attribute of gentility. However, temperance is not a matter of legislation, and just because some persons get drunk is no reason for a law prohibiting everybody from drinking wine — an idea expressed in the fourth book of the *Courtier* as well as in more recent times. One of the most famous of all the world's doctrines on training the youth — Montaigne's essay, *De l'Institution des enfants* — takes a position on the other side of the temperance fence. Montaigne would have his young gentleman be able to fit into the social milieu in which he finds himself. If he is thrown with a group of heavy drinkers, he should be capable of maintaining their pace, for Callisthenes lost the favor of Alexander because he was unable to keep up with the mighty Macedonian in drinking bouts. This does not mean that a gentleman must become in his youth steeped in debauchery, but rather that he should know the mechanics thereof, and then avoid it by his own will: "I wish that in debauchery itself he [the young gentleman] surpass his companions in vigor and solidity, and that he not fail to do evil through lack of force or knowledge, but through lack of desire." [22]

Food was abundant in the sixteenth century and the French had gargantuan appetites. They ate four or five times a day, all classes, though there was a hierarchy of foods and the upper classes managed to reserve for themselves certain delicacies. The tradition of big suppers, starting at four or five in the afternoon and consisting of enormous collections of edibles and entertainment, was a feature of life in the medieval châteaux. These gastronomic bouts usually continued until man and beast — dogs were under the table or in close proximity — lapsed into a state of greasy stupor. Refinements in the instruments for and the technique of eating came in during the sixteenth century, without any appreciable diminution, it must be admitted, in the quantity of food consumed. Napkins, which in the Middle Ages might be passed around rather casually after the meal, made a more frequent appearance in the fifteenth century, and during the Renaissance there was an ultra-refined vogue for changing the napkin after each course. Plates and forks came into general use only in the sixteenth century — in fact, the modern concept of correctness in table service and manners dates from this period. Forks did not replace without a struggle the fingers as mechanisms of transport. In a pamphlet against Henry III, forks at the royal table are berated and offered as further evidence of the King's decadence: "The guests pick it [the food] up with 'forks'; for it is forbidden in that country to touch meat with the hands, however difficult it may be to hold, and people prefer this little forked instrument rather than their fingers to touch their mouths." [23]

Many articles of food consumed by the gentleman of the period would not seem very palatable today. The nobles ate storks and birds of prey as well as the more understandable capons, peacocks, and pheasants. Herons, favored as a bird to be hunted, were prepared specifically for the table, and Francis I had two heronries at Fontainebleau where the birds were bred. The pheasant gradually improved its gastronomic and social position until it dethroned the peacock in the fifteenth century; the pheasant in its turn gave way to the turkey, which became monarch of the genteel table in the sixteenth. There were several varieties of bread fabricated during the Renaissance. In general, the darker breads, which contained barley or oats, were for the peasants. The bread got whiter as it got nearer the nobility. New fruits, like apricots from Armenia, were brought in and Queen Claude, the first wife of Francis I, had a plum named after her. Sugar was easier to get, and liqueurs developed to give further temptation to the gentleman's palate.

The Maréchal de Saint-André, who was first gentleman of the royal bedroom to Henry II and who met his death at the battle of Dreux in 1562, must have been a great giver of entertainments and sumptuous banquets. He was described before the end of the century as a "true Lucullus" who loved "his comforts, his pleasures, and his great luxuries of the table." His château of Vallery was superbly decorated and a center for splendid parties. He was given credit for introducing at the Court too great a luxury of foods, which involved every possible combination of meats, fowls, and fishes, and other pleasant comestibles. Vieilleville has left a description of the superlative splendor of the Maréchal's table,[24] with its abundance of serving dishes in silver and silver gilt and much crimson velours round about. However, Francis I had already set the standard of table lavishness under the direction of his numerous maîtres d'hôtel, twenty-seven of whom were of noble lineage.

An interesting *Mémoire* of the period gives an unbelievably long list of foods appropriate to a banquet, if one was to be given and one usually was. Among the ragouts —and just a few of the dishes will be mentioned — could be chosen stuffed venison, "mock porpoise" (whatever that might be), stag with turnips, and young drakes with cheese from Milan. Partridges could be done in a variety of fashions, or a wild boar might be served with chestnuts. For vegetables, asparagus would be good, or candied cucumbers, or little cabbages very hot. An infinite number of pâtés would be fine — such as pâtés of larks, or artichokes, or snipe, or chestnuts, etc. There could be a large choice of cakes and tarts, since pastry in the sixteenth century was becoming more and more varied. New spices and seasonings were making their appearance also, to excite the gastric juices of the gentleman who fancied himself a gourmet.[25]

Rabelais in his famous *Five Books* — five if we concede him the authorship of the fifth one — gives impressive evidence on the gastronomic habits of the first half of the century. He came from the province of Touraine, the famous region, fertile in foods and wines and châteaux and still known as the breadbasket of France; and with his amazing propensity for exactitude of detail and gigantic lustiness of description, not much that can be eaten or drunk is left out. Though his two primary heroes, Gargantua and Pantagruel, are giants with all appetities fittingly oversized, they are giants who are destined to rule ancestral estates and thus represent, in the midst of much magnifying and satirizing, something of the manners of their class. Grandgousier, he of the large gullet and the father of Gargantua, loved his sausages and hams and smoked beef tongues, and preferred to drink his wine "neat." Everybody in Rabelais's book liked smoked tongue; it must have been a great delicacy. Gargantua, after he got up in the morning and coughed, sneezed, spat, blew his nose like an archdeacon, and generally relieved himself, ate a breakfast of "fine fried tripe, fine grilled beef, fine ham, fine grilled kid, and several excellent thick soups." Farther along in the story, there was prepared for Gargantua, after his destruction of a hostile château, a supper which offered, among other edibles, sixteen beeves, thirty-two calves, ninety-five muttons, two hundred twenty partridges, six thousand pigeons and over twenty other varieties of fowls. Rabelais's most complete catalogue of foods is given in the *Fourth Book*, where Pantagruel and his friend, Panurge, visit the domain of the gluttonous Gastrolastres who bring as offerings to their god, Manduce, page after page of meats, fowls, and nearly one hundred kinds of fishes and crustaceans, as well as frogs and snails. It is a veritable mine of information on the gastronomy of the period, and shows how many different things a man could eat in this age when the consumption of food was definitely colossal. Homage is paid by Rabelais along the way to famous cooks, the inventors of distinguished sauces, and to a dinner beautifully served by blonde demoiselles in the land of the Papimanes — which recalled Guillot's much admired cabaret in Amiens.[26]

The French in the sixteenth century were probably the biggest eaters of Europe, but with their own manners and tastes and little mixture of the social classes at the table. Montaigne, the gentleman of Bordeaux who took a trip around the Continent and told about it in his *Journal*, was surprised to find masters eating with their valets in Switzerland. He noted differences in table service there, too — he would have liked to have a napkin — and in Bâle only two or three platters of meat came with the meal, though there were plenty of shrimps and fish. In Italy bread made from chestnuts was popular, the inns were full of fleas and not full enough of meat for a Frenchman, and every person there washed his hands in the same water. Of more pleasant remembrance was a very nice meal served by the Cardinal de Sans in Rome, with forks resting on a folded napkin. Montaigne himself gave a supper party for everybody at a watering resort in Northern Italy; he was able to invite a large crowd because "a feast in Italy is nothing more than one of our very light meals in France." Montaigne at this entertainment, since he had been ill, ate very lightly — "several pieces of veal and a few pairs of pullets." The Italian ambassador to the French Court, Lippomano, has left a very fine description of the French eating habits of the century. According to him, the French consumed little bread and fruit, though many fruits and salad materials were available because of the favorable climate. The natives of Paris preferred pastry filled with meat, and all sorts of things could be bought already cooked — capons, partridges, hares, etc. — and they were cheaper than their raw equivalents since there was such a tremendous business in cooked foods. Everybody bought them. The mutton was good and two thousand horses arrived in Paris on Wednesdays and Saturdays loaded down with poultry and game, all of which was sold in less than two hours. Butter was plentiful. The fish was not so good as might be expected, but sole, salmon, and sturgeon were abundant in the estuaries of the Loire and the Seine.[27] It is easy to see that under these conditions a gentleman would have had great difficulty in not bursting out of his embroidered breeches.

There had long been discussion and criticism of the upper-class festivals in foods. Before the end of the fifteenth century, a doctor in theology criticized the nobles for, among other things, their excessive expenditures on gold and silver dishes, and their "too sumptuous banquets." Later in the sixteenth century, in a pamphlet on the high cost of living in France, Jean Bodin says that nobody is satisfied with three courses at a meal any more, but that everybody wants "an infinity of sophisticated viands to sharpen the appetite and irritate nature." Giovanni Michel relates that when he came as the Venetian envoy to the French Court, he was received in Paris in the Duc de Guise's mansion, where he was given an apartment tapestried in silk and gold, a bed brilliant with gold and fine embroidery, and a lavish banquet set for fifty persons. They were served a magnificant fish called *brochet*, birds as big as chickens, and splendid wild pigs, as well as other choice comestibles. The service dishes were in silver, the table cloth was changed toward the end of the meal, the guests all washed their hands, and there was a final course of confitures and candied fruits. The ambassador's staff was given the same sort of food in a lower part of the palace, but for them there were only three courses — and confitures and candied fruits were omitted.

Periodic efforts were made to limit by legislation the gastronomic displays of the gentlemen, but without much effect. The great chancellor of Henry II, Michel de l'Hospital, issued an edict with royal sanction that restricted an individual dinner to one capon, one rabbit, and one partridge — but a dozen larks were allowed. In any case, the tendency toward overstuffing at banquets continued throughout the century, supported by the excellent example of Catherine de' Medici. The Queen had a monstrous appetite, which caused her to become fatter and fatter, with consequent doubling and redoubling of the royal chin. Catherine became ill, so the story ran, in 1575 from having eaten too many artichoke hearts and too many rooster combs and kidneys, "of which she was very fond." [28]

But it was wine, despite a few arguments against it, that

gave lubrication and scintillation to the gentleman's gastronomic efforts in the Renaissance. Without it the great banquets would have lapsed into dullness and a stultified stupor, and the participating gentlemen would have dropped on or under the tables. Without it Charles VIII and the Duc de Savoie would not have sat down to dinner and discussed a "variety of matters, among them dogs, and birds, and weapons of war, and questions of love." The ultimate authority on matrimony consulted by Panurge in Rabelais' *Fifth Book* is the Oracle of the Holy Bottle, which is approached through a vineyard that was planted by Bacchus himself and which contained every species of vine, including those of Beaune, Graves, and Anjou. It was wine that gave inspiration, says Rabelais, to such of the ancients as Aeschylus and Ennius, who would drink and then write. When the artists Primaticcio and Cellini got into an argument over an assignment given them by Francis I, Primaticcio suggested that before they come to blows they sit down and have a drink, "according to the custom in France." A distinguished visitor in the Renaissance might be welcomed into Paris with a gift of a flagon of wine — "in Germany, a commonplace present, but in France one destined for princes." [29]

The poets as well as the writers of prose paid homage to the lofty position of wine in the social structure of the Renaissance. Ronsard, the gentleman from Vendôme, is constantly praising the good wine of his country, and would have his page pour out just a little bit more in order that all ennuis might be effaced. Ronsard wrote an epitaph in 1554 for Rabelais which has added nothing to Rabelais' reputation as an ascetic. Rabelais is portrayed in these verses as a big drinker who would rather have some flagons of wine, a sausage, and a ham hung on his tomb than a collection of beautiful lilies. To balance things, Ronsard gives a similar picture of himself in a little *Odelette*, which shows the Prince of Poets enjoying resting from his sorrows by sipping a little wine, while a ham and a bottle that says glug-glug are hanging nearby.[30]

Among the tidbits that might be gleaned concerning the manners and dress of a gentleman of the Renaissance is the quatrain of Melin de Saint-Gelais concerning the use of powder to whiten the teeth. Erasmus, on the other hand, thinks powder is effeminate, nor does he approve of salt or alum, which injure the gums; but he does mention the theory that the teeth can best be kept white by washing them in urine. Around the 1520's earrings were at times worn by the men at Court, either in one or both ears, and apparently nobody said much about it. An important quality for the gentleman of the period — or of any period — was the ability to apply humor to tense situations. Francis I set a pattern for this attitude when, in the midst of problems between the Duchesse d'Etampes and Benvenuto Cellini, he simply laughed. Marguerite de Navarre tells the story of the wife of a gentleman and her husband and a chambermaid: from a shadow cast by a candle on a wall the wife sees the husband kissing the chambermaid. The lady's reaction is simply to burst out laughing. A more serious attitude was taken toward the King's lieutenant and judge — theoretically, a gentleman — at La Rochelle in 1530. The judge stole the money and "clothes of velvet" of those who came before him for trial. He was therefore stripped of his judicial robes of scarlet and imprisoned in the Conciergerie. As for the manners of Frenchmen on foreign soil, they must have been pretty good. The French officers in Northern Italy were reported to have been most acceptable to the ladies of Turin because the Frenchmen operated "under love's most genteel laws." [31]

A vivid and not unbiased opinion on the manners and character of the French gentleman of the later sixteenth century comes from an Italian observer: "The gentlemen of France on the contrary* are more open-handed than elsewhere in the world: they lavish their own money, as well as anybody else's, on horses, banquets, and clothes . . . One of the most striking contradictions in Frenchmen is that, at the beginning of dealings with them, it might be said they are more than men — and at the end that they are less than women. A man might maintain not incorrectly that three qualities are dis-

* That is, as contrasted with French women, who have previously been described as being avaricious.

tinctive of Frenchmen: never to do what they say they will do (some feel that this is more true of the Spaniards), not to write as they talk, and not to recall either kindnesses or offenses. Therefore, in order to deal with Frenchmen, it is necessary to have prudence, patience, and money."[32]

VI

The Gentleman's Education

THERE WAS SOME AGREEMENT in the sixteenth century on what a gentleman's manners and dress should be, but there was much variety of opinion as to what constituted his proper education. All those who had anything to say on the subject approached it with different ends in mind, or from divergent angles. They seem to have been just as uncertain about the appropriate intellectual training of a young gentleman as present-day pedagogues would be. However, one point would appear to have been rather generally accepted: the youthful gentleman of the Renaissance was not expected to be a bookworm. Though he was destined to have some governmental and judicial responsibilities under his king, he was not supposed to be one of Plato's scholar-philosophers, deeply learned and with a taste for every sort of knowledge, in order to serve his state. The second part of Plato's prescription for the ideal governing of the state — namely, that the rulers should be chosen from the best philosophers and the bravest warriors — found more complete acceptance in the Renaissance. The responsibility for the defense of his nation in time of war rested fundamentally upon the gentleman, and this responsibility took precedence over intellectual interests. In fact, though a general culture and knowledge of the world was admirable for the gentleman, his was not the life of the scholar who had begun early the disciplines of a mind intent on burying itself in books and manuscripts. The Renaissance would most surely have denied the Aristotelian dictum that the life of the intellect, based upon education and mental training, would bring the greatest happiness to man. The gentleman lapped up life too vigorously to limit himself to intellectual observations thereon.[1]

In France during the Renaissance it was not likely that a man born in a lowly social and economic situation might rise very far above this state simply by his mental capabilities. It was scarcely an age for the "talented poor," though a man might have a better chance in Italy or England than in France for improving his lot by the intelligent use of his own wits. Those who talked about education in sixteenth-century France, then, aimed their remarks in general at the upper classes. The poor student, who might be studying rhetoric and dialectic in order to discourse on theology, was not under primary consideration. The statement of Thomas Cranmer, made in England in 1539, that a plowman's son should have the advantages of a gentleman's son's training if the gentleman's son was incapable of taking it would scarcely have found full acceptance in France. The suggestion of Cranmer, obviously, does not presuppose the conditions of a true democracy, in that it does not urge that a plowman's son and a gentleman's son of comparable mental endowments are to be given equal opportunities at the same time. The French were unlikely to admit that a peasant could ever evolve very high, even under the most favorable conditions — but there is an occasional parallel to Cranmer's sentiment among the thoughful Frenchmen of the Renaissance.[2]

In that international manual on almost every phase of a gentleman's conduct, the *Courtier*, it is urged that a gentleman should have knowledge of everything, but that he should give the impression of never having worked hard at anything.* Therefore, without any preliminary toil in schools, libraries, and museums, he should be able to discourse easily on art, literature, music, and painting — clearly a difficult feat. Castiglione would prefer, in any case, that his courtier be a cultivated dilettante rather than a scholarly recluse. As for the French, it is suggested in the *Courtier* that they are primarily interested in fighting, though the cultural situation in France is destined to improve under the intelligent young King, Francis I. In any land, certainly, ladies and gentlemen should possess virtues of the mind.[3]

* See Chapter Two.

The universal scholar of the Renaissance, Erasmus of Rotterdam, who could mingle in the courts of kings or turn down a royal invitation, felt that a young gentleman should be trained in piety, should learn early the rules of civility, and should be fashioned in belles-lettres, "so that he may learn by heart and love the *liberales disciplinas*." For Erasmus the real nobility was that of the mind, as may be seen from the following salient passage: "Now, all those are to be regarded as noble who cultivate their minds through the practice of belles-lettres. Let others have painted on their coats of arms lions, eagles, bulls, leopards; the former possess more true nobility, those who could well decorate their escutcheons with a collection of emblems they have derived from the liberal arts." [4]

The attitude of the Court during the fine period of the Renaissance, while not conducive to the combination of gentility and scholarship advocated by Plato, Aristotle, and Erasmus, was not unfavorable to the gentleman's cultivating his mind. As was predicted by Castiglione, with the advent to the throne of Francis I, there was a renewed interest in learning and literature. The young King had been himself well grounded in the classics — especially in the limping elegiacs and subtle amorous philosophy of Ovid — under good tutors at Blois. All the chroniclers of the period agree that he was highly intelligent, and not only encouraged erudition but also liked to associate with men of erudition. He liked to have poets around him and composed a few verses of his own. According to Cellini, Francis I talked to him on occasions in Italian. Most contemporaries admitted that Henry II was less brilliant in mind than his father, though he continued the intellectual and literary patronage begun by Francis I — and this despite the fact that Henry II was first and foremost an outdoor man. Somewhat surprisingly, less than a century after his death Henry II was unfairly credited with sponsoring a court where the best minds turned to the composition of romances full of extravagant visions and poetry full of lasciviousness. Charles IX, who was not robust and little inclined to struggle with the problems of his realm, turned the reins of government over more and more to Catherine de' Medici while he did a little metal work and listened to poets like Ronsard and Baïf. And, rather a strange circumstance, Charles IX dabbled a bit himself in the composition of poetry. In any event, the total atmosphere around Francis I, Henry II, and Charles IX was not hostile to culture and learning.[5]

A considerable revolution took place in the first half of the sixteenth century with regard to the study of languages. It became progressively the fashion for a gentleman to have some knowledge of ancient and modern languages, languages which in an earlier period were learned generally by clerics who intended to use them to carry the doctrines of the Church to benighted lands. After 1500 there was a large number of displaced Greeks in France, and they gave public and private lessons in their native language to a variety of interested persons. Janus Lascaris, patronized by kings and the friend of the great Hellenist, Guillaume Budé, lectured to an elite audience in Paris and organized for Francis I the Library at Fontainebleau. Girolamo Aleandro in 1508 began in Paris his solid instruction in Greek. He gave private lessons and brought in books from the Aldine Press in Venice. And there were other Greeks who came to Italy and France after the fall of Constantinople in the previous century. Though it is doubtful that many gentlemen of the Court ever became very proficient in Greek, it is certain that the study of it had a vogue in the time of Francis I. An unacademic approach to the classic tongue of Hellas was taken by the Platonistic poetess of Lyons, Louise Labé, whose burning sonnets would belie her allegiance to Plato. Of her it was said that she embraced philosophers who came to her salon, simply for the love of Greek. The University of Paris and the theologues of the Sorbonne, who admitted the value of Hebrew, Arabic, and Latin for religious purposes, never accepted Greek. Francis I, undisturbed by such an attitude, seemed to have at one time the idea of establishing in Paris a college for young Greeks. Around 1520 Lascaris was sent into Italy to discuss with scholars there the proposed seminary of Hellenism. The project, with Francis I getting deeper and deeper into political and military difficulties, never came to fruition.[6]

The young gentleman of the Renaissance did not get his learning solely inside the schoolroom. If his family could afford it, he was given private instruction by a tutor, whose teachings might be supplemented by the doctrines of a small college — a college at this time was not normally an institution of higher learning, but rather the equivalent of a modern high school, or *lycée*. Enrollment in a college was not the most desirable procedure. It was preferable for a youngster of genteel ancestry to be sent to some noble or royal court as a page, since it was a young gentleman's privilege to serve in such a position. There he would practice at being a courtier and pick up some formal learning. That this learning was not very deep is suggested by Guillaume Budé when he says in a letter written in 1521, in Greek, to Lascaris that he does not like to waste his time around the Court in an atmosphere of ignoramuses — even though Francis I's courtiers are impressed by Budé's knowledge of Latin and Greek. For the most part, the courtiers are not interested, thinks Budé, in scholarship and are opposed to his plans for improving education in France.[7]

The colleges at the dawn of the Renaissance, in Paris as well as elsewhere in France, were rather miserable institutions. There was no clear line drawn between elementary and advanced instruction, and the subject matter, whatever the theoretical level, was usually puerile. The masters were likely to be brutal and made up in corporal punishment for their lack of intellectual stimulus to their students. The buildings were dark and damp, infested with vermin, and the most rudimentary laws of sanitation were disobeyed. The pupils were kept inside the dim and somber halls for very long hours — as a matter of fact, French children of grammar school age still spend long hours in class. One of the worst, if not the worst, of these establishments was the Collège de Montagu, which was attended by both Erasmus and John Calvin. Memories of the collège de Montagu influenced Erasmus in his decision not to return to France to assist Francis I in the King's proposed educational reform. It is easy to see why these colleges would have little appeal to the genteel classes, or any class, of society.

Rabelais pays his respects to Montagu in an episode where Gargantua is combing his hair with an enormous comb of elephant's teeth after the battle of Vede Wood. With each stroke of the comb objects fall off Gargantua's scalp—they are cannon balls—but Gargantua's father thinks they are "sparrow-hawks of Montagu," or lice, and is surprised that his son has been attending that school. Ponocrates, Gargantua's tutor-guardian, then explains that such is not the case: "Seigneur, don't think that I put the boy in the 'college of lousiness' that they call Montagu. In view of the terrible cruelty and villainous practices that I have known there, I might well have preferred to put him among the beggars around Saint Innocent's. For, slaves among the Moors and Tartars, murderers in a criminal's prison, and certainly dogs in your house, are much better treated than are those poor wretches in that college; and, if I were the ruler of Paris, may the devil take me if I didn't put fire to the place, and burn up the principal and the teachers, who suffer this inhumanity to be exercised before their eyes." [8]

An improvement in educational concepts began to make itself felt around 1525, as a result of the appearance of some professors who were more enlightened and less pedantic than their predecessors. Among them was Georges Buchanan, the Scottish historian and poet who was a royal tutor in his own land and a teacher at the Collège de Sainte-Barbe in Paris in the 1520's; and Mathurin Cordier, who as a teacher of grammar infused such life into his subject that he gave it universality, and through it assisted in developing the more complete personalities of his students. It was he who "substituted a vitality of instruction aimed at the whole man for that gymnastics of nothingness which until then had taken the place of education." Cordier and others paved the way for such an excellent and beloved scholar as Jean Daurat, who, among other things, was tutor of the royal pages, master of the Collège de Coqueret, and mentor of such high-born youngsters as Pierre de Ronsard and Jean-Antoine de Baïf before they became known for their poetry. Ronsard pays affectionate hommage to Daurat when he tells how Daurat "pulled thousands of school-boys around by the ears."[9] In 1530, due to the tenacity and persuasive powers of Guillaume Budé, Francis I established the Royal Lectureships, later to be called the Collège Royal, and still later, as it is today, the Collège de France. This distinguished and world-renowned institution, which celebrated with such fanfare its four-hundredth anniversary in 1930, had rather modest beginnings. The King did not provide at the time a building for the professors who gave the lectures, nor regular pay for their services. Nevertheless, the courses were immediately welcomed by scholars, courtiers, and all categories of students. The newly established organization — nobody knew exactly what to call it — became famous all over Europe. The lectures were open to anybody who wished to attend, there were no fees or system of grades, but there was a great respect for learning and a rejection of the husks of scholasticism. Marguerite de Navarre, the intellectual sister of the King, took a great interest in the institution and the choice of professors, while the general administration of the corporation was under the fine Latin scholar and distributor of royal alms, Jacques Colin.

The "tri-lingual Academy," as it was called by Clément Marot in one of his well-known poems,[10] referred to the professorships of Greek, Hebrew, and Latin. However, in the beginning there were two professors of Greek, two professors of Hebrew, and a professor of mathematics, but none for Latin. A third professor of Hebrew was added in 1531; instruction in the third language, Latin, was not begun until 1534. Shortly thereafter a course in logic, for so long the mechanical mainstay of the Sorbonne's sterile disputations, was offered with a more liberal interpretation of the function of logic in the training of the mind. The first professors included such great names as Pierre Danès (for Greek), François Vatable (for Hebrew), and Oronce Finé (for mathematics). They were followed by distinguished savants like Pierre Ramus, the anti-Aristotelian professor of eloquence and philosophy, and Adrien Turnèbe, the notable Hellenist. The lectures were probably given in Latin, which would have put them out of range of most of the gentlemen around the

Court. In spite of the linguistic difficulties, there was a great vogue at the Court for these courses. Some of them would at times have three or four hundred auditors, among them many courtiers and occasionally the King along with Marguerite de Navarre.

Just as vigorously as he opposed the Collège de Montagu does Rabelais praise the Royal Lectureships. This he does in the much-quoted letter of Gargantua to Pantagruel. Rabelais does not call the Royal Lectureships by name, but he undoubtedly had them in mind since his book was composed during the period of their first great popularity. Also, the program of instruction proposed by Rabelais is recognizably similar to that of the royal professors. It should not be forgotten that Rabelais' giants are genteel giants, ribald and lusty if you will, but destined to carry on family traditions and direct ancestral domains. The program of education that Gargantua suggests to his son, then, is one aimed not at a scholarly recluse but at a young gentleman who will one day have great responsibilities. After making the rather usual paternal statement that conditions are much better now than they were when he was a boy, Gargantua proceeds to elaborate on present-day possibilities for learning and the things he would like Pantagruel to know:

Now all branches of learning are restored, languages are renewed: Greek, without which it is a shame that anybody call himself learned, Hebrew, Chaldean, Latin. Fine and elegant printings — techniques which in my day were invented by divine inspiration just as artillery was created by diabolical suggestion — are available. The whole world is full of learned people, of scholarly teachers, of very ample libraries, and it is my opinion that neither in the time of Plato, nor of Cicero, nor of Papinianus, was there such facility for study. Henceforth it will not be possible to be in any place or society which is not polished by Minerva's wisdom. I see robbers, hangmen, wanderers, and stable-boys of the present more learned than the professors and preachers of my time.

. . . Wherefore, my son, I advise you to employ your youth profitably in study and good works. You are in Paris and you have Epistemon as tutor — a combination which by praiseworthy example and by lively vocal instruction will aid in your indoctrination. It is my understanding and desire that you learn languages perfectly. First Greek, even as Quintilian desires it; secondly, Latin; and then Hebrew for the Holy Scriptures, and Chaldean and Arabic too; and form your style, as for Greek, in imitation of Plato; as for Latin, in imitation of Cicero . . . Of the liberal arts, geometry, arithmetic, and music, I gave you some taste of them when you were still small, around five or six years old. Carry on with the others, and learn all the laws of astronomy . . . Of civil law, I want you to know the good texts by heart, and blend them with philosophy.

And as for the facts of nature, I want you to have curiosity about them: let there be no sea, river, or fountain, the fishes of which you do not know; and the same for the birds of the air, the trees and shrubs of the forests, the herbs of the earth and all the metals hidden in its depths, the precious stones of the Orient and South. Let nothing be unknown to you.

. . . To sum it up, I want you to be filled with knowledge: for, henceforth when you become a grown man, you will have to abandon the restful tranquility of study, and take up horsemanship and arms, to defend my house as well as assist our friends in their affairs, against the assaults of evil-doers.[11]

It would take a giant in mind and body to carry out this program, many details of which have been omitted from the above excerpt. But it is a question of a giant, as the last few quoted lines would indicate, who has a gentleman's responsibility to society. Gargantua's own training, under the direction of his tutor Ponocrates, would possibly have been a little closer to the concept of what was the preferred education of a gentleman during the sixteenth century.

After Ponocrates had changed completely the program that Gargantua had followed under the "précepteurs sorbonagres"* — which consisted of sleeping too late, drinking wine until the soles of the slippers would rise up a half foot, hearing twenty-six or thirty masses, taking too little exercise except with dice and cards, and studying half an hour with the eyes on a book but with the soul in the kitchen — the boy put in a very full day. There was not too much emphasis on books, but enough. Gargantua got up at four o'clock in the

* "Sorbonne-ish instructors" — a jibe at the professors of the Sorbonne, who are *onagres*, "wild asses."

morning, studied some lessons (with reviews of the things learned the day before) involving in particular "the state of man," consumed a great deal of food and discussed the properties thereof while eating, absorbed mathematics by playing with cards, practiced singing and learned to play several musical instruments, spent the afternoon in vigorous exercise, ate a light supper, paid a visit to some "men of letters" or to persons who had traveled in foreign lands, took a look at the position of the stars, said his prayers and went to bed. All this was done under the guidance of Ponocrates, who reviewed the exploits of the day just before they retired at night. If it was a rainy day, Gargantua learned various manual skills like wood-carving, metal-working, etc. Once a month they went to the country — Chantilly, Saint-Cloud, or some such spot — and caught a few quail, crayfish, and frogs, all of which recalled pleasant lines from Virgil and Hesiod. The whole program was as practical as it was well-rounded, even though little provision was made for sleep. Gargantua, in the best manner of a gentleman of the Renaissance, did it all easily and without any strain.[12]

The University of Paris and the theological faculty of the Sorbonne were very powerful in the sixteenth century, but they were scarcely filled with young gentlemen. The University of Paris had at this time between fifteen and twenty thousand students, "almost all of them poor, but who, in the meantime, were trying to improve their minds." Not only were the students stricken by poverty, but so were the professors, who were quite meagerly paid and had heavy obligations. However, a surprising comment comes in 1546 from Marino Cavalli, who states that the title of professor is so honorable that by being one a man "gains in reputation what he loses in money." The masters of the Sorbonne had additional power in their authority to dispose of heretics, whom, says Cavalli, they "roast alive." Many men of letters had difficulty with the Sorbonne, and it is not surprising that the "sorbonniqueurs," or men of the Sorbonne, were exposed to considerable satire. Rabelais has their outmoded methods of teaching logic and rhetoric in mind when he speaks of "Latin verbosination" and when he puts a book in his Library of Saint-Victor bearing the title (in Latin), "Whether a chimera buzzing in a void can devour second intentions." Also, the inside of Pantagruel's upset stomach (Book II, chapter XXXIII) is compared to "the stinking lake of the Sorbonne." The thousands of students, then, in Paris were for the most part poorly instructed and in a bad economic state. It was reported for March 25, 1535 (old style) by an eye-witness of affairs in the city of Paris that, through the King's order and confirmed by the Parlement of Paris, "all poor and indigent students, not having enough to live on and keep themselves up in school, must get out of the city of Paris." There will not be permitted any begging in the streets by the said students — and this was happening just as the Royal Lectureships were getting under way, which seems something of a paradox in educational planning on the part of Francis I. Apparently there was at this time around Paris a professional group of vagabond students just as there were professional beggars. Further evidence of this situation was given by Vieilleville in his description of the La Châtaigneraie-Jarnac duel that took place at Saint-Germain in 1547: the grounds of Saint-Germain were invaded by a mob that came out from Paris to see the activities — and the mob was made up of "students, artisans, and vagabonds." All of which is a sad commentary on the social and economic status of a poor student in Paris in the sixteenth century. But, it can be said again, France at this moment was not a democracy and had no system of public education, nor felt the need thereof. A fine scholar like Charles Estienne, for example, made the assertion that it was not necessary for a farmer to be able to read and write. In any event, the training of a young gentleman was not to be confused with that of a miserable and wandering student.[13]

The Royal Lectureships, with their more liberal appeal to all classes of society through their vitalizing of learning, aroused the immediate opposition of the Sorbonne. The masters of theology accused the new courses of being scandalous, rash, full of heresy, and tinged with Lutheranism. Nevertheless, the embryonic Collège de France continued to receive royal support throughout the century. Another of the educational schemes of Francis I — and one aimed more specifically at the gentlemen of his kingdom — never came to fruition. There was a royal plan, and it is mentioned by several chroniclers of the period, to build across the Seine from the Louvre a super-college for six hundred students, to be educated at the expense of the state in all branches of knowledge. There were to be interpreters at hand for all known languages, and the students were to stay in the institution for fourteen years. Belleforest, who calls Francis I the "restorer of fine learning," says the King would have built that college if he had lived. Mézeray says a little later that Francis I had planned a royal college with 60,000 crowns budget, "in order to take care of and train therein six hundred gentlemen." What measurements of intelligence or gentility were to be used in determining admission to these chosen six hundred are not known. It is too bad that the institution never came into existence, but it is doubtful that it ever would have obtained the world-wide distinction of the Collège de France.[14]

The Renaissance gentleman, with the world widening around him in all directions, became increasingly conscious of the modern as well as the ancient languages. Francis I and Marguerite de Navarre were both excellent linguists; Madame de Châteaubriant, the favorite of Francis I, was said to know Latin and Italian; Marguerite, the daughter of Francis I, was (says Cavalli) "versed in Latin, Greek, and even Italian"; the young Charles de Brissac (later a marshal of France) studied Latin with the royal princes on the Loire; Lucrezia Borgia was a fine lady who spoke "many languages," and Catherine de' Medici, in addition to her native Italian, spoke "good French." In Rabelais's idealized Abbaye de Thélème, where everything was conducted with civilized gentility, there was not a person "who did not know how to read, write, sing, play harmonious instruments, speak from five to six languages." Some sort of linguistic prize should have gone to Monsieur Parisot, grand master of Malta, who not only was a tall and handsome captain, but spoke French, Italian, Spanish, Greek, Arabic, and Turkish — "without any interpreters." Brantôme makes a strong plea for a knowledge of foreign languages on the part of gentlemen in official positions. He recommends this in particular for ambassadors and others who have international responsibilites; otherwise they will be like "calves who speak only the language of calves." An ambassador might well know Spanish, Latin, French, and Italian. Since other languages — the specific languages are not named — are so difficult, if a state official is ignorant of them he is to be excused. Monarchs like Francis I and Charles V have been very gifted in languages, and Marguerite de Navarre in foreign tongues "knew more than her daily bread." A discourse in a different language, when the occasion is appropriate for it, will add a touch of gentility and gallantry. A person who speaks a foreign tongue should speak it well enough not to be laughed at, and this requires practice. However, when an idiom is handled well by a man who is not native to it, he will be "loved, honored, and esteemed" by everybody. Brantôme then boasts a little of his own proficiency in Spanish, and considers that he got along quite well with Philip II because the King of Spain was pleased that a foreigner could speak so fluently the language of Castille.[15]

Toward the end of the century many theories were offered concerning the type of education appropriate to a gentleman. Montaigne has much to say on the subject, and he is generally opposed to the encyclopedic gulping down of knowledge suggested by Rabelais. Montaigne is not bothering about the education of the vulgus — "and most of the world is made up of this species" — but rather wishes to improve the training of young gentlemen. His longest essay dealing with the subject, *On the Training of Children*, is dedicated to Madame Diane de Foix, Comtesse de Gurson, who is about to give birth to a child and the assumption is that it will be a son. The education of girls is another matter. It is from this essay that comes the much-quoted remark of Montaigne on the choice of a tutor for the prospective small gentleman: the tutor should have a head that is "well-balanced rather than well-stuffed." Montaigne is strong for good tutors rather than for studying in the colleges. He considers that he was himself very lucky in having teachers who did not disgust him with books but inspired in him a love for learning. It is easy to understand how scholars like Georges Buchanan and Marc-Antoine Muret, whom Montaigne describes as his "private instructors," would have aroused in him a desire for books and knowledge. As for the colleges, Montaigne defends them no more than did earlier writers, when he comes out with the following strong denunciation: "I do not want this child to be imprisoned in a college, I do not want him to be abandoned to the choler and melancholy disposition of some wild school-master; I do not wish to corrupt his mind by keeping him on the rack and at work, in the fashion of the other youngsters, fourteen or fifteen hours a day, nor do I wish to spoil his generous impulses by contacts with incivility and barbarism." Children are genteel when they enter the colleges but they come out brutalized. Montaigne says that he himself attended the collège de Guienne, the "best in France," for six years and came out of it at the age of thirteen "without any profit."

As for the materials to be studied, Montaigne would not have a boy stuff his head with Greek and Roman authorities, and become one of those "college-bred Latinizers." It is better to play with a bat and ball than to become too impressed with the infallibility of the ancients — but Montaigne's own facility in Latin must not be forgotten, nor his easy excursions into the literature of classical antiquity. Later he admits that Greek and Latin are valuable, "but you pay too dearly for them." A foreign language that is to be spoken should be learned early, for otherwise "the tongue will not be [illegible]le to wrap itself around it." Knowledge should never be [illegible] 'low and vile hands," but philosophy and "this great world" should be primary objects of study. The young gentleman will be benefited greatly by travel, though he should not go to foreign lands "just to learn the number of steps in the *Sancta Rotonda*," or the length of Nero's face on a medal. It must be remembered that, as Plato said, both the body and mind should be trained. At Padua, where there were fine schools for fencing, dancing, and horsemanship, Montaigne found around one hundred French gentlemen. In his estimate, this was too large a number, since it prevented other French gentlemen from arriving there and "gaining knowledge of foreign lands." He does not believe that the "well-born" should become involved in "rhetoric, the judiciary, or logic — and other such trashy articles on public sale." Montaigne comes back again to attack the materials and methods of teaching in France: "I return willingly to this matter of the futility of our method of instruction. It has for its purpose not to make us good and virtuous, but learned; it has had some success in that. It has not taught us to follow and embrace prudence and virtue, but it has impressed on our minds their derivation and etymology. We know how to decline virtue, even if we know no affection for it." In view of the inadequacy of formal instruction in France, Montaigne thinks it is a splendid thing that so many of "our good families" have opened up their houses to youngsters for training and experience, the result of which is something like a "school for the nobility."[16]

Some very spirited and practical advice on the education of a gentleman comes from two of the toughest old warriors of the Renaissance, Gaspard de Tavannes and François de La Noue. Tavannes was a young page at the court of Francis I, was captured at the battle of Pavia, later served well as a soldier under Henry II, and died in 1573 shortly after the Massacre of Saint Bartholomew. Tavannes was the friend and companion of Francis I's son, Charles, Duc d'Orléans, and was supposed to toughen up Charles, who in his early years was accused of being effeminate. The two of them managed to make considerable noise around the Court and through the narrow streets of Paris before the death of the young prince, who was struck down by an infection at the age of twenty-three. François de La Noue, it will be remembered, lost his left arm in the Religious Wars and rigged up an iron mechanism to replace it, a technique that enabled him to sit a horse in battle. Henry IV is reputed to have said in 1591 at La Noue's death that he had lost a man of great vigor and honor. From Tavannes and La Noue, then, would not be expected a bookish educational program destined for a genteel recluse.

The sons of a wealthy gentleman, says Tavannes, preferably should follow the career of arms. Theology and jurisprudence are also open to gentlemen, but they are not to take up an ignoble profession like medicine. Several unworthy men have entered the judiciary because of the ignorance of the nobles. Therefore, in preparation for these legitimate careers, young gentlemen should have faithful instructors, both in private and at the universities, until the age of twenty-three years — a surprisingly advanced age. The guardians and tutors of the youths should be honorable and God-fearing men, and if the requisite qualities can not be found in one tutor, two should be obtained. The young pupils should "learn to talk well, gain a general acquaintance with all knowledge and especially with history, in order to be of service in matters of State." The art of war and military exercises are important, but it is useless to try to make a soldier out of a monk.

Tavannes does not recommend the study of languages and literature for the young gentleman since "stories and tales induce lying, tragedies cause fear, and poets suggest luxurious indolence." It is better to read the Bible or real history than fiction. Languages are not in reality knowledge, and the time spent on them could be better employed in learning "histories, precepts, strategies, and the conduct of war." If a child is to study Latin, however, it should be begun at the age of two, so that it will seem like a native tongue. Instruction should be varied according to the child's capacities, but very early he should be given toy soldiers and toy fortresses to indoctrinate him, by the use of playthings, in the art of war. But never let it be forgotten that novels and poetry are the "poison of youth."

Conversation is profitable unless the youth hears a lot of dirty words, which are "knives that cut deep into the natural goodness of young persons." Bodily exercises of all kinds are valuable, but it is useless for a young gentleman to waste time with musical instruments. The years between sixteen and nineteen are very important in the life of a youth, because it is then that he is most susceptible to training for war. Gentlemen should take more interest in the development of their own sons, who as pages at Court are likely to have servile and ignoble duties to perform. They learn many vices, too, by traveling in Italy. Tavannes believes that the genteel upper classes are superior to the lower classes in virtues both of the mind and the body. A gentleman inevitably begets a gentleman. Any mixture of classes will produce monstrosities and infirmities — a doctrine previously enunciated by Plato.[17]

La Noue laments the decline of virtue in his time and the general growth of corruption. One of the reasons, he feels, for this situation is the little care that is being taken now in training young gentlemen in honorable pursuits. The pages at the Court learn many externals of manners and the proprieties of dress, but they become dissolute in speech and depraved in actions. It is inadvisable, therefore, for boys of good families to serve long and uninterrupted periods as pages. Foreign travel, also, has its plus and minus values for the young; it is undoubtedly good for the learning of languages. Italy is a place where many genteel things may be acquired, but Germany is a crude spot. In all journeyings among foreigners, unfortunately, "with the roses are found a number of thorns." Some young gentlemen are sent to study in the universities, but this is a mixed blessing, and a number of fathers think their offspring can learn more at the Court, especially when they consider "the crude and simple manners of the students in comparison with the gentility, courtesy, and skill of these young gentlemen who have made only two trips to Court" — and here would appear to be something of a contradiction in La Noue's attitude toward the educational possibilities of the Court, unless he does not intend for this second group of gentlemen to act as pages.

A keynote in La Noue's planning for the youthful gentlemen of his day is a suggestion that there should be set up over the land of France several academies for the training of the young nobility. Among the cities chosen for these institutions would be Paris, Lyon, Bordeaux, and Angers. In addition to these cities, academies could be installed in many of the châteaux that dot the landscape, in those where "the kings go infrequently or not at all," like Fontainebleau, Plessis-lès-Tours, and Cognac. Many types of exercises, both of the body and the mind, would be given in the academies. Ancient and modern books that teach virtue would be read, and mathematics, geography, and fortification would be studied, as well as "some of the vulgar tongues, which are very useful for a gentleman — to know as much of them, I mean, as he can put into use." Some of the bodily skills taught in the academies may require instructors to be brought in from Italy. All these procedures should assist in checking the flood of "universal corruption" that has been inundating the nobility of the present day — La Noue's *Discours* were published in 1587 — and bring young gentlemen back to a realization that their primary function is war and the protection of "true honor." [18]

Books have their place in the gentleman's education, but that place is limited. Even Ronsard gets tired of having his head buried in a book, and asks in one of his odes: "What's the use of studying except to get bored?" On the other hand, Ronsard admires a patron of letters like Jehan du Thier, who took time out from his official duties to buy copies of Pindar and Simonides from two wandering Greeks. In Rabelais's *Second Book*, Panurge tells his friend, Pantagruel, not to spend the whole night studying learned tomes but to take twenty-five or thirty drinks and go to bed. Works of fiction, specifically those dealing with chivalric adventure, were popular early in the century. Marguerite de Navarre says in her forty-ninth tale that it is from the books of the Round Table that a genteel warrior learns what is an honorable action toward a weak opponent. The stories in prose of Lancelot, Merlin, and Tristan were popular as late as 1560. Interestingly enough, a French translation of the famous Spanish romance of chivalry, the *Amadís de Gaula*, became the veritable breviary of the court of Henry II. This adaptation of the *Amadís*, done in four profusely illustrated folio volumes between 1540 and 1556 by the seigneur des Essarts, was praised in an ode by Du Bellay, in an epigram by François Habert, and by the scholarly Etienne Pasquier in the seventh book of his researches on France. Nevertheless, most of those who give advice on a young gentleman's education dislike the *Amadís*. Montaigne says he very fortunately avoided the *Lancelot du*

Lac, the *Huon de Bordeaux*, and the *Amadís* — trashy books which amuse the youth of France. Tavannes does not think that Roland and Amadís are of any benefit to the young.[19]

It is La Noue who gets most excited about the *Amadís*, and its bad influence on the youth of the land. With the decline in popularity, around the middle of the century, of the medieval romances like the *Lancelot*, or *Perceforest*, such things as the *Amadís* took their place. In the time of Henry II pedagogues used the *Amadís* like a textbook, and youngsters were trained to "amadiser de paroles," or talk in the manner of Amadís. Though the French translation of the *Amadís* is better than the original (since the Spanish language is "too simple"), says La Noue, the book is still too full of fanciful things like magicians and enchantments, which inflame and excite the imaginations of the readers. Everything in the book is too unrealistic, like one knight's killing two hundred adversaries, and "when a gentleman has spent all his life reading the books of the *Amadís*, he will be neither a good soldier nor a good guardsman." [20]

The gentleman of the Renaissance was, then, only a modest intellectual, and that is all he was expected to be. There was no complete agreement, obviously, on the program of his instruction. Symphorien Champier thought that a young noble should be able "to read and, also, write." Charles Estienne felt that a master of an estate should "philosophize" and not spend all his time running around to banquets and getting drunk. Ronsard believed that one should not imitate too closely the speech of the Court, where the ladies and gentlemen were concerned more with other matters than with the perfection of the French language. Scholars might be attached to an ambassador's mission, but it was better for the first representative of France on foreign soil to be a man of arms rather than a man of erudition. The gentleman was no closeted scholar. By training and experience, he was more at ease outdoors with a horse, and indoors with a woman, than with a book in either place.[21]

VII

Life in the Country

THE SIXTEENTH-CENTURY GENTLEMAN, though he liked to make his mark at Court, was still very much attached to the land. The period from the beginning of the century until the outbreak of the Wars of Religion just past its middle was a fascinating in-between period for the nobility. It was the interlude that separated the last powerful feudal barons of an earlier era from the nobles of the later seventeenth century, when the nobility was chiefly a decorative background for the King. Before Richelieu and Louis XIV there was in reality such a thing as the country gentleman, an independent personage with roots sunk deep into the soil from which he derived a robust vitality and confident vigor. Within the limits set by the monarch, he still had considerable power: as a provincial governor, or as a *bailli* or seneschal, he carried out the King's commands in the provinces. He was responsible for public order, and distributed justice in the lower courts to the commoners and underprivileged. He had hunting rights denied the commoner, and special dominion over the construction of pigeon houses, dovecotes, windmills, and wine presses. It was not a very democratic arrangement, but the gentleman in exchange for privileges and exemptions from taxes might be called upon to lay down his life in time of war.* In any case, the country gentleman on his estates lived in close contact with the people around him, in a relationship that was for the most part satisfactory to all concerned, and he had both the privileges and responsibilities of an aristocrat. He was likely to be a very busy man from morning till night in a series of activities that were infinitely varied.[1]

* See Chapter One for other details. Cotgrave says a *bailli* is a "magistrate appointed within a Province . . . to execute justice, maintain the peace, and preserve the people from oppression, vexation, and wrong. . ."

The gentleman of the sixteenth century distrusted cities and was ill at ease in their compressed and narrow streets. He had difficulty in dealing with the merchants therein, the aggressive bourgeois who devised more and more means of making money. The smell of the city, the accumulated debris of its streets and the filth of its open sewers, were shocking to a genteel nostril. The King himself had set the fashion early in the century of getting out in the open country as frequently as possible, a move that irritated the burghers who liked to have the Court in town. Montaigne, himself a country gentleman, in his essay *On Odors* says that the beautiful cities of Venice and Paris lose favor with him because of their olfactory irritations, Venice because of its marshes, Paris because of its mud. The cities, moreover, were dependent on the country for their supplies of meat, vegetables, fruits, and grain. Normandy and Burgundy helped to keep Paris fed, and the Seine with its heavily laden supply boats was a teeming artery of traffic. With the steady movement of incoming provisions, there were frequent traffic jams and collisions on the river. In 1519, so it was said, a boat from Corbeil to Paris, loaded with "grain, flour, wine, and people," was bumped so hard by another boat that it sank. However, with its overcrowded river, with all its smells and decadent vegetables, Paris was the throbbing heart of a growing nation, the "glory of the Muses," the "glory of France and one of the most notable ornaments of the world." But a gentleman did not want to be cooped up inside her walls.[2]

Much evidence has come down, both in writings and in edifices still preserved, as to what sort of a house a Renaissance gentleman lived in. France had long been a land covered with châteaux, some of which were great stone fortresses, with thick walls, drawbridges, portcullises, and other devices for resisting invaders. Bastions of this nature were Loches, Chinon, and Langeais — one of the last of the fortified châteaux, built in the fifteenth century, and still in a fine state of preservation; but their military value was greatly reduced in an age that was perfecting the use of gunpowder and massed cannon. They had always been uncomfortable as dwellings, with their dark and cold interiors, though they were impressive settings for ceremonials. The Renaissance château, for its part, was not expected to be able to resist a siege; it was designed for pleasant and civilized living. Many ideas concerning luxury of décor had been brought up from Italy along with the necessary artists and artisans to put them into operation. This did not mean that turrets, crenelations, and portcullises disappeared completely during the sixteenth century. A noble liked to keep on his house these mementoes of medieval warfare simply as decorations, since they indicated the antiquity of his family. And if a wealthy bourgeois could manage to acquire the remnants of an old château with some lingering beams of a crumbling pigeon house near it, he might with a little restoration lay the foundations of the life of a noble for his son.

As for the royal châteaux, Charles VIII imported hundreds of Italian workmen in 1492 to labor on Amboise. The job was finished by Francis I, the great Renaissance builder who had his hand in the construction or renovation of eight or nine châteaux or palaces, among them Fontainebleau, Saint-Germain-en-Laye, Madrid "two leagues from Paris toward the West, near the river Seine," Azay-le-Rideau on the river Indre, and Chambord. Androuet Du Cerceau, the sixteenth-century engraver who has left a large collection of engravings of the notable châteaux of the period, says that Francis built La Muette in the woods around Saint-Germain-en-Laye because he wanted a place where he could see the end of the chase. Chambord, the beautiful towered château nestling today in a flat forest, was formerly on a detoured branch, now dry, of the Loire river. The more than eight hundred different types of salamanders carved in the ceiling of the main hall of Chambord are constant reminders that Francis I was there. Chambord was not much of a winter château, but was a favorite place for the royal hunts. The stables held some twelve hundred horses, and the top deck of the building, which was open, would hold over one thousand persons. From this upper deck the ladies of the Court could follow the hunt in all directions. Anet, the château given by Henry II to Diane de Poitiers, was also a fine place for hunting. Two châteaux of the Loire valley, Chaumont and Chenonceaux, are particularly associated with Henry II, Catherine de' Medici, and Diane de Poitiers. Chaumont, which sits on a promontory affording a magnificent view of the Loire, has been almost too perfectly restored. It looks like a fortified château, externally, but its interior is deceptively modern. Catherine de' Medici managed to give it to Diane de Poitiers in exchange for Chenonceaux. Chenonceaux, the jewel of the Renaissance, is approached by an avenue of plane trees, five hundred twenty-five yards long. It sits astride the river Cher, and contains many reminiscences of Diane de Poitiers, including her signature. Most of the furnishings of these châteaux have been taken out to various museums. Azay-le-Rideau, however, still has much of its interior equipment. Several Renaissance chests are in the halls and two sixteenth-century dressers are in the bedrooms, which are hung in damasks from the sixteenth-century silk mills at Tours. As for objets d'art, Azay-le-Rideau has six Bernard Palissy porcelains and four small Cellini bronzes. Over it all linger the shades of Renaissance ladies and gentlemen.

Spectacular as they are, it is not from the royal châteaux that we find out about the gentleman's life in the country during the Renaissance. Though the gentleman might well be invited to participate in the celebrations that took place in a setting like Chambord or Chenonceaux, he scarcely lived in such an abode. His mansion or manor house was a habitat much more modest than these princely installations for the relaxed moments of royalty. Some quite specific information on a sixteenth-century manor house has been left by Charles Estienne in his *Agriculture et maison rustique*. Estienne endeavors to cover all possible phases of a gentleman's comfortable existence in the country, in that his book contains "every thing that can be required to build a country house, to feed and care for animals of all sorts, to maintain vegetable and flower gardens, to look after honey bees, to plant and cross every sort of fruit tree, to prepare meadows, fish-pools and ponds, to cultivate the grain-bearing land, to create the vineyards, to plant the tall trees and shrubs, to build the warren, the heronry, and the enclosure for the wild animals," — and to all this is added a brief discourse on hunting and falconry. It was the late "King Francis I, patron of knowledge," who encouraged the bringing in of several plants, herbs, and trees never before known in France, says Estienne in a preliminary epistle, and thus encouraged a gentleman to live on and improve his land. The house, after the title to the property has been cleared, should be placed on rather high ground. It is very important that the site of the house may be satisfactory to the gentleman, because he will most likely live in it the year around and not be able to change his domain with the seasons in the manner of a prince. In France there is much good soil, but that of the provinces of Anjou, Maine, and Touraine is the best. Touraine, in fact, is "deservedly called the garden of France." The house should not be so large as to be a burden; but the master of it should live in it rather than in the city.

The country house should be set on a square of ground about an acre and one half in size, and this plot will be enclosed with walls eighteen inches thick and ten feet high. In the middle of the terrain will be a pond, and beyond this a well. There will be in the center of the front wall, which "will face toward the setting sun," an entrance gateway wide enough to let in a cart of hay. In front of this gateway will be eight or ten acres of open land. As you enter to go into the enclosed area, there will be at the left the farmer's lodging and at the right the stables for the horses and cattle as well as a room for the servants. The master's house will be directly opposite the gateway on the other side of the square, and the main entrance to it will be approached by a flight of no more than eight steps. The main floor of the house will be a story above the kitchen and the special quarters for two or three personal servants, all of which will be at the right of the main entrance on the ground floor. The master may also have his den and bedroom on the ground floor. The main windows of the house will face toward the east, and not on the courtyard. The house will have plenty of room for any friends or passers-by who might drop in. There will be privies for the occupants of the house and the lower seats thereof will be used by the farmer and his helpers. Adequate space will be available for chickens, geese, pigs, gardens, orchards, and pastures.

The master of the domain — Estienne calls him the "father of the family" — will look after everything. He will be gentle with his servants, and issue no commands to them in anger, yet he should not become too familiar with them, or they will hold him in contempt. The farmer in charge of operations should be a mature and reliable man, who is willing to work from morning till night, and who is not interested in amusing himself at the village nearby or at a country fair. He needs no education, but should be simple and truthful — and Estienne goes on with many more details. It is obvious from Estienne's suggestion that he expects his country gentleman to live in close association with his farmers and servants, in paternalistic oversight of them, but not on a basis of social equality.[3]

The ideas of Estienne on the country gentleman and his house were restated and somewhat modified toward the end of the century by Olivier de Serres in his *Théâtre d'agriculture et mesnage des champs*. He covers all the points treated by Estienne and gives a little more complete advice on the cultivation of vineyards — "since it is also necessary to drink in order to live, and since wine is the most general and salutary of beverages" — and on the raising of pigeons. Serres feels that there should be covered sheds for wine presses, and two or three cellars to hold the wine. Also, seven or eight extra bedrooms in the house should be made comfortable for any season of the year — "for nurses, maids, schoolmasters, or friends happening by." Another touch of delicacy is added by Serres: on the north side of the house there should be two sets of privies, one for the male servants and one for the female servants, "out of consideration for modesty." The kitchen might well be placed on the main floor, above the ground floor, next to the general living room, because the master can then watch things more closely. He will be better served, as a matter of fact, if he eats in the kitchen. This was the attitude, Serres points out, of the Connétable Anne de Montmorency, who said that a "gentleman having attained as much as five hundred livres revenue" starts putting on airs and dining in the dining room, at the mercy of his cook. As long as he eats in the kitchen, a gentleman is sure of getting the best portions. The "father of the family," however, should have affection for his subjects even though he orders them about, and should act honorably toward everybody. Serres' book concludes with several designs for gardens, based upon the horticultural plans of some of the famous châteaux.[4]

The ideas of Estienne and Serres on the construction of a gentleman's house were not simply the idle imaginings of men who liked to write. Many abodes of the country gentlemen of the sixteenth century were built in the manner prescribed by these two proponents of genteel rural comforts, and a number of the structures are still standing. The valley of the Loire, with its fertile black soil and network of meandering smaller streams, was most encouraging to a gentleman who wanted to build a fine house during the Renaissance. It was favored by kings for the creation of princely châteaux as well as by gentlemen for their more modest dwellings, and it is thus understandable that the Loire valley better than any other area of France might give today evidences of architectural tastes of the past centuries. As recently as 1934, the Baron Karl Reille published in Tours a series of drawings, with brief commentary, of some two hundred châteaux and genteel houses of the region.[5] Many of these follow the specifications set down by Estienne and Serres. In the autumn of 1948, I myself spent about a month radiating in all directions from Tours — with the help of a little Renault automobile — looking for present-day remains of a gentleman's house of the Renaissance. A very near approximation to the concepts of Estienne and Serres was found in the mansion of Azay-sur-Cher, only about two kilometers from Tours. The house is set in a squared area, enclosed by walls of the prescribed height and thickness. Each side of the square is about one hundred seventy-five feet, and the house rests in the center of one side. On going through the gateway toward the main house you find to the right and left, stables, sheds, and appendages. A pond, evidently a satisfaction to several ducks that were dipping in and out of it, is just outside the walled area to the left. The house itself is marked at the corners in good Renaissance and medieval fashion by towers, sixty feet apart. There is a graceful approach to the main gateway, more than two hundred yards long. On this particular day in autumn, a quiet operation that would have pleased Estienne was going on: the farmer was driving through the gateway with a cartload of hay.

A little more than three kilometers west of the village of Suèvres is the fine gentleman's mansion of Dizier. Its right-hand tower as you face it must go back to the fourteenth century, judging from its crumbling crenelations; also, there are remnants of a moat and there was once a drawbridge. Some later man of the Renaissance added a façade more in keeping with his age, with a main floor entered by mounting a flight of ten or eleven steps — a few more than suggested by Estienne, but this threshold looks "restored." There are a dining room and salon on the main floor, both commodious — with twenty-foot ceilings — but not unreasonably large. On the ground floor, to the right as you face the entrance steps, are the kitchen, pantry, and storage rooms — as is proper for a country home. The kitchen contains a very old and very sizable fireplace, which must have consumed a large amount of wood. The grounds are pleasant, with a stream running along one side of the house. In the back, as you look to the left, there are the remains of a pigeon house. It must have been very satisfactory to live at Dizier.

Then there is the compact little manor house of La Roche, some ten kilometers slightly northeast of Amboise, two hundred meters off highway N751. It is now owned by an American, but its rounded turrets are pre-Renaissance and the octagonal tower in the center of the house is reminiscent of Blois. It has a neat little courtyard and gardens sloping down toward the river. Between Langeais and Tours is Chatigny, with its towers of stone and brick that give a checkerboard effect, and its Renaissance façade on a small inner court. This comfortable property is still owned by the descendants of its original genteel possessors, according to the gardener who took a suspicious look at the little Renault from the top of a stone wall. The family was not then in residence, he said after a few puffs on an American cigarette, but the "bourgeoise" was there and would be able to give something of the history of the place. The person referred to so casually as the "bourgeoise" turned out to be a highly intelligent preceptress and graduate of the Sorbonne; she stopped reading André Gide a few minutes to talk about Chatigny. It would be a pleasure to say a few words about the great house sitting down in a small valley of Touraine, with smoke curling out of its tall chimney at the close of the day. Its main gate was open, through the enclosure of the walled square, each corner of which had a small watchtower. There was no possibility of getting further information on the mansion, unfortunately, because of a post-Renaissance dog that in the best tradition of his ancestors was protecting the castle of his master.

Some fifteen kilometers from the town of Mer is the rather intimate château of Talcy, built by Bernard Salviati, the cousin of Catherine de' Medici and father of Cassandre de Salviati, the inspiration of Ronsard's first sonnets. The ancestral home of Ronsard, La Possonière, in the province of Vendôme, was thus not too far away from one belonging to one of his beloveds. There is much that is fascinating about Talcy, with its small courtyard and colonnade of octagonal columns. The kitchen is on the ground floor and has a fireplace ten feet wide. The bedrooms are of reasonable size, about twenty feet by twenty feet, and there are still in them some handsome beds of the sixteenth century. The beds and heavy chests were likely to be the most splendid pieces of furniture in the Renaissance house. In the lower courtyard of Talcy is its famous wine press, which dates from 1520. It is made of enormous chestnut timbers, and still works. On the opposite corner of the yard from the wine press is the pigeon house, even now in a good state of preservation, which once housed over fourteen hundred pigeons. It is impossible to leave the Loire valley without mentioning the big château of Villandry,* with its magnificent gardens that go back to the Renaissance and ear-

* Jean Le Breton, a wealthy citizen of Blois, acquired Villandry in 1532 and rebuilt the château, which had further renovation — mostly unsatisfactory — in the eighteenth century.

lier. The boxwoods are still beautifully kept, and contain an allegory of love with many hearts in intricate design, one division of the older garden having two *D*'s in boxwood, back to back, in honor of Diane de Poitiers.

Many other Renaissance country estates in other parts of France had the main house follow the general pattern suggested by Estienne. Such a place is La Hérissaie, the ancestral home of the teller of tales, Noël du Fail, in Brittany. However, there was a very good reason for such a blooming of spacious houses in the land adjacent to the gentle bends of the Loire. In this section is an abundance of excellent building stone. Lippomano, the Venetian, spoke of this stone in his sixteenth-century report on France. When it is first cut, it is rather soft and manageable, but after it is put into a building and the winds, sun, and rains have struck it, the stone becomes very hard "like that of Istria." Lippomano says that this stone is replacing wood and mortar as a building material in France, though only the nobles erect fine houses; the bourgeois in the cities are too stingy to spend their money. In any case, this same stone is today cut out of the sides of the hills in the region of the Loire basin for new construction, or used for repairing historical châteaux, as was being done in 1948 to Chambord.[6]

The gentleman in the country must have had a hard time keeping warm. He would not have been too comfortable in the city, for that matter, though the urban houses and rooms therein were smaller. Part of the reason for tapestries, or sometimes straw mats, on the walls of a château was to cushion it against the wind and assist in keeping the feeble heat inside. As has been indicated, there was no lack of size to the fireplaces. It was just impossible to heat a large and drafty room, clammy with the winter's moisture, with a fireplace. In the efforts to do it, the supply of wood was so decimated for centuries that France has never recovered from it. Many of the fireplaces in the châteaux (as at Langeais or Chenonceaux), were handsomely wrought and beautifully ornamented with arms and emblems; but they were not effective in combating the cold. Montaigne said he much preferred a Swiss stove to a French fireplace — among other advantages, there was much less smoke to contend with.[7]

Much information concerning the life of a Renaissance country gentleman has been preserved in the diaries, journals, and account books * of the period. Probably the most complete of these is the *Journal* of Gilles de Gouberville, which in some twelve hundred pages describes every possible phase of Gouberville's life on his estates in Normandy from 1549 to 1562. There are details in it on foods and cooking and the reading of the *Amadís* in the kitchen, the growing of apples, illegitimate children (who were treated with consideration), dogs and medicine (Gouberville had to do a little doctoring from time to time), all sorts of amusements, and a trip to see the King at Blois in 1556. Gouberville must have been a man of limitless energy and zest for living. The *Journal* of the Comtesse de Sanzay offers a wealth of detail concerning the internal furnishings of a country place. The countess, who was married in 1571, began in 1572 to procure furnishings and equipment for her château in Normandy, La Motte-Fouqué, which had a forest around it of about two thousand acres. First she bought — and very appropriately — two bed canopies with embroidery on a sky-blue background, four white Spanish rugs, two dozen small dishes, two dozen larger ones, eight platters, three dozen plates, several pots, pitchers, and cauldrons, as well as one hundred pounds of pewter. In 1573, she bought a tremendous amount of cloth to make napkins, aprons, tablecloths, and sheets, along with two hundred sixty pounds, at "eight and one half sous a pound" — the countess always gives the price of everything —of goose feathers for the beds. In 1574, she purchased five steers, nine cows, twelve sheep, five or six fat pigs, barrels of wine and cider, sugar, pepper, ginger, and twenty pounds of herring. In 1576, wine became more expensive; so the countess laid in a supply of cider which had gone down in price. The Comte de Sanzay, who was a gentleman of the King's chamber, went to Paris in 1580 and came back with a nice little coach,

* Many have been published; one of the most recent is Montaigne's "day-book," his *Livre de raison* (Paris, 1948).

which cost a little more than one hundred crowns with the harness included. In 1581, the countess accompanied her husband to Paris — it took them nine days to reach there at a speed of eight to fourteen leagues a day — and there she got some gold buttons. Heavy furniture — beds, buffets, chairs, etc. — was purchased in 1586. There were many visitors to the château in the 1590's, which necessitated the hiring of another cook, for twenty-five livres and a pair of shoes. The countess periodically renewed her own wardrobe in Rouen. The count died in 1601 (all funeral expenses are listed); so the countess sold the château to a nephew.[8]

The men of letters during the Renaissance constantly praise the pleasures of living in the country. Some of their homage may be an affected ruralism, but much of it is sincere. Du Bellay, far away in the marble city of Rome, would like to see the smoke curling over his own slate roof and to sip the sweetness of Anjou. Ronsard, periodically disgusted with the Court and its intrigues, would like to go fishing and taste the new wine; or, maybe, with some apricots, melons, artichokes, and strawberries (with cream), stretch out on the bank of a small stream and relax. "I would rather see," says Ronsard, "a beautiful meadow tapestried in color, or hear the murmur of a chattering brook, and go to sleep in the green grass, than be at Court and beg in vain for a false hope of favor that slips through the hands." In *La Salade*, a delightful poem to his friend and fellow-poet, Amadis Jamyn, Ronsard sings the praises of getting together the makings of a salad, with a little perusal of the "ingenious Ovid," out in the country and away from the Court. Happy is he who in his own ancestral home, says Ronsard in a *Discours* to Odet de Coligny, far away from the tumult and falsity of the Court, "cultivates his own small heritage."[9]

A full picture of the life of a country gentleman is given by Nicolas Rapin in his poem, *Les Plaisirs du gentilhomme champêtre*. In sixty-five stanzas of five lines each Rapin praises the life of the gentleman who is removed from the pomp and grandeur of the Court, and has his hunting, crops, dogs, wine, and moderate food. He will have a house "without sumptuosity," some woods and a meadow and a pond, a warren, and no "grand Seigneur" too close by to interfere with his affairs. While going through the fields he may meet a shepherd lass who is amenable to a little amorous dallying, but it is especially satisfying to find in the house at the end of the day a "non-importunate wife" who has supper all ready along with a smiling face. It is fine for him to have three horses in the stable, about a dozen dogs, and a hawk or two. His repasts with friends will be on the modest side, with quantities of fruits and herbs, and no one will have the hiccoughs which come from the overstuffing of more pompous banquets. After his temperate sessions at the festive board, there will be no need for drugs, doctors, and apothecaries. Simple partridges, capons, and pigeons will take the place for him of arrogant peacocks and pheasants. On occasion, of a winter's evening, he may well read a book and learn therein what he should do to follow the "beautiful road to virtue." He will not have to take the trouble to curl his hair every morning, or sweeten his breath, or be constantly changing his velvet and satin clothes. His shirt will not need to be starched, nor will he have to appear at fancy parties alternately as a Venetian nobleman and an ancient Roman. Freed from all this courtly display, the gentleman in the country might well live to be one hundred years old. And in this manner does Rapin, along with many other poets of the Renaissance, restate the theme of the Latin poet, Horace,* on the advantages of living in the country.[10]

One of the most colorful, certainly, of the Renaissance country gentlemen was Jacques du Fouilloux, the great hunter, who called himself a "gentleman of the district of Gastine, in Poictou." The manor house of Du Fouilloux, in the commune of Saint-Martin-du-Fouilloux near the ancient town of Poitiers, has now almost gone back to the soil, and the fountain of water in the courtyard, where once famous hunting dogs quenched their thirst, has in more recent centuries been dishonored by grunting pigs. But the stories concerning Du

* Horace's famous ode, beginning *Beatus ille . . .*, devotes some seventy verses to the joys of living in the country.

Fouilloux linger on even today in the environs of Poitiers. Du Fouilloux was born in 1521 and ended his lusty career on this earth in 1580. He was brought up by his uncle, after the death of his mother and his father's remarriage in 1526. In a poem that Jacques wrote, *Adolescence*, he tells us that at the age of twenty he left his uncle's château to seek adventures of his own — for, like a three-year-old wild boar that goes out to shift for himself, so does a man at twenty break away from family restrictions. In the words of Du Fouilloux: "One fine morning I went away from there, forgetting nothing except to say good-bye. I took my hound and wandered off, with my bottle hanging at my side." It was after this severing of connections with his relatives that Du Fouilloux's exploits really began. Many of them were procreative, for he was said to have fathered around fifty children, some legitimate, more illegitimate. He never abandoned the demoiselles who had fallen victims to his blandishments, but made proper monetary provisions for them; also, he had a kindly affection for his not inconsiderable number of bastards.

One of the taller stories, with a wide circulation, about Du Fouilloux, concerned his giving to a pretty peasant lass a bright red apple. Though she did not know it, the fruit contained a liberal portion of Du Fouilloux's own personally-concocted aphrodisiac. The maid did not eat the apple immediately, but put it aside; it was later thrown out inadvertently into the backyard with garbage for the pigs. A rather cumbersome sow consumed the fruit and came charging into Du Fouilloux's room in the middle of the night. The noise was tremendous, and the whole house was awakened before quiet could be restored. In 1554, Du Fouilloux married the daughter of Monsieur Berthelot, counselor for the Parlement at Poitiers, and assumed, relatively, a more responsible attitude toward the directing of the affairs of his estates. He had the reputation, incidentally, of being a thoroughly honorable man in business dealings, and he never wished to hurt anyone; women were his major problem.

Madame du Fouilloux, most understandably, became a trifle irritated at her husband's numerous infidelities. Her complaints became louder and louder, and more and more frequent. Whereupon Du Fouilloux, so the story ran, put her in a big cradle and rocked her until she was quiet. This incident, true or not, had such broad circulation in its day that at least two of the century's storytellers picked it up. Guillaume Bouchet in his collection, *Les Serées*, repeats it without mentioning any names. However, Béroalde de Verville, in his *Moyen de parvenir*, tells of the cradle-rocking and attaches it specifically to Du Fouilloux, a slightly unusual procedure. Though writers of tales in the century, especially Marguerite de Navarre, mixed fact and fancy in the relation of their yarns, in most cases the persons involved are not called by name. Du Fouilloux is also mentioned in the *Moyen de parvenir* in connection with certain exploits at the fair of Fontenay, a fair that was quite popular with the nobility of lower Poitou. Du Fouilloux is listed as one of a "joyous troup of gentlemen of the region" who were stirring up things at the fair. As for Du Fouilloux, that rollicking gentleman and mighty hunter, he would scarcely have been bothered by being put in a storybook; nor did he seem to be disturbed, in his busy career, by the breaking of the seventh and other commandments. But he did write in his spare time the best treatise of the century on the hunting of the stag and other animals, assuming undoubtedly that through the intervention of Saint Hubert and Saint Eustache, the patron saints of venery, he would take his place with other good hunters in Paradise.[11]

It would not be correct to regard Du Fouilloux as an ideal gentleman of the sixteenth century, but he surely had many of the qualities, good and bad, of the country gentleman; and he was more highly placed than certain civil and judicial officers who were known somewhat derogatorily during the period as "gentlemen of the city." His amorous excursions and marital delinquencies had no effect on his acceptance by royalty, since he always joined the King's parties that passed through Poitiers. The forests around Du Fouilloux's house were full of all sorts of game, and it must have appealed to a regal visitor to hunt a stag or wild boar under the guidance of an expert. Among his other abilities, Du Fouilloux was supposed to have remarkable eyesight, and to be able to see the movements of a wary animal at an incredible distance. His estates probably could not have accommodated a royal party of fifteen thousand that stayed for six weeks or so — which happened to Jean de Laval in Brittany in 1532 when the King dropped by his property of Châteaubriant. Nevertheless, Du Fouilloux most likely had plenty of dogs in his kennels — Charles IX himself, in his little book on hunting, *La Chasse royale*, had advised that on a country estate an acre or so with a brook should be set aside for the kennels — and a few things to eat and drink when royalty passed by.[12]

There were other gentlemen and other estates. Vallery, one of the "private houses" listed by Du Cerceau and the property of the Maréchal de Saint-André, was a trifle too luxurious to be regarded as the manor house of a country gentleman. It was superbly and lavishly decorated, and the site of many splendid parties. The great château of Brissac in Anjou was almost completely destroyed during the Wars of Religion, with the exception of two sixteenth-century towers. René de Brissac bought the seigniory of Brissac in 1502, which seigniory gave to the new master control of the château, a pond, several windmills and water mills, and some farm lands, as well as of the beautiful ghost of Charlotte de Maulévrier, slain by her deceived husband in 1470. He also was in charge of the administration of justice and the operation of fairs and markets in the area. Such dominion — that is, the control of the miller as well as the mill — was progressively reduced during the century, except as a gentleman functioned as an officer of the King. The gentleman in the country was no longer a feudal baron, and by 1560 the Third Estate felt free to complain to the King about the carelessness of the gentleman's hunting habits, particularly his invasion of fields that had been recently planted or which contained vineyards. And in 1560, according to the *Mémoires* of Guillaume de Rochechouart, everything was changed and terribly expensive. The price of land and the price of wheat had both gone up, and if a gentleman got more for the products of his lands, the increase in the cost of living offset it.[13]

Much was to be said, then, for living in the country just as there was much to be said for being at Court. The gentleman in the country certainly had the advantage of the open air, and spent an enormous amount of time on horseback. Montaigne, in fact, quotes Tasso as saying that French gentlemen have much frailer legs than Italian gentlemen because the former are on a horse so many hours of the day. The French gentleman unquestionably could chase the stag all day if he so desired. This could happen even at Blois — unless he had to put on his pretty clothes to go see the Queen's sponsored production of Melin de Saint-Gelais' translation from the Italian of the tragedy *Sophonisbe* — where Andrea Navagero said in 1528 that there were gardens and a forest eleven leagues by four, and "many species of wild beasts abound therein." And the gentleman in the evening might wander back to his own house where a grateful wife had prepared for him a bed with spotless sheets and coverlet, a jug of wine, some candied nuts and preserved fruits, as was done in Marguerite de Navarre's tale of the lady who won her husband back from a hussy.[14]

All in all, the gentleman who dwelt in the country during the Renaissance at its best period was in a most favored position. He could live pleasantly on his estates, exercise considerable authority in his province, and — if he were clever — still spend some time at the court of his King.

VIII

Sports and Diversions

THE GENTLEMAN OF THE RENAISSANCE was strong in body. In an age that was so demanding of all his energies, he had to be. There had come to be in the sixteenth century a wholly different attitude toward the human body from that held in the Middle Ages. In previous centuries in France, despite the formidable exploits of the heroes of medieval epics, the physical side of man's life on this earth was minimized and his terrestrial moment was primarily a preparation for the eons of being after death. The cult of the Virgin, the construction of magnificent cathedrals, the emphasis on allegory and didacticism in literature, the preference for Biblical and saintly subjects in painting and statuary, all symbolize this point of view.* Even pagan characters, if they were treated, were covered with a coating of moralization, or, if they were represented visually, with several layers of clothes. In the late fifteenth-century editions of French adaptations of such writers as Ovid and Virgil, there are many woodcuts used for illustrations — of, among other personages, Helen of Troy and the goddess Diana. Both are dressed in Mother Hubbards and several layers of petticoats. In the Louvre a fifteenth-century representation by Francesco di Giorgio (1430–1502) of Europa riding the Jovian bull shows her sitting demurely sidesaddle in a modest full-length gown. The sixteenth century changed all this. The *galerie François Premier* at Fontainebleau has sixteen frescoes done by Primaticcio and Rosso — there was no real school of French painting in the Renaissance, so the artists largely were Italian imports — most of which are based on the legends of

* It is true that the feudal baron, like the Renaissance gentleman, was lusty and earthy; but the baron did not live in a cultural and artistic atmosphere so openly favorable to the paganism of the ancients.

Ovid. In one of them, Europa is riding her bull, her hair flowing in the breeze, and there is only one silken streamer at her waist to offer wind resistance. In the *galerie Henri II* at Fontainebleau, dominating figures are the goddess Ceres, with a beautiful bosom and a bunch of flowers, and the undraped god Pan. The Louvre has four notable paintings by the sixteenth-century artist, Guido Reni, of events in the life of Hercules — and not a mighty muscle is hidden. The human body, then, in the Renaissance was not something to be ashamed of. A fine masculine torso or a subtly-rounded feminine breast received quite openly critical admiration. The most beautiful statue of the French Renaissance, the nude Diana of Jean Goujon, with a stag resting contentedly by the goddess, was very possibly modeled from the delicate corporal lines of Diane de Poitiers herself. The classical admonition was that the body, the proud container of the soul, should be kept in good condition; this idea was accepted during the Renaissance.[1]

Francis I and Henry II set the standard among their gentlemen for athletic prowess and energy. They both had constitutions of iron, and a great interest in outdoor activities. The "great King Francis" was a fine figure of a man, and physical exercises had made his body very robust. He was accomplished at wrestling, though Castiglione thought this was not a very good sport for a gentleman, since he would lose caste if he lost to someone beneath him in rank. In any case, Francis I from his infancy liked all types of games — ball games, impromptu snowball fights, jousting, simulated attacks on châteaux, etc. He liked dogs and hunting, and was always on a horse. His son, Henry, was probably an even better athlete. Henry was "all muscles," and was ready at any time for any sort of formal or informal sport. If it happened to snow or freeze at Fontainebleau, the King led the Court in a little snowballing or sliding on the ice — "and he always liked to have the ladies around to see the performance." The dark-skinned Henry was an excellent jumper and was especially good at the broad jump. He could do between twenty-three and twenty-five feet, so the story ran, which would put him in the class of champions. His only rival at this specialty was the Admiral

Bonnivet, who in trying to follow the leaps of the King one day fell in a deep ditch full of water. Henry also loved horses, hunting, and jousting — and his love for the last cost him his life. Poor little Francis II, King for less than a year, was not around very long, and Charles IX, though he had the elegance of the Valois and an appreciation of the sporting interests of a gentleman, was not very strong. Henry III was more at home in a beauty parlor than on a stag hunt. It is a strange thing that the three royal sons of Henry II and Catherine were all frail, anemic, or uninterested in the outdoor sports of a gentleman, for the Queen Mother was a sportswoman in her own right, whether indoors or outdoors. She liked dancing, ballets, riding, and hunting. Completely at home on a horse, she first attracted the attention of Francis I before she was Queen because of the dash of her riding and the ease with which she swung a leg over the saddle-bow.[2]

The hunting of the stag was probably the most engrossing of a gentleman's sporting activities. Other animals, such as the wild boar and hare, were pursued with horse and hound, but the stag was the favorite and was surrounded with the most complete ritual. Erasmus thought that so much ceremony in connection with the slaying of an animal was silly, but there was much doctrine written down on the subject. An annual item in the royal budget was for hunting; the figure for 1535 was reported to be forty thousand crowns and by 1546 had been increased to one hundred fifty thousand. Kings, scholars, and huntsmen all wrote on the question of stag-hunting and the training of dogs therefor. In chronological order, among a number of writings, is Budé's *De Venatione*, a little treatise in Latin on venery, which appeared around 1529; it was translated later into French by the good Latin scholar, Louis Le Roy. The most popular manual was Jacques du Fouilloux's *La Vénerie*, which came out in 1561 and had a number of later editions. Charles IX's *La Chasse royale*, which treats of the nature of the stag and the raising of dogs, was not put into printed form until the seventeenth century. From these manuals as well as from comments by men of letters — poets like Saint-Gelais, Jean Passerat, and Ronsard have much to say about dogs and hunting — a good deal of information can be gleaned about the way a crowd of gentlemen on horseback, accompanied by a large collection of dogs, pursued and destroyed a stag during the Renaissance.

A gentleman of skill does not want, according to the manuals, to waste his time on a small and inferior stag, but prefers one that is completely mature, and this noble stag should have at least ten points. There are many signs that will indicate the fully grown stag — his tracks, which will be wide and show a hollow in his foot, his dung, and the general trail left through the wood in a path visible to the expert. The most competent huntsmen will already have examined the terrain and located several likely stags. They will have done this with their crafty and persistent bloodhounds, which have very keen noses, made more so by the insertion of a little vinegar into their nostrils. If this preliminary examination has been done late in the afternoon and the hunt is set for the next morning, a huntsman should go at dawn and climb a tree in the area to try to see the stag. A good huntsman must have excellent eyesight, since by this means he can help the dogs. At any rate, the various stags have been staked out, the terrain to be covered pretty well marked off, and the king or grand seigneur is in the woods with his party. The huntsmen show to the king or grand seigneur the several examples of stag dung, give descriptions of each particular stag, and the great nobleman picks out the stag he prefers to hunt. After this momentous decision has been reached, everybody relaxes and has a drink.

Eminent preparations have been made for the bibulous and gastronomic phases of the hunt. The keeper of the wines arrives with three horses laden, says Du Fouilloux, with "materials for moistening the gullet" — barrels, flagons, and bottles of the best wine the country provides, all properly cooled. Tablecloths are spread near a fountain or brook. The cook comes up then with a light repast — hams, smoked tongue, pigs' snouts and ears, sausages, backbones, slices of beef, and cold loin of veal. Everybody stretches out on cloaks, and there is much eating, drinking, and laughing; and if there is some "woman of reputation" in the environs she may be called in for the pleasure of the company. Eventually the question of the stag comes again to the fore, but nobody rushes into it.

The bloodhound is finally put on the trail of the chosen stag and the full pack is let loose to the sound of trumpets. The dogs must follow only the noble stag, though he will try to confuse them by all sorts of ruses, like mixing up his own scent with that of a smaller stag. Or he will cross streams of water, or even join flocks of domestic animals. In these circumstances, the bloodhound must straighten out the trail and get the pack back on it. A good hunter can tell from the bark of a mature dog whether he is on the right scent or not; and if he is, the hunter should sound three blasts on his horn to call other dogs in to help. Finally, the stag is brought to bay and then he is very dangerous. If he is standing in a stream of water it is best to approach him in a boat; if he is on land it is preferable to slip in behind him with a knife. In either case, the stag has reached the end of the road.

Death is sounded and the dogs and the company are recalled. The dismembering of the stag's body is highly ritualized. The right foot is cut off and presented to the king or grand seigneur. The stag is then turned over on its back and is shorn of its testicles; next the hide is removed. However, before the carcass is cut up, the huntsman puts aside his knife and has a drink — in fact, the whole party takes a little time out for "drinking, laughing, and good cheer." The valets of the dogs, which are all tied on leashes, during this process will not be having an easy time holding the noisy pack in check. The body of the stag is finally cut apart in keeping with an established formula, with the various segments distributed according to plan. The grand master of the hunt, for example, receives the stag's brisket. The backbone is given to the valet of the bloodhounds. As for the dogs, they are given the vital organs of the animal. The first bloodhound gets the heart, and the least able dogs get chunks of bread dipped in the stag's blood. All of this is done under the guidance of a designated huntsman — and thus ends the play in which the leading actor was predestined to die. Du Fouilloux does not think that it is obligatory to wear a green costume for the hunting of the stag, and a gray one for hunting the wild boar, although tradition has had it this way. He would leave the matter of color to the fancy of the individual, but he does lament the fact that few huntsmen nowadays know how to blow a trumpet correctly or how to handle dogs, in the manner of the Duc d'Alençon and the seigneur de Montmorency. The present generation of hunters is only interested in killing the stag and not in the fine methods of venery.[3]

The wild boar is a rough beast and not to be hunted with the best pack of dogs, because a number of them will most certainly be killed. The boar lives to be twenty-five or thirty years old, but a four-year-old animal is a tough proposition and worth hunting. The size of a boar can be judged by his tracks, etc., even as a stag. A boar is always dangerous, and out of a pack of fifty dogs used to corner him, not more than ten will return to the kennels uninjured; and many will be dead, victims of his ripping lower teeth. The dogs, and horsemen accompanying them with swords, will have to combine to kill the boar. The hunting of the hare is a much more pleasant sport "for gentlemen" because it is not so expensive and it provides a nice relaxation to watch the maneuvers of this clever little beast. He may hop into a pond, hide in the ivy, or join a flock of sheep to get away from his pursuer. There is "little pleasure" to be derived from the hunting of the fox, which is done with short-legged basset hounds. However, if a gentleman decides he wants to do it, he should take along half a dozen men with spades to dig the animal out of holes, while the gentleman rides in a cart with a pallet in it and bottles of wine hanging on each corner post, a supply of ham, smoked tongue, and other good "gullet armor" * — and a young demoiselle aboard to keep him company. Under these more favorable conditions, the hunting of the fox becomes a rather delightful diversion.[4]

* *Harnois de gueule*, a favorite expression of Du Fouilloux, is defined by Cotgrave as "mouth armor," or "bellie furniture."

For many of the types of hunting done by the gentleman, there was a need for dogs — and the gentleman loved his dogs. The raising of dogs was a gentleman's privilege, and adequate space was gladly provided by him for the kennels, well fenced in and with two or three posts covered with straw. The manuals give much advice on the care the dogs should receive. The valets who are to look after the dogs should sleep in the attic above and these guardians should be trained in all they need to know "to be worthy to stay near the dogs." The hunting dogs are to be distinguished according to their color — white, tawny, gray, and black. The first of the famous white dogs, says Du Fouilloux, was Souillard, given by a poor gentleman to Louis XII. Souillard had many famous descendants, especially after he was reinforced by Francis I with a tawny strain. The tawny canines are good dogs, particularly for hunting the stag, but they do not have the endurance of the whites. The gray dogs are very satisfactory for a gentleman to own because they will work any sort of game. They are spirited dogs, not afraid of water, and can be trained to obey the voice and trumpet of their master. The most ancient line is the black dog, blessed by Saint Hubert himself. Since this species is not very fast, it is better for wild boars and foxes. Many of the qualities of a good hunting dog are native, but he must be carefully trained. When he is a youngster of some six or seven months, he will want to run after everything; so care should be taken that he does not chase rabbits — an excellent piece of advice, as all trainers of dogs know. He will learn his profession best if he hunts with older dogs that are not too easily fooled by the wiles of the animal being pursued. The writers and poets sang the praises of hunting dogs. Jean Passerat wrote a poem entitled *Le Chien courant*, or *The Hunting Dog*, in which he mentions the famous dogs of his time, and outlines the ideal qualities of such a dog. Much beloved dogs of the century were Francis I's childhood playmate, Hapeguai, which died in 1502, and Courte, whose royal master was so bereaved at her death that he had her skin made into a pair of gloves.[5]

The kings and "the great gentlemen" fixed the pattern for

hunting in all its forms. Fleurange says that he and Francis I as youngsters set traps "to catch stags and wild beasts." Budé states that Francis I was the master of the pursuit of both the stag and the wild boar, and that the King deserved comparison with the great huntsman, Orion. No one rode a horse with such "incredible speed" as the King, who dashed over mountains, through forests, thickets, and bushes with just one arm raised to protect his face and eyes from the branches. As for a fuming wild boar, the King would slay him with a thrust of the sword, while Budé watched from a safe point of refuge. The King's wild riding cost him an eye injury from a branch of a tree on a hunt at Blois in 1519, which caused his mother considerable worry. Henry II also liked very much to pursue the stag and, according to Giovanni Capello, hunted at least twice a week. The royal offices that were connected with hunting were high in their honorary and influential implications. For example, Claude de Lorraine, the first Duc de Guise, was grand master of the royal hunts under Francis I and his son François, the second Duc de Guise, was grand master later in the century. Both were expert in hunting and the training of dogs.[6]

Falconry, though not the favored sport it was during the Middle Ages, was still practiced and the owning of falcons was a gentleman's privilege. The gift of a falcon from one gentleman to another was a notable gesture of courtesy during the period, and the Crown's office of grand falcon-master was highly honorific and no sinecure. The grand falcon-master, with his fifty assistant falcon-masters, had the responsibility for the sale or exchange of falcons throughout the realm, and early in the century the expense attached to the operation was more than thirty-six thousand francs annually. A gentleman kept a few hunting birds whether he himself hunted or not; like the sword, they were external symbols of living the life of a gentleman.[7]

A falcon was not easy to train, though one that was taken quite young out of the nest was an easier proposition. To teach him his duties, a hood would be placed over the bird's head to keep him at rest, and frequently he would be starved. Sometimes a line would be attached to a leg, and then he would be released for limited flight. Of he might be encouraged to proficiency in his profession by the use of a wounded partridge on which he could pounce easily. In any event, through kindness and patient discipline, he gradually learned to carry out the hunting demands of his master. It was better if two falcons could be trained to work together, so that they would not fight in mid-air. A large amount of space was needed to teach the birds the proper techniques. In the more wealthy or royal houses, the leather hoods of the falcons would be garnished with gold and pearls. Each bird wore little silver bells on his legs and a copper ring on which was the name of the owner. To fail to return a lost falcon to his master was a very ungenteel trick.

A great variety of birds and small animals might be hunted with falcons — like herons, cranes, kites, partridges, quail, and hares. The male falcon was about one third smaller than the female and would be used generally to hunt the lighter birds like quail or partridges. It was not considered sporting to take a heron or kite too near the ground. The falcon should be held on the wrist under his hood until after these birds have been flushed. There were many varieties of falcons. The goshawk, sparrow-hawk, merlin, and gerfalcon were "wrist birds," since they could be trained to return to rest on the hunter's leather-covered wrist. The lanner, saker, and hobby came back to a bright red bird made of cloth that could be seen from a great distance. The gerfalcon was the most esteemed of all these hunting birds. From the letters of Louis de Brézé, grand hunts-master for five years until 1495 and later husband of Diane de Poitiers, can be seen the high regard a gentleman had for his predatory birds. Brézé, in a letter from Blois to René de Savoie in 1519, says he has lost a saker and it causes him "great displeasure." And to that fine hunter, Anne de Montmorency, Brézé writes in 1529 that he is sending him a falcon, caught just four days before and not yet, therefore, ready for the field. Later Brézé laments in a letter to Montmorency that a fine black saker named Giron, given to him by the King, has died.[8] Rabelais pays a little homage to falconry when he has his idealized Abbaye de Thélème equipped with "paragons of birds," which include every species of falcon.

Other techniques were employed for destroying unsuspecting birds and animals in the fields, but dogs and falcons were the primary adjuncts to the process. Early in the century, leopards had been introduced for the pursuit of rabbits, and there were cages at Anet to hold the predatory beasts, but they never became a standard part of a gentleman's hunting equipment. Nets and other snares were set at times, but they were too passive and a trifle unsporting, like seining for fish. There was little if any wing shooting in view of the inaccuracy of the blundering weapons of the period; still, a gentleman insisted that he be the sole bearer of an harquebus, and that the weapon be kept out of the hands of the commoner. Benvenuto Cellini, he of the easy hyperbole, claims that he shot a number of geese outside Florence with his very dependable carbine. One of them was brought down in flight and Benvenuto could pick them off easily at around one hundred yards — which can be consumed with a lump of salt. It is pleasant to note that the Renaissance knew that most satisfactory of hunting animals, the bird dog. He was called a *chien couchant*, a "setting dog," and Ronsard praises him in a delightful poem, *La Chasse*, where the setter — he must be a setter though he acts a bit like a pointer — sniffs out the field rapidly with his unerring nose and goes straight to the covey of partridges; then, "raising a leg and stiffening his tail, and stretching forward, he holds himself firmly planted until he sees the spot where the game is huddled down covered with a drag-net." All of which might be compared to shooting quail on the ground or catching trout with worms, but the quarry had few inherent or legal rights in the Renaissance.[9]

Close to hunting in popularity with the gentleman of the lustier years of the sixteenth century was jousting in its variety of forms. The Middle Ages had had a great taste for tourneys, in which large groups of knights in heavy armor hammered away at one another with broad sword and mace. It was very much like war and a man could be seriously injured in such exhibitions; also, if he were conquered, he lost his horse to the victor. Some refinements were added to tourneys in the fifteenth century: rules were codified, judges were present as well as beautiful ladies, and prizes were given to the winners. Balls and gala festivals were held in connection with many tourneys, and participants therein were supposed to be gentlemen. In the early part of the century, Symphorien Champier, the erudite doctor in Lyon, had a few words to say about tourneys and jousts, the primary purpose of which was to "make young gentlemen fit for war." Two avowed enemies should not be allowed to compete against each other, the beginning of activities should be signaled by the heralds with blasts on the trumpet, and no one whose name is not inscribed on the roll should be allowed to enter the lists. All weapons and armor must be previously inspected by the judges and there will be a great fanfare when the king and ladies enter the stands. The victors who have been given the prizes — a jewel, a sword, or a helmet — by the judges will be conducted around the lists to a fanfare of trumpets, and if the victor is a "prince or a nobleman capable of doing it," he owes a banquet to the ladies and knights assembled. The Chevalier Bayard in his early years was very fond of tourneys; at the age of seventeen he participated most successfully in one at Lyon, and received the approbation of the ladies present for his accomplishments. The following year Bayard himself staged a tourney outside the village of Ayre in Picardy, beginning on the twentieth of July. After it was proclaimed in advance to the sound of the trumpet, some forty-six gentlemen entered it. On the first day, on horseback, there were three clashes of lances and twelve with swords, for each knight; and for the winner, there was as a prize a "golden arm bracelet enameled in his colors and worth thirty crowns." On the following day there was to be combat on foot with lance and battle-axe until the judges picked a winner, to whom would be given a "diamond worth forty crowns." In the evening at the end of the first day Bayard gave a big supper party in his lodging; there were many ladies present and much good cheer. After supper there was dancing, "and several other amusements," until one o'clock in the morning. Everybody slept late the next day, and then went to Mass, after which the gentlemen promenaded with the ladies, "talking about love and other pleasant topics." The second half of the tourney finally got under way around two o'clock in the afternoon and was completed around seven. The judges decided that Bayard had won his own tourney. He gave the prizes in genteel magnanimity to two other doughty knights.[10]

Bayard's tourney, it should be remembered, took place a little before the beginning of the sixteenth century. With the succeeding years the vogue for such mass competitions began to wane, though such a game as the *pas d'armes*, which was usually an imaginary attack on a château, continued in popularity. One group of gentlemen would be the defenders behind a simulated fortification, while another group would be the attackers. This pastime could get quite rough, depending on the weapons used, and it will be remembered that Francis I almost lost his life at it when he was struck in the head by a fireplace log at Romorantin. However, as for the confused medley of clashing horsemen, or the general combat on foot at the barrier, where two groups of knights stood on each side of a barrier up to their navels and smashed at one another with sword and axe — these crude types of amusement gradually passed out of the picture.

Jousting, a single combat between two knights, was more of a sporting proposition. The primary point of it was to shatter a jousting lance * and not to incapacitate an opponent, and skill played a part as well as brute force. The champion was the man who smashed the greatest number of lances against an adversary's chest. According to Champier, a gentleman who had shattered as many as twelve lances in one day would not be allowed to ride again in the arena until the next day. The standard jousting lance was about five meters long, with a slightly blunted iron tip. It was a somewhat lighter weapon

* The adversary might be unhorsed in the process of shattering; but with the lighter jousting lance of the Renaissance it was not necessary to unseat an opponent to gain the victory.

than the lance used in actual warfare, since it was intended to be broken. There was sometimes a small iron hook on the right side of the breast-plate of the armor to support the handle of the lance. Examples of armor, lances, decorated helmets, and other jousting materials may be seen today in the Musée de l'Armée in Paris. The jouster, when he was so heavily laden with his equipment, needed a small stepladder to get on his horse. The shock of the impact of the lance against the rider was tremendous; so he leaned forward and gripped his mount with his knees in order to avoid being unhorsed.

Riding along a barrier became increasingly popular during the first half of the sixteenth century. The jousters rode at each other from opposite sides of a wooden fence about a meter in height, with the barrier at the left of the charging horse. The right-hand side of the armor was therefore lightly reinforced and the ventilation of the helmet was also on the right-hand side. The target for the lance, which might be crisscrossed with bone and wood, was thus on the left side of the armored chest of the gentleman. As can be visualized, it was easier to keep the horse on a straight course if he raced along parallel to a barrier; also, there was a better chance to score a clean hit on the target. A milder version of jousting was to smash the lance against a fixed shield or target, but this was disdained by more ardent horsemen. One could also "courir la bague," or thrust at a ring with the lance while riding full tilt.

Francis I and Henry II, by enthusiasm and by example, encouraged these simulated man-to-man combats among their gentlemen. The eighteenth-century historian of the city of Paris, Henri Sauval, states that jousting areas during the period of the Renaissance were set up all over the city — in a courtyard of the Louvre, on the rue Saint-Antoine, in the "place des Anglais in front of the Jesuits," and from the rue Saint-Paul up to the Bastille. Jousting, with its variants, was a normal part of any royal ceremonial or celebration, even though occasionally a gentleman might get killed at it. Fleurange tells how Francis I and seven captains (including Fleurange) as the defenders in an armed combat took on all comers at the marriage of Louis XII and Mary of England. It was a notable job of defending, because more than three hundred valiant men of arms were present. And François de Lorraine, Duc de Guise, later in the century with only one knight to assist him undertook a combat at the barrier (then a somewhat outmoded amusement) against some fifty attackers — and withstood them. The Duc de Nemours, who lived from 1531 to 1585, was also expert at these warlike games, whether on foot or on a horse. He was really "the flower of all chivalry, beloved of everybody around, especially the ladies." The prowess of Henry II has been variously catalogued. Ronsard in his poem, *Avant-entrée du Roi*, written for the entree of Henry II into Paris in 1549, pictures the blare of trumpets, the horses charging in their shining harness, the smashed lances flying up to the heavens. However, the favors of the ladies and the thickest of armor will not prevent a knight from toppling to the ground, "if my great King strikes him with a lance." As has been seen, the death of Henry II in 1559 from a broken lance caused the sport of jousting to become unpopular in France. The royal residence and jousting grounds of the Hôtel des Tournelles (nowadays the Place des Vosges) were, after the death of the monarch, abandoned by Catherine de' Medici.[11]

Of the less violent sports that might attract the interest of a gentleman, the most popular one in the Renaissance was the *jeu de paume*, the "game of the palm," and it might mean anything from the elemental palm-batted ball against a wall to the more complicated racket-and-ball game played on a covered court, with a net and other obstacles — or an approximation of the very elaborate game of court tennis. Charles VIII, it will be recalled from the chroniclers, bumped his head so violently as he was looking in on a *jeu de paume* at Blois that he died from the blow. It was just about the end of the fifteenth century that the naked palm was covered with a glove to strike the ball, a splendid improvement and still welcomed today by all those who play handball. As for the balls themselves, the French made excellent ones out of leather stuffed with the hair of animals; they were so much in demand that at times an unscrupulous dealer would make a profit, before he was caught, on balls filled with sand or rubbish.

Etienne Pasquier, that mine of information on so many affairs of the sixteenth century, gives some details on the history of the game. He says that the "tennis-courts, where we take our amusement with rackets and not with the palm of the hand," were once named *jeux de paume*. "When tennis-courts were introduced throughout France," says Pasquier, "people did not know anything about a racket, and they played simply with a ball and the flat of the hand — a thing which I discovered in an old book in the form of a diary, which I make use of often in my researches." He goes on to state that from the first game with the naked hand came the game with the gloved hand; then some clever fellow put cords or tendons across the glove so that the ball could be "thrown better" — this sounds more like jai alai — and with less "pain." Finally from that point "was introduced the racket such as we see it today." [12]

The long racket, or "long palm," was an instrument strung with parchment and quite expensive. The shorter racket, or "short palm," strung with cords became the more popular instrument for playing the game. The sixteenth century saw the enclosing of walls for the sport, and the invention of a net across the court to replace an earlier cord with fringe hanging down from it. A prodigious number of specially designed halls for the contest were built during the sixteenth century. Every château had one and there were hundreds of them in the city of Paris, which would indicate that the game appealed to all classes of society. With the decline in popularity of the diversion in later centuries, some of these indoor courts were turned into theaters, and thus the sport "gave back to belles-lettres what its parchment covered bats had taken away." [13]

As for the technique of play in a match of *jeu de paume*, some idea of that was given by one Henry de Sainct Didier, who calls himself a "Provençal Gentleman." Sainct Didier's little manual, which he describes as a "treatise on the practice of, and certain points worth knowing about, the game of the palm," was published in 1573. It was appended to a more elaborate manual on the use of the sword, "the mother of all weapons." Since there are similarities in the methods of handling a sword and those of manipulating a racket, says Sainct Didier, the two treatises may be studied together. For example, there are forehand and backhand strokes with a sword just as there are with a racket. The author insists that his study on the *jeu de paume* is very elementary, and not intended for the "learned and skillful." Nevertheless, he has in it several astute observations that smack more of gamesmanship than of sportsmanship. If rackets are to be tossed to see whether you or your opponent is to be "inside" or "outside," let him toss his because it may have its strings loosened in falling. If it turns out that yours is to be tossed, it is advisable to have on hand a second inferior racket that is used just for tossing. For excellence of play, a good racket is necessary and not one that is all banged up. If there is a preliminary choice of rackets — evidently from several furnished by the club — try to choose first, so as to get the best one and the lightest one. In the *jeu de paume*, it is a good thing to have a light racket and a heavy ball.

Sainct Didier, along with his rather spurious ethical approach, has some good tactical suggestions for the player. It is always better whenever possible to take the ball on the volley and not wait for its bounce, which may not be true — all of which is somewhat anticipatory of the "big serve and volley" tactics of contemporary lawn tennis. If the ball is missed in the air, or strikes the wood of the racket, it is not an "accident" but an "error." Another important thing, says Sainct Didier, is to keep your eye on the ball all the time. If you watch your opponent, whether he is serving or you are serving, you will get tricked, but not so if you watch the ball. And a final point: wear heavy shoes two or three hours before the match so that when you change to some lighter in weight you will be "more nimble and dextrous." Sainct Didier's rather clumsily written manual is not lacking in practical advice, though some of it, obviously, is not very genteel.[14]

From all the records, the *jeu de paume* remained one of the favorite games throughout the century. Francis I and Henry II were both excellent players, and a very fine hall for the game was fixed up in the Louvre. The young Dauphin, François, after a game of tennis in 1536 drank water and died. Some said it was because he was overheated, others intimated darkly that he had been poisoned. A young gentleman could linger many hours around one of the halls, and did. The game progressively became an instrument of gambling, and wagering thereon was quite general. At the end of the century, one of the best players was the first of the Bourbons, the "vigorous gallant" himself, Henry IV.[15]

All sports involving a considerable expenditure of physical energy were popular with Frenchmen during the sixteenth century, and the French of this period were perfectly willing to go out into the midday sun to participate in them. Several games did not have too high a social rating but gentlemen still played them. Such a game was *soule*, a kind of primitive football, with a large ball filled with hay or air. And there was the game of *crosse*, which had a ball batted with a crooked stick; and *mail*, in which a wooden ball was knocked over any available terrain with a mallet. Wrestling was practiced by all classes and was not an upper-bracket sport, though it was said by Fleurange that Francis I won a bout from Henry VIII on the Field of the Cloth of Gold. Castiglione, it will be remembered, catalogues some of the proper exercises for a gentleman in the first book of the *Courtier*: they are hunting, swimming, tennis, and vaulting — but tumbling and rope-climbing are not for the man of gentility. On the other hand, Rabelais's Gargantua indulged in two hundred seventeen games, indoors and out, and most of them have been identified. Montaigne believed that the cultivation of the physical being was very important for the young gentleman — "indeed games and exercises will be a part of the training: running, wrestling, dancing, hunting, the manipulation of horses and arms." Such a program will make a "tough and vigorous youngster," but he should not try too hard at games like chess or tennis or he will become tense and not do too well; and, besides, such amusements are not very important. Erasmus, that great sage, wants his genteel youth to remember that games are for fun and not for gain, and that they reveal your true character. Therefore, they should be played in good humor without argument over the referee's decision — and, a doubtful point, an inferior opponent should be allowed to win from time to time.[16] Visual evidence of what was esteemed to be some of the appropriate physical training for a young Renaissance gentleman may be seen today in Rosso's fresco at Fontainebleau of the centaur Chiron teaching the young Achilles to swim, joust, etc.

When it came to indoor diversions the gentleman had a fairly wide selection from which to choose. If he were at the Court, he might attend a ball twice a week, to the music of violins imported from Italy. There were brief concerts, too, in the King's chambers nightly after supper. Music, in fact, was something that a gentleman could legitimately interest himself in, though he should not become professionally proficient at it or it might soften too much his warlike propensities. However, it was allowable for him to play an instrument like the lute, even as did Melin de Saint-Gelais, but he should not struggle over it. Catherine de' Medici encouraged dancing and many of the ladies at the Court, like Marguerite de Valois, were good at it. The Queen also staged many spectacularly ornate ballets, which made a large dent in the royal exchequer and should have provided considerable entertainment in compensation therefor. As for the professional theater, there was none about which a gentleman, as in the seventeenth century, could offer his supercilious criticisms. Private performances of comedies and tragedies at the Court became fewer and fewer after the outbreak of the Wars of Religion. According to Pierre de L'Estoile, a traveling troup of Italian actors, I Gelosi, did establish itself in Paris momentarily during the reign of Henry III, and it was a scandalous thing for the King to allow such vulgarians to remain in the city.[17]

As for dice, card games, and chess, it was all right for a gentleman to indulge in these if he did not do them to excess, but as the century progressed everything became a trifle excessive. Chess was considered by Montaigne a triviality — one is inclined to wonder how well he played it — and Pasquier, it will be recalled, saw a symbol in the game. The knight's ability to check the king from so many unexpected directions should warn a monarch that the nobility, if hostile, could make its resentment felt in a variety of ways. Edicts had to be passed, quite understandably, against gambling and dice in public places. And it was said that late in the century a group of Italians in the Louvre won thirty thousand crowns from the King of France in a dice game, which could not have happened in a "well policed realm." [18]

The gentleman of the Renaissance found travel a very relaxing diversion. He roamed a great deal over his own land, sometimes attached to the ambulatory court of his King, and he had a curiosity about foreign lands. Explorations in and importations from the New World attracted his attention, and he became increasingly cognizant of areas closer around him. England and the British Isles, strangely enough, were not a great field of interest — this was to come in later centuries — but between France and other countries in Europe there were numerous genteel contacts. And the Frenchman of the Renaissance, somewhat unlike Frenchmen of more recent periods, felt that a few things could be learned from foreigners and that there might be some elements of civilization outside France. In particular, there was an interchange of ideas and culture between Italy and France, with France doing the greater part of the borrowing, especially during the first part of the sixteenth century. Many of the gentleman's excursions outside his own domain were official — ambassadorial, military, or in attachment to the high clergy in Rome; others were made simply to see the country.

Travel was not so easy in the Renaissance as at the present time, and there were no travel agencies to smooth out the rough spots or make advance reservations. As for the roads, even if France was supposed to have the best in Europe, they still were not good. A gentleman would normally make his journey on horseback, and a poor pilgrim headed for some shrine would make his on foot, but it was not advisable for either to travel alone. Though a limited service of horse-drawn coaches came in before the end of the century, they would have been used very seldom by a gentleman in his peregrinations. He preferred to have his own good horse with a saddle on it.

One of the chief problems encountered in voyaging was the number of robbers that infested the travel routes, ready to attack a party suspected of having gold, jewels, or other valuable possessions stored in a chest or pouch. France seems to have had her liberal share of these highwaymen, some of whom Cellini met on his trip from Rome to Paris in 1537 to go into the service of Francis I. The artist went from Rome to Padua, where he got three horses to continue his journey into France. He and his companions went through Zurich, Lausanne, Geneva, and then left Switzerland for France and spent four days at Lyon. The trip from Lyon to Paris was very agreeable, says Benvenuto, "although at La Palice a band of adventurers, whom we escaped only by showing great courage, wished to assassinate us." Cellini mentions later in 1540 the bandits around Grenoble who do not hesitate to "assassinate on the main highways." Giovanni Michel said in 1575, in confirmation of Cellini's experiences, that between Lyon and Paris a traveler was in constant danger of being "robbed and maltreated." He managed himself to avoid difficulty only because he was in the company of several gentlemen. Lippomano in 1577 circumvented certain "Provençal ruffians" that waited for travelers between Tarare and Roanne by going through Burgundy on his way to Paris. His party had no difficulty on this route, though it was a very muddy road.[19]

The most complete and fascinating record of a gentleman's traveling during the Renaissance was kept by Montaigne in his *Journal de voyage*. The *Journal* is concerned with a trip that lasted from June 22, 1580 until November 30, 1581; Montaigne was accompanied by his youngest brother, Bertrand-Charles, seigneur de Matecoulon, the seigneur de Casalis (possibly Montaigne's brother-in-law), and Montaigne's very efficient but anonymous secretary. After leaving the château of Montaigne near Bordeaux, the party went through Lorraine, a corner of Switzerland, the Tyrol, Venice and its surroundings, the Papal States, Tuscany, Milanais, and Savoie. The main purpose of the expedition was the visiting of various watering resorts in search of a cure for Montaigne's kidney stones; in this respect the operation was a failure, but Montaigne's commentary on what he saw during the more than seventeen months of the journey is astute and refreshing. Many of Montaigne's reactions would be shared by any six-weeks tourist of today.

A few details from the *Journal* will be illustrative. In Bâle, in Switzerland, they find good food, fine stoves, poor sleeping quarters, and a doctor who dries flowers. There are a number of pretty fountains around, which makes it more attractive than a French city. A guidebook would have been helpful in Germany, which is a more expensive place than France. The Germans are pompous, choleric, and drunken; but they are not traitors and thieves. At Sterzing they have round loaves of bread, and see many houses of gentlemen in the valley. They relax pleasantly at Brixen, and Montaigne remarks that people are prejudiced about foreign countries and want to judge everything according to the "usage of one's own village." From Bolzano on the frontier of Italy, Montaigne writes to his friend, François Hotman, and comments on how a traveler in a foreign country is at the mercy of innkeepers, profiteering guides, and interpreters. In Italy, generally, things are less expensive than in Germany, and in Padua there are splendid schools of fencing, dancing, and horsemanship, all very popular with a number of French gentlemen who are there. They reach Florence, which is smaller than Ferrara, and inspect the stables of the grand duke. Also, in Florence they see a number of strange animals, including one "the size of a large mastiff with the shape of a cat, all black and white striped, which they call a tiger." The animals in Florence are all mixed up with the standard attractions for the modern visitor — the masterpieces of Michelangelo, the Duomo, etc. In Rome, Montaigne found too many Frenchmen, and was greeted many times, as he wandered about the city, in French. The streets of Rome remind him of Paris but Rome, though much smaller than Paris, is more beautiful because of its fine squares, streets, and houses. On going north again, they discover bedbugs in a hostelry in Florence; so they sleep on a table. They visit many baths, which do little to alleviate for Montaigne the painful passage of a small kidney stone; also, he is suffering from a violent toothache. They hear that the roads between Milan and Genoa are infested with thieves; so they avoid Genoa and go to Turin, thence through the pass of Mont-Cenis on to French soil. It has been a long trip.[20]

IX

The Gentleman at War

IN TIME OF PEACE PREPARE FOR WAR, become inured to the rigors thereof through long days of hunting over rough terrain and marshes, and remember that the only ruler not easily deposed is an "armed prophet." The foundations of a state are good laws and solid weapons, and when war comes it should be waged by native soldiers under the leadership of their own princes, and not by imported mercenaries. Italy has been oppressed by foreigners because she has been militarily soft, but France would be a difficult land to conquer because of the toughness and independence of her nobility. In fact, one of the best ordered kingdoms of the time is France as a result of the nicely balanced relations between the nobles, the people, and the governing powers — and all this was said early in the sixteenth century by that most realistic of political philosophers, Machiavelli.[1]

The preferred vocation of a gentleman of the Renaissance was unquestionably that of arms, if he had any aptitude at all for things military. Most of the games and sports that he played in his youth were destined to equip him for a life in the field. In his background was the opinion of the ancients that a warrior's early training should prepare him for his profession — with enough education to "humanize" him — and that citizen soldiers are the best since they will have too much pride to show cowardice and run away. Although the cowardly soldier will lose caste and be reduced to the rank of an artisan, said Plato, the bravest warriors will receive rewards and responsibilities. Castiglione, too, felt that his courtier should be trained in arms as well as in letters, that making war is an honorable pursuit, and that Frenchmen are more interested in military matters than in erudition.* The French themselves during the Renaissance were practically in unanimous agreement that it was better for a gentleman to be a soldier than a scholar.[2]

Valor, and value, and virtue, and force are all blended in the creation of a gentleman — and "the proper, sole and essential life for one of the nobility in France is the life of a soldier." This was the belief of Montaigne, a gentleman who wielded a pen rather than a sword, though it has been said that the great essayist had aspirations toward glory in arms. When the cause is good, war is the "most noble exercise that a prince, or a gentleman, can have," says Fleurange, who was himself a captain in the field. And the Prince of Poets, somewhat apologetic for toiling up the steep inclines of Parnassus rather than enduring the rigors of service in the cohorts of Mars, states that death in battle for one's prince or homeland is better than death on a bed of fever, or from poisoning. Glory and honor come to the "brave and valiant captains" and the memory of those like Lautrec and Bayard, among others, will last on for centuries. The young gentleman, then, should be trained for this career in arms, which will bring him immortality and protect the land of his ancestors. Genteel and prosperous families, says Tavannes, if they have three sons, "ought to put two of them in arms." The descendants of sturdy fathers, toughened like the Romans under the weight of heavy armor, thus will be the great captains and leaders in the field. There they will set the example of bravery for their soldiers, and avoid excesses of gambling, wine, avarice, and women. The young gentleman will be careful even of the manner of his speech, and talk like a soldier rather than like a pedant.[3]

For the Renaissance the highest nobility was the nobility of the sword, and the gentleman who was the master of the "mother of all weapons" could legitimately feel superior to a noble who had been given his title by an edict of Parlement. No legislative process could create a nobility comparable to that based on military exploits. The judicial nobility, the "nobility of the robe," should not be rejected, thinks Pasquier,

* See Chapter Two.

but those gentlemen who fight for their land and endure the hardships of war should be given added distinctions. So "our gentlemen who rest the principal claim of their nobility upon arms" can quite correctly look down on any urban claim to gentility. Foreign observers on French terrain in the sixteenth century confirmed the fact that a gentleman's greatest contribution to his nation was in the métier of a soldier, and "any noble, seigneur, or prince who does not love and seek for war is little esteemed." Though a young gentleman of the Renaissance might not be born always with a silver spoon in his mouth, he was, said Lippomano, "born with a sword in his hand."[4]

The two great French kings of the Renaissance, Francis I and Henry II, were never able to gain any final victories for France against that astute master of political and military manipulation, Charles V, the Holy Roman Emperor. And Henry VIII of England, though he made occasional forays across the Channel, for most of the time sat ponderously balancing the power and watched Charles V and Francis I bump their heads together, almost in prophetic anticipation of the Wars of Religion in France and the Spanish Armada buffeted in the gales off the Isle of Wight. Francis I and Henry II, for their part, gave personal leadership to their armies and brought France nearer national unity. The story was often told of how Francis I went to the wars in Italy as a precocious lieutenant general at the age of seventeen, was dubbed a knight in the field, and was captured at the battle of Pavia in his bright and shining armor. Henry II in his time dissipated much energy in Italy, but did extend the French frontiers to the East, winning the siege of Metz, losing an army at Saint-Quentin, and seeing Calais taken from the English in 1557. Peace came in 1559, symbolized by the well-publicized marriages of Henry II's sister Marguerite to Philibert-Emmanuel, Duc de Savoie, and of his daughter Elisabeth to Philip II of Spain. These ceremonies marked the end of a strenuous period in French history; during the preceding fifty years never had the gentlemen of France, frequently under inept leadership, fought so gallantly for their King and their native land.

The sixteenth century saw a number of changes begin to take place in the art of war. The offensive and defensive weapons of the Middle Ages — the lance, sword, crossbow, and heavy armor on a mounted knight — became less and less effective against the long-range attack of artillery. Nevertheless, in the earlier years of the century, the gentleman on horseback was the primary military strength of the nation. He was the solid kernel of the two permanent armed forces of France — the king's ordonnance companies or *gendarmerie*, and the Royal Household Guards, which included the very decorative "hundred gentlemen." The ordonnance companies, which formed something of a select core of the regular army, constituted the preferred service for the gentleman destined to become a professional soldier. The main attacking power of the ordonnance companies was the "man of arms," who was in "complete armor and on a great horse." He was a gentleman who had volunteered his services to his king, and he was supposed to have a minimum age of around twenty years. He was expected to have ready for use at least three horses, two for service and one for his baggage. He carried a lance and, after the first impact, fought with a sword in the event that the lance was shattered or lost. The man of arms became a "fully equipped lance" when he was supported by archers and light cavalrymen. A fully equipped lance composed of eight men was in accord with the ordonnance of Francis I on June 18, 1526. The archers were young gentlemen who were admitted to the companies at around the age of eighteen. They were normally former pages who had been brought up in the military atmosphere of the Court and would after a year or more of service become men of arms. However, as the century progressed, the ordonnance companies had in them many commoners who had previously served well for several years in the infantry. This situation was recognized by the nobles in 1580 when they complained in their report to the King at the meeting of the Estates-General at Blois that the ordonnance companies as well as the infantry were being infiltrated by "farmers and other persons of little quality." There was at the same time complaint on the part of the nobility about the inadequacy of the royal allowance for the upkeep of a man of arms.[5]

The ordonnance companies in the sixteenth century comprised around three thousand lances, which made an effective force. These men of arms and supporting units were divided into about one hundred companies, which were normally commanded individually by some important gentleman. The potency of the man of arms decreased considerably as the century advanced because of the appearance of more modern weapons; in the second half of the century he began to carry a rather erratic pistol instead of a lance. He was still too heavily armored to move very fast. The introduction of the harquebus in 1509 had a gradual effect upon the technique of warfare, and increased the importance of the foot soldier. The *arquebuse à fourchette*, or harquebus with a rest, was put into use around 1531, and made for more accurate and less tiring shooting of the gun. The general result, too, was the recruiting of greater numbers of infantrymen, though they were never as well recompensed for their services as the man on a horse. In 1534 Francis I issued an ordonnance for the creation of seven infantry legions of six thousand men each from the provinces. Of this force twelve thousand were to be equipped with harquebuses. The legions, which were supposed to be called out twice a year, proved unsatisfactory and fell into disuse in the second half of the century.[6]

Despite the many theoretical objections on the grounds of loyalty and patriotism to the hiring of mercenaries, all nations did it in the sixteenth century as war became more and more mechanized. There were, for example, fifteen thousand lansquenets, or German footmen, with Francis I at Marignano. And treaties permitted the hiring of men in Switzerland. A professional man of war, normally a gentleman of somewhat modest origin, would be deputized by the Crown to procure an exact number of mercenaries. He then would hire them in companies of from three to five hundred men, completely organized from captain to fife-player. Though these men might lack the urge of defense of their homeland, they made no problem of demobilization and readjustment to civilian life at the end of a campaign. They simply were available for some other war. It was the gentleman, in any case, who provided the leadership and inspiration for victory in the field. According to the chroniclers, the mercenaries could be unreliable in the fierce heat of battle: such was the situation at Marignano but the victory was won, nevertheless, by the dashing Francis I, who wrote to his mother about it on September 14, 1515, and entered Milan "at the head of eight hundred men of arms and twenty thousand French and German foot soldiers." Lautrec's loss of the battle of La Bicoque in 1522 was blamed on the defection of the Swiss. Part of their lack of interest in the conflict must have been caused by the disappearance of four hundred crowns due the army in back pay. It was said that Louise de Savoie, queen-mother and sometime regent of the realm, had put the coins in her own coffers so that she might bask in their golden glow.[7]

The armies of the period were certainly larger than any corporal's guard. The Bourgeois de Paris gives a complete breakdown of the troops under Francis I as the King left for Milan in 1523: there were with him 1370 French lances (or men of arms), one company of whom was commanded by Bayard; 390 Italian lances; 10,700 French foot soldiers; 30,000 Swiss, German, and Italian infantry — and these numbers do not count "the adventurers" or the lances set aside to guard the frontiers. There is no indication as to how completely the lances were "furnished," but it was a sizable force. The King proceeded with this army as far as Lyon, where he turned it over to his lieutenant general, Admiral Bonnivet (an admiral at the time seldom saw the sea), who took it on into Italy. The army of Philippe Chabot in 1536 was catalogued as follows: 12 ordonnance companies or 810 lances; 1,000 light cavalrymen; 12,000 legionnaires from the King's recently created legions; 2,000 French foot soldiers; 6,000 German lansquenets; 3,000 Italian infantry; corps of artillery (numbers not given); and 800 construction men. It will be noted that this army differs from that of Francis I in 1523 in that it has in it fewer men of arms with their lances, and in that it recognizes the growing importance of artillery and engineering

1. *Francis I*

2. *Marguerite de Navarre*

3. *The Duchesse d'Etampes*

4. *The Admiral Bonnivet*

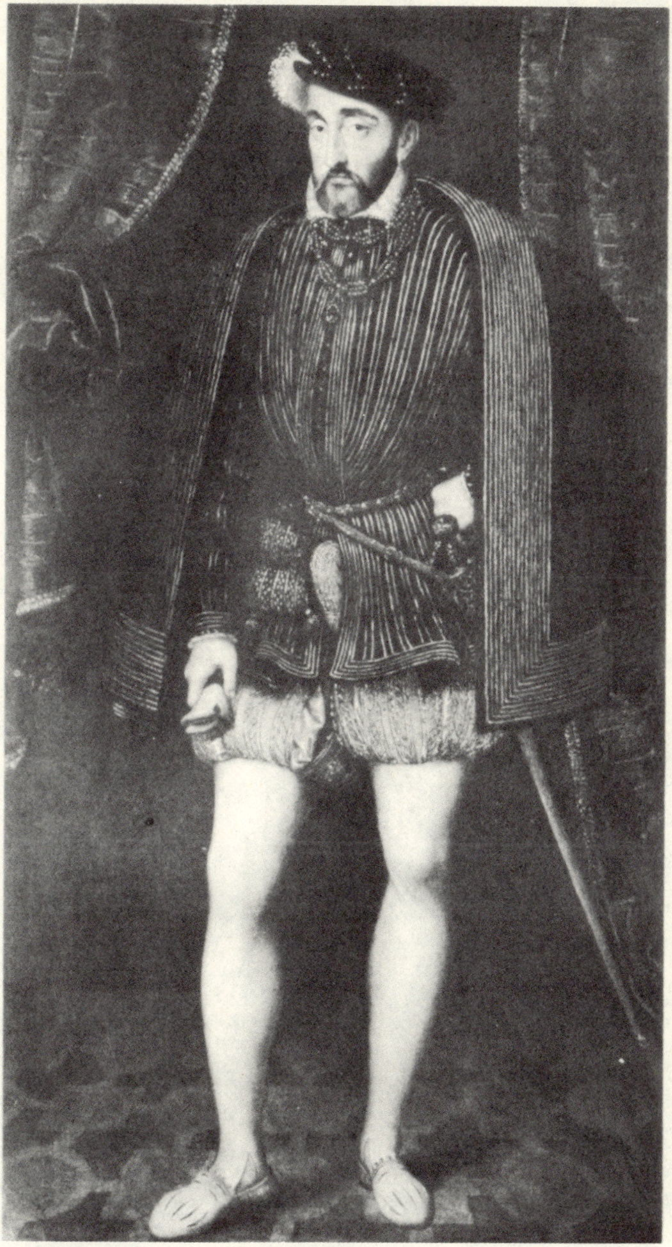

5. Henry II

6. *Diane de Poitiers*

7. *Catherine de' Medici*

8. *Mary Stuart*

9. *Francis II*

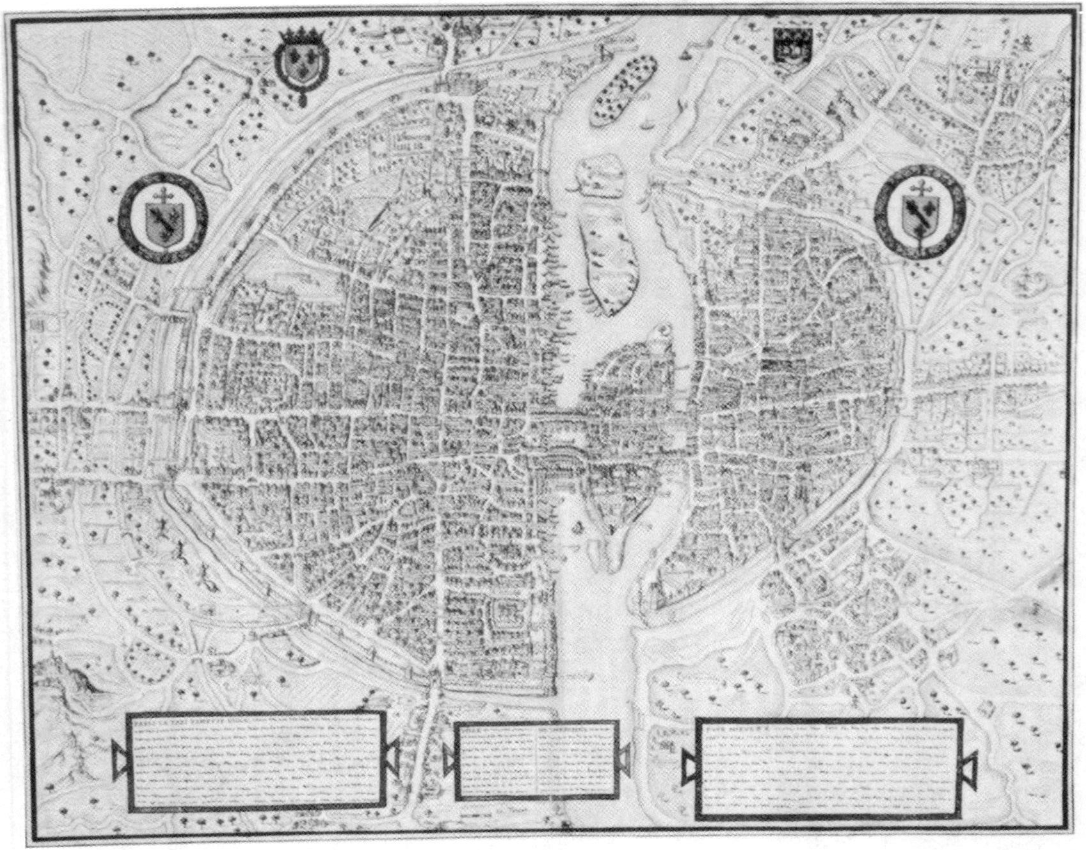

10. *Map of Paris*

11. *Fresco at Fontainebleau*

12. *Renaissance chest*

13. Book binding with monogram denoting Henry II, Catherine de' Medici, and Diane de Poitiers

14. Sixteenth-century medallions of Henry II and Catherine de' Medici

15. Catherine de' Medici on horseback

16. Montgommery in jousting regalia

17. Henry III

18. Guardsmen from the period of Henry III

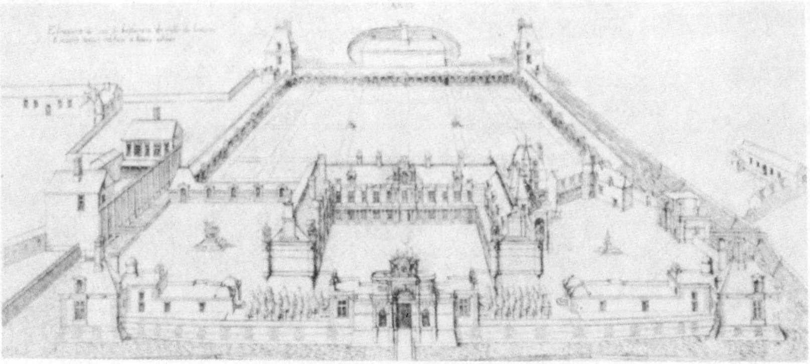

19. *Anet, the château of Diane de Poitiers*

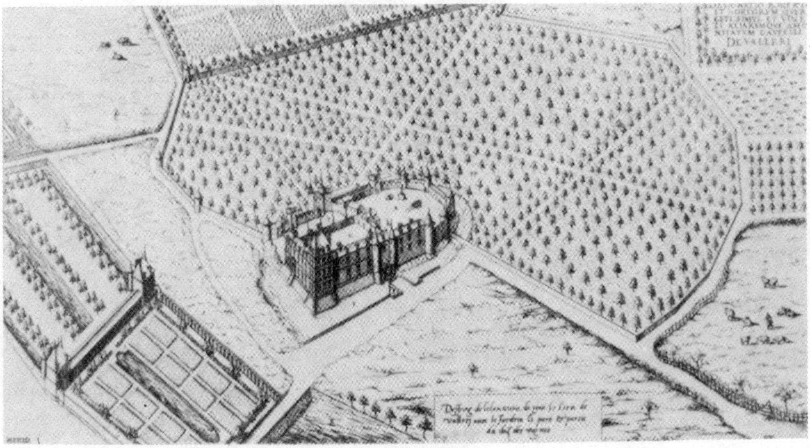

20. *Vallery, the château of the Maréchal de Saint-André*

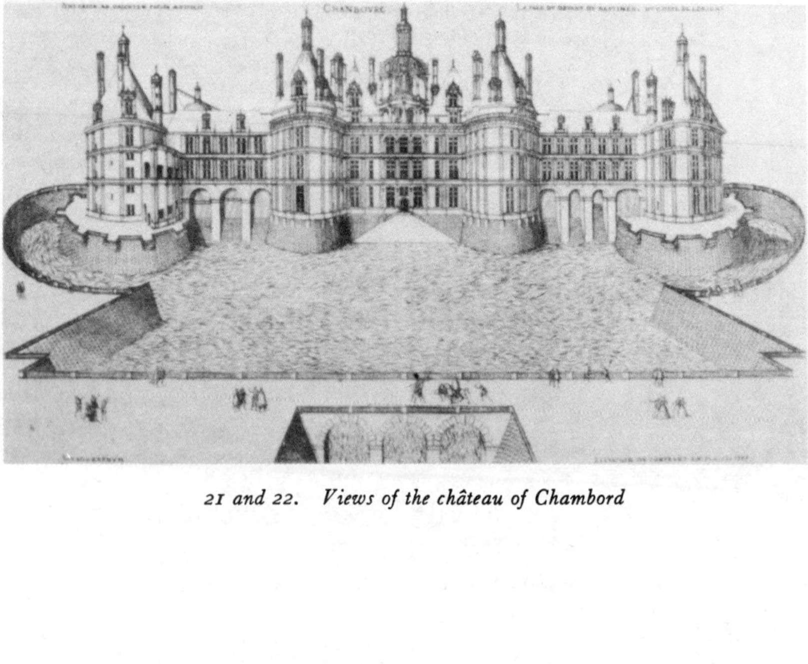

21 and 22. Views of the château of Chambord

23. *Joust between Henry II and Montgommery which resulted in the death of the King*

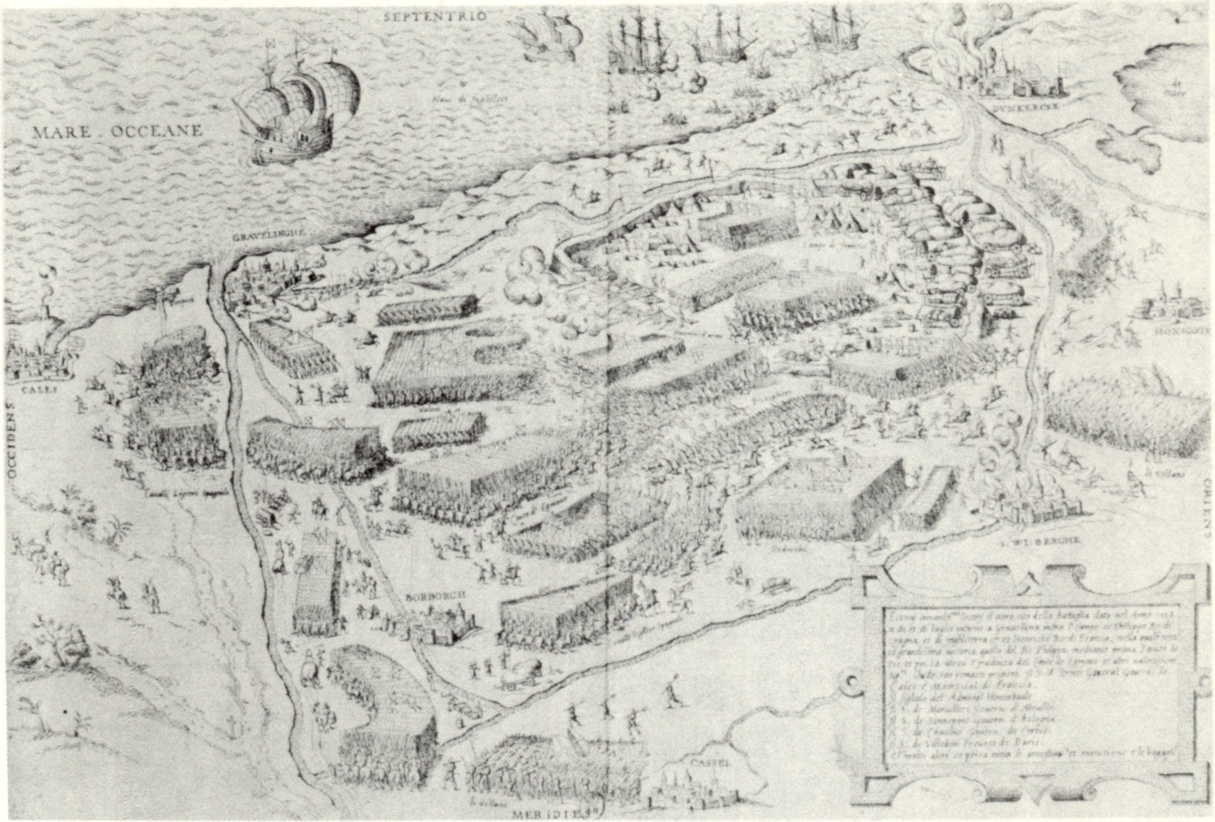

24. *French and Spanish forces in battle along the Channel coast in 1558*

25. The La Châtaigneraie-Jarnac duel

26. The Chevalier Bayard

operations. There is to be an increasing recognition of gunpowder as the century goes on. At the siege of Metz in 1552, for example, Charles V threw twelve thousand cannon shot at the city in a space of two weeks — which for the time was quite a massing of artillery.[8]

Artillery, though it did not completely displace the pike for an infantryman or a lance for a gentleman on a horse, did make warfare less personal and less sportingly genteel. Rabelais, who considers the invention of printing as a "divine inspiration," looks upon artillery as coming from a "diabolical suggestion." The parallel developing in the sixteenth century of printing and artillery caused other comments, which put printing on the side of peace and artillery, naturally, on the side of war. Montaigne said that the French should not be so proud of "the invention of our artillery and printing" since other nations had been using them centuries earlier. However, the Italians were paying homage to French skill in gunmaking as early as 1535, when Marino Giustiano said: "Artillery in France is in a fine condition and of varied calibers. I saw some pieces made recently in Paris, among which there were one hundred cannon and double *couleuvrines* of a more ductile and less breakable metal than ours. The French use less bronze, which reduces the expense and makes transportation easier." It was true that the mobility of French artillery assisted in the winning of the victory at Marignano just as confusion as to the position of the guns ten years later in 1525 brought about the defeat at Pavia and the capture of Francis I. The King got out in front of the artillery, according to Du Bellay, and "that was one of the principal causes for the loss of the battle." Brave captains like Bonnivet, Bussy-d'Amboise, and Louis de La Trémoïlle fell at his side as the King was surrounded by rowdy soldiers, despite his own valiant efforts and those of his gentlemen. He finally was able to surrender to a gentleman of appropriate rank, the Count of Lannoi. Many sixteenth-century *couleuvrines* — the cannon that shot a projectile a little more than four or five inches in diameter and took its name from the handles on it shaped like a snake (*couleuvre*) — are still preserved today in the Musée de l'Armée in Paris, including one with Francis I's salamander at its base and a fleur-de-lis toward the end of its eleven-foot barrel. And at the siege of Rabastens later in the century that tough old soldier, Blaise de Monluc (who has seen, he says, as much shooting as "anybody today alive"), praises the work of two artillery officers, who took over the firing of their battery from their cannoneers for five days and in six or seven hundred rounds did not miss more than ten times.[9]

Despite the noise of the guns, some of which boomed "like thunder," warfare through the reign of Henry II offered occasions for genteel actions and courtesies. War was scarcely a twelve-months-in-the-year operation. By mutual agreement hostilities lasted regularly from the beginning of Spring in March until the cold and wetness appeared in October; then both sides tried to get comfortable for the winter. Machiavelli believed that some of the reasons for Italy's national weakness were an unwillingness to wage war in winter, a concentration on cavalry rather than infantry, and a disinclination to patrol at night or attack the enemy under cover of darkness. However, in the early sixteenth century this attitude was not the sole property of the Italians. It was still the period when fighting was the occupation of a gentleman, and, though he might die gallantly from the thrust of the blade of a worthy foe, he did not want to do it impersonally in the middle of the night. There was much that was chivalric and courteous in the interchanges between enemies during non-fighting interludes, regardless of major national issues involved. Just before the battle of Ravenna in 1512, the Duc de Nemours and the Chevalier Bayard were taking an early morning ride around their camp. They encountered a group of Spanish gentlemen, their enemies, enjoying a similar breath of matutinal air, and bowed to them very politely. The Spaniards returned the greeting with even greater bowing and salutations, and then there was an exchange of introductions. When the Spanish captain, Pedro de Pas, learned the identity of Bayard, he exclaimed: "And would to Heaven there might be peace between your master and mine, so that we might chat a little together, for during my whole life I have had great admiration for your bravery." Shortly thereafter the furious battle of Ravenna was joined, in which the Duc de Nemours lost his life. And when Bayard was slain in 1524 everybody was stricken with grief, including his enemies, the Spaniards. The Spanish officer, the Marquis of Pescara, paid him great homage and said that he would give up a "half gallon of my blood" and not eat meat for two years in order to have Bayard in good health and "my prisoner." Though it was fortunate for Charles V not to have any longer such a warrior as Bayard against him, said Pescara, it was saddening to think of the loss that his death meant for "all chivalry." [10]

Some years later in 1553 a forty-day truce was arranged between the French and Spanish in the Piedmont. During the period, the French and Spanish commanders, the Maréchal de Brissac and Domp Ferrand respectively, indulged in elaborate courtesies and dinners, each with his full staff of officers, on a neutral spot between the lines. Brissac and his men appeared at the meetings in battle dress, with horses and weapons gleaming and shining. The Spaniards were dressed in velvet and jewels, "gilded like chalices." On seeing the two groups Domp Ferrand told Brissac, taking him by the hand, that the Spaniards were "adorned like maidens" while the French were "dressed like soldiers," thus showing that the best raiment for a fighting man is that in which he gains "glory and honor." In any event, there was tremendous bowing, scraping, and embracing among the two delegations. Both came on the field to a fanfare of trumpets and the trumpeters vied with one another in their spirited display. Dinners were arranged on all sides, and while the two commanders talked, their officers strolled around together chatting and laughing at one another's jokes. After it was all over the fighting started again. And even the stern Monluc could relax a bit at Christmas. In 1554, the Spanish commander in Northern Italy, the Marquis of Marignan, was tightening his blockade against Monluc and the French troops. Nevertheless, on Christmas Eve Marignan sent Monluc as a little token of the season "half a stag, six capons, six partridges, six flagons of Trebian wine and six loaves of white bread for a party the next day." Monluc found this quite a legitimate procedure and explained the situation: "All these courtesies are very genteel and praiseworthy, even among the greatest enemies, if there is no understanding between them, as was the case with us; he was serving his master and I was serving mine; he wished to add to his reputation [as a soldier] and I to mine. It is to act like Turks and Saracens to refuse little courtesies to one's enemy; it is not necessary, however, that they be so large or of such nature that they may hamper or delay your plans." [11]

A gentleman of the earlier Renaissance might go wandering over the country hunting a battle just for the excitement, or as though he were playing a game. It might easily be a risky diversion, but many did it. A gentleman could well be mystified by the deep purposes and causes underlying a war, and have to leave such matters "to the more learned" — thus spoke François de Rabutin, who was in an ordonnance company of the Duc de Nevers in the time of Henry II. But a lack of understanding of the major problems of military and political strategy did not prevent a gentleman's seeking out the spot where there was shooting and the clash of arms. At the siege of Metz in 1552, the French commander, François, Duc de Guise, issued a general order for all soldiers to stay in their own barracks and specifically limited the movements of these wandering gentlemen: "And realizing that the French nobles are accustomed to rush toward the spot where things are happening and a siege is taking place, that a goodly number of them would retire into this city, where, if they had no one to whom they would be particularly responsible, they would take up their lodgings wherever they liked and enter into all operations that would be under way, out of which often more inconveniences have been seen to result than good effects; for this reason the order is given that all gentlemen and others who might wander in for their own pleasure must choose one of the cavalry or infantry captains in the city to serve under him, and take up lodging in his quarter, follow and accompany him on all sallies, forays, and operations that will be undertaken by him, obeying his orders just as though the wanderers were being paid and had given oath to the King; and they will enter into no other undertaking, under threat of being thrown out of the city." It is evident that the Duc de Guise did not care for the contributions of casual gentlemen who, with some unattached soldiers, wished to fight a private war. But François de Lorraine, the second Duc de Guise, was a good fighting man, if the *Mémoires* of his friend Claude de la Chastre can be credited, and gentlemen liked to serve under him. The King sent an army in 1556 down into Italy under the leadership of the Duc de Guise. La Chastre lists the various company commanders on the expedition; and in addition to the organized combatants, he points out that there were "a goodly number of seigneurs and gentlemen in royal service, and others quite young who had come on this trip, as much out of hope of seeing and learning something (for the Frenchman is naturally curious) as because the Duc de Guise was greatly admired and supported by all the nobility." [12]

A gentleman went to war sometimes, it was claimed, in a lesser capacity than that to which his rank and experience would entitle him — instead of being fully armed on a horse, for example, he might be a more modest archer. The Spaniards suggested that this was done many times for the purpose of escaping a heavy ransom if captured, since the amount of money demanded for redeeming a prisoner would depend upon his rank. The Maréchal de Brissac had a good answer for this accusation: the gentleman of France goes "gaily" and "voluntarily" to war to serve "his prince and his fatherland," out of a feeling of honor. If at times he serves in a minor position of command, it is in order to learn a soldier's profession better under some good captain; a gentleman is not concerned simply with enhancing his own reputation as a military commander — a point of view somewhat different from that of Monluc.[13]

As for the question of ransom, it was a vital matter for the young sieur de Vouillon, whose older brother was master of the King's wardrobe and in rather a satisfactory position at Court. In 1559, just before the signing of peace between the French and Spaniards, Vouillon managed to get himself captured at Saint Quentin. His ransom was set at two thousand crowns, which Vouillon did not have. He was permitted by the Duc de Savoie, who was then fighting on the side of the Spaniards, to go to Paris to collect the sum from friends and relatives, and return within a specified time. Before Vouillon's trip could be completed, though he did it according to agreement, the war was over and the erstwhile enemies were having a gay and bibulous time in Brussels. The social season could not have been more brilliant, with two royal weddings in the making to cement the friendship between France and Spain. The Duc de Savoie, who was to marry Henry II's sister, Marguerite, was giving a big party for a group of French noblemen. Vouillon, out of breath on a tired horse and without the ransom money that he was unable to raise in Paris, arrived in the middle of the celebration and offered himself as prisoner to the Duc de Savoie. The Duc sent him word that he had not yet finished dinner, and that he would look after the little matter of locking up Vouillon sometime later. Vouillon did not wait around, but got on a horse and rode off to Paris, with the statement that he had kept his word and now considered himself free to escape. The affair, after the festivities had calmed down a bit, was deliberated by several captains, "both French and Spanish." They agreed that Vouillon had fulfilled his part of the bargain as a man of honor, and that in the end he had legitimately reclaimed his liberty.[14]

War may have had its sportsmanlike qualities during the Renaissance, but thousands of gentlemen, and the soldiers who fought with them, died from its wounds and diseases. On the whole, there was little confidence in medicine or the doctors, despite the admitted abilities of a skillful surgeon like Ambroise Paré. In comparison with modern techniques and equipment, the ministrations given to the sick and wounded during the Renaissance must have been pitiful indeed. Du Bellay says that though the French gained some victories around Naples in 1528, more than half the army there was destroyed by maladies; the Maréchal de Lautrec was himself a victim of disease, and it would be better to find a healthier climate to carry on a war. Pasquier gives a little more of an historical background on Neapolitan maladies: "On the trip that Charles VIII made into Italy, the greater part of his soldiers through having slept, unfortunately, with immodest women contracted a contagious malady, which we have called *mal de Naples*, because that was the place where it began; and the Italians have called it the French disease, inasmuch as the French were the first who had it." The debate over the nationality of syphilis has gone on for a long time, but there was certainly no cure for this impersonal scourge during the Renaissance.[15]

Doctors were distrusted by those who most admired the profession of arms. Tavannes felt that surgeons had inflicted tremendous damage, and "the razor posing as a friend has done more harm than the bullets of the enemy." Montaigne spends a very long essay, *De la Ressemblance des enfants aux pères*, in an attack on the futility of medicine and the ignorance of doctors — poor Montaigne with his inherited kidney stones. Even Melin de Saint-Gelais, in the midst of his pleasant verse trivialities for the Court, has a quatrain against the doctors. Mézeray recounts the legend of the seigneur de Laval, who was wounded in the thigh while hunting a "wild beast" in Brittany in 1531. The seigneur died a few days afterward "through the ignorance of his doctors and surgeons," who always talk a great deal but are not of much assistance in time of need. There is a balancing story on the plus side for the greatest of the Renaissance surgeons, in connection with the fighting around Boulogne in 1545: "The wound that François, Duc d'Aumalle received in an attack made by the enemy was a very remarkable thing. He came back from the fight having in his head the iron tip and a wooden segment of a lance, which had entered at an angle between the right eye and the nose and come out in back between the nape of his neck and his ear. It was necessary for the surgeon, who was Ambroise Paré,* to pull it out with pincers; in spite of everything, happy to relate, he got well."[16]

* The great doctor, Ambroise Paré, served as royal surgeon under Henry II and later under his three sons. Paré wrote extensively on diseases and the techniques of surgery. Much of his knowledge was gained from treating soldiers on the battlefield.

Even when he was in the best of health and in full armor, the gentleman of the Renaissance was not a very large man. The ideal of the Renaissance, descended from antiquity through the Italians, was that it was preferable for a man to be moderate in size. Men that were too big were likely to be clumsy and lacking in grace. On the other hand, a man should not be so small as to be unimpressive. For a gentleman to be completely acceptable as to physique, he should strike a golden mean of size. Montaigne considered that he was a little below the norm in height and thus would be ill-equipped to occupy a position of authority. To be a leader, a gentleman should be rather tall and carry himself well; it is terrifying to the enemy to see marching at the head of a column a captain of "fine and imposing stature." A gentleman's prime claim to handsomeness is in the harmony and balance of his figure. If he does not have this, perfection of individual details like the eyes, teeth, nose, or lack of bodily odors will not make him attractive.[17]

Francis I was approximately six feet tall and well proportioned. Henry II was probably a trifle under his father in height, but very agile and graceful in movement. Not only are these measurements suggested by various chroniclers, but they are confirmed by the armor of the two kings preserved today in the Musée de l'Armée. Francis I, or at least a set of the King's armor, is sitting very elegantly astride a horse in the *salle François Premier* at the Musée; it is so lifelike that if the visor of the helmet were opened, the royal countenance might be expected to appear. The highly ornamented *Armure aux Lions*, with the helmet bearing the face of a lion, also suggests that its wearer (possibly Francis) was around six feet. The armor of Henry II, black and damascened with silver, and bearing the interlaced *H*, *C*, and *D*, shows that he was a moderately tall and slender man. However, the armor of the Connétable Anne de Montmorency indicates that he was rather a big and burly fellow. His helmet has a hole in it where he was shot in the jaw by a pistol at the battle of Dreux. On the basis of his armor displayed in Paris, Othon Henri, prince of the Palatinate, must have been the biggest man of the sixteenth century.

Many of the gentlemen who went to war were much smaller. There is considerable evidence among the chroniclers of the period on the question of a man's size. Commynes in his *Commentaires*, when he tells of the death of Charles VIII at Amboise, says that the King bumped his head against the top of a door, "although he was quite small." Brantôme says that Bayard was a man of moderate figure, "but very handsome and erect"; and La Châtaigneraie, who fought the famous duel with Jarnac in 1547, was also of modest height. The seigneur de Vandernesse, who died fighting in Italy early in the century, was a gentleman "small in body but great in courage." [18]

It is quite understandable that a gentleman could bump his head against the top of a door in the sixteenth century, and he did not have to be very tall to do it. The doors, particularly those of the interiors in the châteaux, are neither very high nor very wide. At Langeais, for example, the doors connecting the various ceremonial and private rooms as well as those entering the towers are slightly more than six feet in height. At Blois, the door leading from the guardsroom into the gallery of honor of Henry II is a trifle more than seventy inches high and a little over thirty-three inches wide; and another one out of Henry II's first gallery is a few inches more than six feet in height, but only twenty-six inches wide. On the next floor at Blois, the doors into the workroom of Henry III are small openings: one is half an inch under six feet, one that leads into the hall where the third Duc de Guise was assassinated is an inch over six feet, and a third one is only sixty-eight inches high. A gentleman had to be both careful and agile to get through these crevices. Not only were the royal châteaux ill-adapted for the easy movements of a tall man, but the same situation also was true for the manor houses. In the fine gentleman's mansion of Dizier, the doors of the right wing (as you face the main house), entrance as well as interior on the ground floor, are just about an inch over six feet. It would not have been possible for a large gentleman to put on his fighting clothes and march off to war through these doors. That a gentleman was moderate in size, however, is confirmed by the small apertures through which he could pass.

The gentleman of the Renaissance, after he had rendered his service in the field, liked to receive therefor his honors and rewards. In that he was no different from the present-day soldier with his pride in medals and battle stars, and other recognitions for valor in combat. In the sixteenth century even as now, there was complaint about too many awards being made, and that they frequently were given for social rather than military virtues. The sixteenth century was not without its warriors who showed up better in courtly attire on parade than they did in the battle dress and mud of a campaign. But the real gentleman-soldier won his ribbons by brandishing a sword rather than by waving a silk handerchief or a plumed hat.

At the turn of the century, the exploits of a young gentleman who had distinguished himself in battle might have been seen by an older gentleman, who was a knight by virtue of his valor in arms. The older knight, in recognition of the younger man's soldierly qualities, could make him on the field of battle a knight of the sword. But by the time of the Renaissance and with the many abuses in chivalric recognitions, the kings of France took away the privilege of one knight's being able to create another knight. The King himself bestowed, or delegated the authority for bestowing, the orders of chivalry. Before the end of the century, a member of the order of chivalry was not necessarily a distinguished soldier. Royal favor played a greater part in the granting of the honor than battlefield accomplishments, and no longer could a great captain on the basis of his own judgment pin a ribbon on a valorous young gentleman. Naturally, there were no awards for the mercenaries or the soldiers in the ranks. They were paid for their services.

In the first half of the century, a gentleman who became a knight of the Order of Chivalry was attached to the Order of Saint Michael, which had been created by Louis XI in 1469. Symphorien Champier said in 1525 that "the kings of

France make chevaliers in the name of Sainct Michiel." The Order of Saint Michael, which began with thirty-six knights, became during the Renaissance more and more crowded and there were many complaints about the ease of entry into it. Brantôme has a long discussion on the fashion later in the century of military awards being made to a gentleman for non-combat duty, and says that such was not the case under Francis I, who himself gained his knightly spurs in the "battle with the Swiss" at Marignano and by his own request was made a knight in the field. And the ceremony was not administered by any armchair general, but by a doughty outdoor soldier, Bayard, who was at the time merely a knight of the sword and not a member of the Order. Francis I thus became a "chevalier of chivalry," a distinction that could be won by bravery alone. Later, as automatic head of the Order, the King made Bayard a knight of the Order. Unfortunately, as a result of ignoring valor in the field, says Brantôme, there are more chevaliers today than formerly there were squires, "so great are the abuses in the granting of chivalry." Vieilleville states that he was made a knight of the sword in 1536 when he was twenty-five years old, but not a knight of the Order, which honor was reserved for "seasoned captains" — a situation that was different from today (Vieilleville died in 1571) when there are more "chevaliers than wielders of swords." Castelnau in his *Mémoires* tells how the Duc de Guise in 1559 made eighteen knights of the Order, which was too many and caused the Order to lose prestige; and though Guise made eighteen friends, he lost that many or more among those gentlemen to whom the eight-pointed cross was not awarded! Montaigne, in his excellent essay, *Des Récompenses d'honneur*, says that rewards for valor can not be bought and that "formerly" the Order of Saint Michael was the highest honor to which the French gentleman could aspire. By 1577, according to Lippomano, the Order of Saint Michael had been given to so many persons, "nobles and commoners, too," that there was no distinction in belonging to it, and the finest gentlemen of France sought to avoid its ceremonial day.[19]

At the end of 1578, Henry III founded the Order of the

Holy Spirit in an effort to restore an element of exclusiveness to chivalric orders. In a highly ritualized series of ceremonies, the King created twenty-six new chevaliers. There were five days of Masses and vespers, with the twenty-six favored gentlemen dressed in cloth of silver and wearing swords. The King first took the oath kneeling before his confessor, received the grand cloak and grand golden chain of the Order, a book of the hours, and a chaplet of ten Pater Nosters and ten Ave Marias. Then he sat in a gold chair and dubbed the other chevaliers. The next day there was a church ceremony, in the presence of the Queen and the ladies at Court, at which the knights wore cloaks of black velvet bordered with fleurs-de-lis in gold. After the High Mass, they all received communion, following which there was a fine banquet. The King sat at a table alone, but with the knights near him, the Queen and the great ladies were in another room, the ambassadors and prelates in another, and the King's council in still another. This happened on January 1, 1579. The statutes of the Order were read two days later. All the knights were pledged to prayers and Masses, and confessions at least twice a year — and they had to pray for the King every day. All of which is a far cry from creating a knight in the dust and sweat of battle. The Order really had little connection with the fighting qualities of a gentleman. Before many years had passed, it was "mocked and held in little esteem," and was looked upon as a "mark of favor and not of honor." [20]

The gentleman, then, might not always receive a bright and shining medal for his services in time of war, but that did not mean that his King was ungrateful or that his exploits were unremembered. The story of Bayard's gallantry, for example, was chronicled many times during the sixteenth century and it was not forgotten that he died facing the enemy. The writers of the period, both in poetry and prose, recalled the great captains and their techniques of waging war. Montaigne lists some of "the most rare" men of the century, and heads the list with "the Duc de Guise who died at Orléans and the late Marshal Strozzi." The Italians conceded that France had some fine military leaders and listed among them the first Duc de Guise, the Duc de Nemours, the Maréchal de Brissac, the Prince de Condé, and Blaise de Monluc. Monluc himself, who in his unyielding spirit held honor and glory most high, catalogues many "brave and valiant captains" who have died for France — men like Lautrec, Bayard, Foix, Brissac, Strozzi, Guise, and others — and hopes that one day his own name may be worthy to be added to the roll. And on the other hand, the chroniclers treat fully the treachery of the Connétable de Bourbon, who turned against his native France and was snubbed by Bayard, it was said, even when the Chevalier was dying.[21]

In the period of the Renaissance it was the gentleman who set not only the pattern of personal bravery but also maintained an element of decorum in the operations of the armies. Vieilleville, when he was a lieutenant with the Maréchal de Saint-André at an uprising around Bordeaux in 1549, was very careful to pay for all lodgings and punish any of his men who were found guilty of pillaging. Full protection, or at least moderately full protection, was also given the feminine population of the city. In Brissac's general orders for his campaign in Northern Italy in 1551, company commanders were required to make periodic checks on the equipment of their men, and all soldiers under battle conditions were obliged to carry strapped on their persons enough bread for two meals. Punishment was promised for those men who "blasphemed the name of God or the Virgin," and anyone guilty of desecrating churches or raping women would be put to death. As for the young gentlemen in his command, who have been mumbling and complaining a bit, Brissac tells them that he expects from them a "concordant and affectionate obedience" even though they are as yet inexperienced in military affairs. The youthful Prince de Condé replies graciously that the complaints have come from "courageous youth not yet tamed to the discipline of a soldier," but that they want to serve their commander and their King. Brissac accepts this explanation and says that they will have as spectators of their faithfulness and loyalty the monarch himself and the spirits of the great captains of the past.[22]

The gentleman of the Renaissance by tradition and training was prepared many times in his life to ride off to war. He was expected as a symbol to provide for his men a high order of bravery and inspiring leadership.[23] He had to be able to control human beings rather than guide machines.

X

The Code of Honor

A GENTLEMAN MIGHT WELL DURING THE RENAISSANCE risk his life many times for France on the field of battle; he had a fair chance also of risking his life a few times on the field of honor. The privilege of having a personal honor to defend was, in fact, limited to the genteel classes. A commoner could scarcely receive an insult of sufficient gravity to involve the intricate formalities of a duel. In many respects he was lucky in being in this position, since the problem of what constituted a besmirching of a gentleman's honor was infinitely complicated in the sixteenth century even as it is today. However, under certain conditions that had been more or less defined by tradition or the mores of the Renaissance, a gentleman had to draw his sword or be accused of cowardice. Many of these situations would seem trivial in the present age and some of them seemed silly, in theory, at that time. It was difficult for a gentleman to use logic in order to avoid a combat imposed upon him by the code of honor.

Honneur was a term in good usage in the Renaissance and its connotations have not changed too much since then. As a personal attribute, it meant that the possessor had a sense of courage, honesty, justice, and dignity. Some thought it was a question of having inward virtue. *Honneurs* were external "prizes of virtue"—the Aristotelian concept—and incorrectly would fall on any but the good. *Gloire* was the outside appearance before other men, but it must be maintained untarnished; *honneur* would thus be linked with "character," and *gloire* with "reputation." It was in defense of both his *honneur* and *gloire*, which reflected his inner qualities of virtue, that a gentleman could be called upon to fight. By extension, he might have to defend the honor and reputation of a friend or relative, maybe of a man or more possibly of a woman. The meaning of the words in Italy, which had so much influence on the concept of dueling in sixteenth-century France, were a little different. *Virtù* was more of an external and vigorous quality, and might well mean valor and bravery in combat. Machiavelli speaks of princes who acquire power *per vie virtuose*, or through valorous ways, and says they are able as a result to retain it with ease. For Castiglione, *virtuoso* implies both high capability and versatility in accomplishing the matter at hand. The Italian term for honor, *onore*, with its derivatives, seems to have been at the time a trifle less honorable than the French, *honneur*. In the elegant and violent Italy of the century, *onore* was somewhat parallel to *virtù*, and suggested the quality by which a clever and unscrupulous man could accomplish his ends without regard to the rights of others. Such an "honorable" man was Machiavelli's ideal prince, who was to be both a lion and a fox, and appear to keep faith but break it when it was advantageous to do so. The French historian, Lavisse, whose opinion may not be completely unbiased, speaks of *onore* as being the "art by the aid of which a man of cleverness accomplishes a difficult action, profitable to his own interests, without any scruple of morality or humanity." Cellini recounts the story of how he killed a man with a dagger, and was accused of thieving and counterfeiting, and other misdeeds. He managed by intrigue to get himself cleared of all charges, and afterward, he says, "my reputation as an honorable man shone forth brighter than ever." It is clear that the Italians did not help the French very much in defining honor and virtue. In Renaissance France, the milieu of the gentleman pretty well determined the practical code of honor that would demand the unsheathing of a sword. And this knightly honor had to be defended at all costs, even in spite of the edicts of kings and the threat of royal punishments.[1]

The removal by individual combat of a slur, fancied or real, on a gentleman's honor was not an invention of the Renaissance. It had happened many times in medieval France. These affairs of the Middle Ages which were fought in full armor, with lances, swords, daggers, and battle-axes, were not very popular during the Renaissance. Nor was the *duel judiciaire*, or duel fought by judicial decree, wherein God was supposed to intervene on the side of the innocent man and make him victorious. In the more pagan atmosphere of the Renaissance, it was believed that divine inclination was most likely to be on the side of the more skillful swordsman. The sword, in fact, the carrying of which in the sixteenth century was one of the marks of the gentleman, was the principal weapon used in the period for the defense of his honor. It became, in keeping with the refinements of the Renaissance, more elegantly chiseled and damascened, and could well be the gift to a young seigneur of some attractive demoiselle at the Court. In using it, he no longer in most cases had the protection of a layer of steel over his chest, but rather the fragile weaving of a silken doublet, behind which, "very near, was the beating of his heart." The Italian gentleman at this time had the reputation of being a fine swordsman, and excellent in individual combat if not in warfare. The French learned the Italian technique of fencing — the Italian schools of fencing were visited by the French gentleman in his travels — but the thin Italian rapier was never considered during the Renaissance in France to be a completely legitimate weapon. Many thought that fencing was a tricky sort of skill and inconsistent with true honor and virtue, since the instrument used in it was not one that a gentleman could take with him into battle. A gentleman with the highest sense of fair play, then, would scarcely choose the slender instrument of fencing in fighting a duel, even though he might be very adept in its use. "I have seen the nobles," says Montaigne, "flee the reputation of being good fencers, and hide away when they learned fencing, it being an art based on subtlety and not on true and solid virtue." Henry de Sainct Didier, in his *Treatise on the Sword*, illustrates very fully many details of Italian techniques of swordplay — positions of the feet, thrusts, points of attack, etc. — by means of over one hundred woodcuts of a combat between the "Lieutenant" and the "Prévot." There is amazing variety in the poses and the costumes, but the sword is always a very heavy and solid weapon, and never looks like a fencing foil.[2]

When the code of honor had been sufficiently broken as to demand a duel, a series of rules and formalities came into play. These varied somewhat in the sixteenth century from those of earlier periods, which might allow commoners not only among the spectators but occasionally among the combatants. In the fourteenth century, for example, Philippe le Bel issued an edict concerning the regulations of dueling. It was forbidden in it that any spectator be armed or on horseback: if a gentleman were caught on a horse by the marshals, he would lose the horse, and if a commoner were caught on a horse, he would lose an ear! One of the early sixteenth-century treatises on the duel is that of Symphorien Champier, *Du Combat appellé Duellum*, included in Champier's study on the origins of the nobility, published in Lyon in 1535. Champier says a duel has to be fought when there has been "an imposition of crime which can not be proven," since no witnesses were present. The encounter that results from such a situation should be staged under the King's auspices, and the combatants should arrive at the dueling ground early in the morning, with their seconds. If by chance the affair is between a noble and a commoner, the commoner may be required to have his hair cut; but not the noble. Even though the combat may be between mixed social classes, the weapons must be the same, because "the contestants must be equal in the eyes of Justice." As a result of the events leading up to the duel, one man is the challenger, and the other the defender. After the preliminaries have been completed, the heralds sound forth: "Come on to the field and do your duty"; and the two antagonists are admitted to the enclosure by the marshal. They then bow before the marshal and he asks them if they believe in the Father, Son, and Holy Ghost. If the answer is in the negative, the combat is called off, and one or both of the combatants may be punished "as heretics." However, if the religious tests are passed and the two opponents have sworn they have no devices of sorcery on their persons, they go back to their chairs, and on signal come out fighting; if the weapons they use are a shield and big stick, it is a rather low-class duel. The defender, if he is not defeated by the time the stars appear, "or should appear," is adjudged the victor on a time basis. The conquered man may well be taken to the gibbet and given further punishment, since God has shown that he was guilty of instigating the whole affair. The concept of Champier is, obviously, a not very lofty version of the duel by judicial decree.[3]

By the time of Francis I, there were many influences to protect a gentleman against the wild claims of just anybody who might want to challenge him to a duel. If the challenger were in any way smeared with dishonor, or an unrecognized bastard, or had himself already been conquered, or belonged to the lower ranks of society, a gentleman did not have to accept his challenge. But, if there was doubt about any of these derogatory conditions, a gentleman might be forced into a duel to avoid the accusation of cowardice. Francis I, even if he approved of most of the artistic elegances favored by the Italians, never was very tolerant of duels. Though some were fought during his reign, they were not with his authorization. And the rumored duel between Francis I and Charles V never took place. Du Bellay and Brantôme, in the long question of which monarch was supposed to be afraid of the other, both say that Francis I challenged Charles V. Du Bellay says that heralds were exchanged in 1527, while Brantôme states that Charles V was too old and, besides, they could not agree as to whether the affair should be on foot or horseback. Modern historians, on the other hand, have suggested that Francis I ignored the challenge of the Emperor. In any case, Francis I shared the feeling of men like Henry IV and Richelieu that dueling was contrary to the best interests of the state. To avoid useless personal combats, tribunals were set up to regulate affairs of honor. However, a gentleman who had really been insulted did not want to cast his honor into the complex mesh of legal processes. The sword was a much quicker and more satisfying instrument of satisfaction.

In addition to the law's obstacles to dueling, the Church spoke out strongly against it. The Council of Trent in 1545 offered a deposition against duels as being an artifice of the devil, and proposed that all participants in and spectators of them be excommunicated and refused burial in consecrated ground. Francis I opposed this proposition, although he agreed with its provisions, because it had the Church intruding in temporal matters.[4]

Therefore, in spite of royal and religious edicts, duels continued to be fought in France. Other nations may disapprove of the custom, admits Brantôme, but any Frenchman who tacitly suffers slanderous or lying words to be spoken about him is not a true noble, "in the words of King Francis I." The formula of challenge, or *cartel de défi*, issued by a gentleman to a slanderer or liar, could be both bombastic and incisive. One taken from a sixteenth-century manuscript runs as follows: "Seigneur, each and every time that you have said or written, or caused to be said or written, anything opposed or prejudicial to my honor, just so many times have you lied in your throat, and in denying it you have lied again. I do not wish to make use of threats in writing, since I consider that more suitable to a vile and low person than to a chevalier, but I shall hold myself in readiness, if you are not afraid to appear, to talk to you with a sword in my fist." Brantôme has a rather arrogant and confident phrasing of a cartel: "Monsieur, you are such an insignificant thing that, were it not for the insolence of your words, I should never be able to remember you. The bearer of this will tell you the place where I am waiting, with two swords the choice of which will be yours. If you have sufficient assurance to reach the spot by your own strength, I shall relieve you of the necessity of remembering the way back." The language of cartels made them quite a literary form in the sixteenth century, and the poets frequently wrote amorous cartels, with a full quota of dueling terms in them.[5]

The most famous duel of the century, and one that will be most illustrative of the demands that could be made on a gentleman under the code of honor, was that fought between Guy Chabot, baron de Jarnac, and François de Vivonne, seigneur de La Châtaigneraie. This affair, which was a long time in the making, attracted the attention of many chroniclers of the Renaissance. The incidents leading up to the duel occurred during the reign of Francis I, but he would never allow it to take place while he was alive. Henry II did permit it, and dignified it with his presence, during the first year after he became king. Five contemporary manuscripts, all of them identical with the exceptions of a few variations in copying, give eyewitness accounts, from the heralds who were there, of the preliminaries before the combat and of the combat itself. Their story is a long one and full of intricacy of detail, but the main thread of it deserves retelling.[6]

Jarnac and La Châtaigneraie were gentlemen at the court of Francis I, and they were great friends. Jarnac was a favorite of the King, who called him familiarly, Guichot. La Châtaigneraie was well liked by the Dauphin, later to be Henry II, because of his "native attractiveness and perfection, fine stature of body, generosity of heart." Both men were good swordsmen but La Châtaigneraie was reputedly the stronger blade. In view of their friendship for each other and their position of influence at Court, "several" persons became jealous of them and wished to break them apart. The method they used to cause a breach between the two friends was one of the most vicious — the spreading of gossip: "Without having any regard for the consequences, they decided to put on Jarnac the accusation that he had boasted to La Châtaigneraie of having slept with his step-mother." Jarnac's father, Charles Chabot, who had remarried in 1546, was one of the first to hear this scandal, and was ready to fight, himself. The rumor shortly thereafter reached the ears of Jarnac, who proclaimed immediately that "whoever had said that he had boasted of having slept with his step-mother was wicked, and ill-fated, and had lied." La Châtaigneraie quickly took up this refutation of Jarnac, and, feeling certain that he would be victorious in any conflict that might ensue with Jarnac and feeling confident that he had the sympathetic support of the new King, Henry II, began to issue cartels. It should be remembered that Henry II did not share his father's antipathy for duels.[7]

La Châtaigneraie lashed out at Jarnac in three cartels, which were sent, in order to make them more emphatic, to the King himself. In the first cartel, La Châtaigneraie said: "Sire, having heard that Guichot Chabot was recently in Compiègne, where he stated that whoever would have said that he had boasted of having slept with his step-mother was wicked and ill-fated: on which point, Sire, with your permission and pleasure, I shall reply that he has wickedly lied, and will lie every time and just as many times as he says that I have said something that he did not tell me. For he told me and retold me several times, and boasted that he had slept with his step-mother." This cartel caused a furor at Court, and La Châtaigneraie was accused of "attacking a lady's honor," especially that of one who was highly respected; so he wrote a second cartel for his justification: "Sire, in the quarrel that exists between Guichot Chabot and me, up to the present I have considered the preservation only of my own honor, without bringing into play that of ladies, of whom I am traditionally the defender rather than the accuser, even of the one about whom there is a question in our quarrel. But granting that, for my own justification it is indeed required that I state that the said Chabot had his will with his step-mother, and that he told me he slept with her and bestrode her." All of which was much worse than the first cartel, and added more fuel to the flame. Jarnac replied that La Châtaigneraie was lying through his teeth, and asked the King to set the spot for the duel, with the statement that "La Châtaigneraie does not have a mouth so blatant but that I shall stop it up with a pound of steel." La Châtaigneraie in his third cartel to the King requested that a ground be chosen. The King, having consulted with the "princes, sieur de Montmorency, the Constable of France, the sieurs de Sedan and de Saint-André, marshals of France, and other seigneurs, chevaliers, captains, and important personages of our retinue," decreed that the duel was to take place within forty days from this edict, dated June 11, 1547, at Saint-Germain-en-Laye, in a "closed field." The penalty for defeat in the combat might well be the loss of nobility for the loser and his descendants, and the deprivations of rights, preëminences, privileges, and prerogatives that the nobles customarily enjoyed. Both Jarnac and La Châtaigneraie accepted the King's stipulations.[8]

On June 12, 1547, La Châtaigneraie sent Jarnac a cartel: "Guichot Chabot, I am indicating to you the choice of the field which the King has been pleased to send to me, and on which I wish to prove to you through the offensive weapons you may choose — but let them be in keeping with a gentleman of honor — that you told me you slept with your stepmother and bestrode her." La Châtaigneraie, whose duty it was to provide the weapons designated by Jarnac, asked that he be informed within four days of the latter's choice. Jarnac drew up a formidable array of offensive and defensive weapons, a list of which was read out to La Châtaigneraie by a herald on June 16. La Châtaigneraie was amazed at the collection and said: "Jarnac wishes to combat my ingenuity and my pocket-book." However, he managed to assemble an adequate variety of arms and armor, and the duel took place on July 10, 1547, in the presence of the King and his assembled ladies and gentlemen.[9]

The day was a Sunday, and the enclosed field was set up in the park adjacent to the great château of Saint-Germain-en-Laye. La Châtaigneraie, the challenger, had as his second, monseigneur le Comte d'Aumalle; and Jarnac, the challenged and thus the defender, had as his second, "monseigneur le grand écuyer." * With the rising of the sun, the herald proclaimed the fight and said "no one is to prevent the completion of the present combat, nor aid or interfere with the combatants, on penalty of death." La Châtaigneraie then came out of his lodging, led by his second and three hundred of "those of his company," who were dressed in his colors of white and incarnadine, and they went up to the enclosed field to the sound of trumpets and tambourines. La Châtaigneraie entered his pavilion to the right of the entrance gate to the field; there he was to stay until the duel was signaled. Jarnac arrived at the field from his lodging, led by his second and one hundred twenty of his company, dressed in black and white, and disappeared in his pavilion. The examination and approval of weap-

* He is not identified further by the heralds.

ons by the seconds took hours, and the Comte d'Aumalle protested several times about the long delay. Finally, each contestant was allowed a regular sword (and only one more if the first one broke), a long dagger tied to the thigh by cords, and a short dagger thrust in the left boot. The combatants were brought on to the field by their seconds and companies, and swore before the King on the Holy Scriptures, which were on a "square of velvet and cloth of gold reaching to the ground," that they had on their persons no secret weapons, charms, magic words, or incantations that would give an unfair advantage. The herald announced, "by order of the King," that during the combat none of the spectators was to speak, cough, or spit, or make any movement with the foot, hand, or eye that would aid or interfere with either of the contestants. La Châtaigneraie and Jarnac, having been given their weapons, sat down in chairs opposite each other and awaited the herald's signal.[10]

The herald from Normandy came forward and cried out: "Let the noble combatants proceed," and the fight was under way. It was a very brief affair, in comparison with the many hours and days of preparation that had gone before. In the words of the herald, "there were several great thrusting as well as cutting attacks, one of which on the part of the said Jarnac struck the calf of the left leg of the said La Châtaigneraie as he made a thrust at Jarnac; and Jarnac struck another blow on the same calf of the leg." La Châtaigneraie fell to the ground, evidently with the tendons in the calf of his left leg severed, and was unable to rise. Jarnac leaned over him and said, "give me back my honor." There was no reply; so Jarnac advanced to the King with the statement: "Sire, I give you La Châtaigneraie; take him, Sire, and may my honor be given back to me. It was our youth that caused all this." The King made no response; so Jarnac knelt down to say a prayer and then returned to La Châtaigneraie, still stretched out on the ground. Jarnac asked La Châtaigneraie again to make acknowledgments, but La Châtaigneraie raised himself on one knee and tried to lift his sword and shield, whereupon Jarnac said, "don't move or I'll kill you." La Châtaigneraie made an effort to rise, saying "then kill me," and fell back. Jarnac returned to the King and asked again to be considered a man of honor, since there was no gentleman at Court more ready in any capacity to serve his King. The King still answered nothing. Jarnac went back once more to La Châtaigneraie, still stretched out on his side with his sword lying on the ground, and said: "Châtaigneraie, my old comrade, recognize your Creator, and let us be friends." Then Jarnac assumed an attitude of caution: "While charity was advising him to forget his feeling of enmity, caution counseled him to take no chances; so he reached out with his sword for the sword * and the dagger, which had slipped out of its scabbard, of La Châtaigneraie." Jarnac handed the weapons over to a herald and asked the King, "for the love of God," to recognize the defeat of La Châtaigneraie; Monseigneur de Vendôme and the Connétable de Montmorency made the same request, since it was necessary now for La Châtaigneraie in all mercy to be removed from the field. Jarnac next addressed himself to "a certain great lady"—probably Diane de Poitiers—in the stands, and the King, "moved to pity," finally listened to Jarnac and said to him: "You have done your duty, and your honor is hereby restored." [11]

The bleeding La Châtaigneraie was borne from the field by the heralds and four gentlemen, and put into his tent on the outside. Jarnac, despite the suggestion of high noblemen, refused to be carried off in triumph, but threw himself on his knees before the King, who embraced him saying: "You have fought like Caesar and you have talked like Aristotle"—which was a somewhat ambiguous remark and tinged with irony. Despite the King's attitude, Jarnac was full of honor throughout the land for having conquered La Châtaigneraie, "who was esteemed bold, strong, and skillful, as to tell the truth he was." So ended the heralds' account of the Jarnac-La Châtaigneraie duel. It will be noted that in it there is no mention of the death of La Châtaigneraie, which occurred within a few hours at Saint-Germain-en-Laye; the account does include some of the elements of court intrigue that led up to the

* It was now lying on the ground.

tragic affair. Later chroniclers added further details and explanations.[12]

In keeping with the demands of the code of honor, it is more than obvious that after a certain point had been reached the Jarnac-La Châtaigneraie duel had to be fought. Jarnac could not possibly have ignored the arrogant and scandalous cartels issued by La Châtaigneraie. However, it was the original planting of the seeds of evilly-flowering gossip that really produced the mixture of farce and tragedy, which ended in the blood-soaked dust of Saint-Germain-en-Laye. Jarnac was married to Louise de Pisselieu, the sister of the Duchesse d'Etampes, the favorite of Francis I. There was no love lost between the Duchesse and Diane de Poitiers, who had possibly caught the eye of Francis I and who was most certainly already the preferred of the Dauphin, later Henry II. Rumor had it that there was a father-son rivalry for the delectable Diane and that the situation was something of an "incestuous liaison." Therefore, in the emotional convolutions of high-placed feminine rivalries, a story as a counter-irritant was spread concerning Jarnac and his stepmother. Even the Dauphin himself was supposed to have helped it along, and then to have passed over the responsibilities of the resulting duel to La Châtaigneraie, the good friend of Jarnac. Monluc thought that loose feminine tongues brought about the unnecessary fight between friends, and that the King should "stop up the mouths" of ladies who talk around the Court: "A babbling woman caused the death of Monsieur de La Châtaigneraie. If he had been willing to believe me and five or six of his friends, he would have straightened out his affair with Monsieur de Jarnac in some other way; for he fought against his conscience, and lost his honor and his life." Vieilleville, after speaking of La Châtaigneraie's great overconfidence about his certainty of winning the fight and the advance preparations made by La Châtaigneraie for a big banquet to celebrate his victory, maintained that the gossip all started from confusion over the word *entretenir*, which normally meant in the sixteenth century, "to chat with," "to entertain," but which might have an extended meaning, "to entertain intimately." According to Vieilleville, when Jarnac spoke to La Châtaigneraie of having "entertained" his stepmother, the latter was "so impudent and unrestrained" as to give a bad interpretation to the term. Also, the King was partly responsible for the duel "through having himself interpreted in the wrong way this word *entretenir*, on which the quarrel was founded." [13]

There is little doubt that everyone was surprised at Jarnac's victory. Through the sober and factual account told by the heralds comes the note of the King's amazement and of his desire to wash his hands of La Châtaigneraie, who had been overconfident and performed so badly that he was very nearly allowed to bleed to death on the field. The position of the King in the whole affair was far from admirable, and the publicity attached to it caused it to be the last duel in France to be dignified by the presence of the monarch. Jarnac showed up well in the tragic drama: as a gentleman he wanted, after the victorious thrusts of his sword, to have the King make official the restoration of his honor; and then he wanted a reconciliation with his friend, La Châtaigneraie, who preferred to die rather than take anything back — also the privilege of a gentleman. It would have been a legitimate tactic, too, for La Châtaigneraie to have slashed out at Jarnac while he was looking the other way, if the recumbent La Châtaigneraie could have reached his sword and had had the strength to lift it. Jarnac as the practical gentleman put the weapons out of reach. The affair added a new expression to dueling for use in later centuries: a *coup de Jarnac*, which came to mean a clever and unexpected thrust,* destined to bring death in the morning or maybe late in the afternoon. And the poet in formal strophes and antistrophes sang a song, *La Victoire de Guy de Chabot, seigneur de Jarnac*, wherein it was shown that the exploits of a coward are soon forgotten and the empty bombast of the spoken word may be cut away by the sword.[14]

Although the Jarnac-La Châtaigneraie duel seems a tragic comedy of errors when looked at in the light of reason, it was relatively one of the more sensible affairs of honor of the

* At present, a *coup de Jarnac* means a "treacherous blow."

period. In the second half of the century, with the progressive decadence of standards at the Court, duels were fought over the most trivial of trivialities. Bussy d'Amboise, one of the best swordsmen around the court of Henry III, became involved in swordplay with a good friend because they disagreed as to whether the design in a lady's silken sleeve was shaped like an *X* or a *Y*. It was fashionable also during this time to fight duels in nothing but a chemise, or in the moonlight. Bussy d'Amboise and a friend, in 1579, "in a quarrel over nothing," fought two other courtiers (all four in no armor but their thin shirts) with sword and dagger. In this double duel the later pair were "cruelly beaten and wounded." The seigneur de Givry and the Comte de Soissons, "at the court of our King," became involved in an affair of honor over dancing with Mademoiselle de Grammont. Givry would lead the charming lady on to the floor, where Soissons, who outranked him, would take her away. After this happened twice, Givry challenged the Count, and it looked as though another episode was to take place on the well-worn dueling grounds of the Pré-aux-Clercs in Paris. The intervention of royalty prevented the combat, though everybody agreed that Givry had been perfectly correct in his attitude. But despite the King's interdiction, a great number of France's gentlemen in the decades previous to the tougher policy of Henry IV died in futile and far-fetched duels. As for Bussy d'Amboise, the most swashbuckling figure in the lavender glow of Henry III's court, he died at the ripe age of thirty in an amorous ambush, "having very little fear of God." Though Bussy fought valiantly against some dozen men posted by the seigneur de Montsoreau, with whose wife Bussy had planned to spend the evening, the odds were too great for even such a renowned sword as his.[15]

In the reign of Henry III, when the ordonnances against dueling were ignored "even as all other good ordonnances in the realm of France," one of the most fantastic duels fought was that between three of the King's dandies and three courtiers attached to the Duc de Guise. However light may have been the cause of the conflict, the results were quite destructive. The sober Pierre de L'Estoile has left a description of what happened: "On Sunday, April 27, 1578, in order to settle a quarrel born of some small incident the day before in the courtyard of the Louvre between the seigneur de Quélus, one of the chief dandies of the King, and the young Entragues, whom they call Antraguet, a favorite of the House of Guise, the said Quélus with Maugiron and Livarrot, and Antraguet with Riberac and the young Chomberg, found themselves at five o'clock in the morning at the Marché-aux-Chevaux (formerly Les Tournelles, near the Bastille-Saint-Antoine), and there they fought so furiously that the handsome Maugiron and the young Chomberg fell dead on the spot. Riberac, from the thrusts that he received there, died the next day at noon. Livarrot, from a heavy blow that he received on the head, was ill for six weeks but finally recovered. Antraguet came out of it safe and sound with a small injury, which was only a scratch, on the arm. Quélus, author and aggressor in the affair, languished for thirty-three days from the nineteen wounds that he received, and died on Thursday, the twenty-ninth of May." The combat received much publicity at Court, and Quélus was visited every day by the King, who offered a reward to any surgeon who could patch up his favorite and bring him back to life. Henry III cut off and preserved the blond tresses of the dead Maugiron and Quélus — all of which, says L'Estoile with admirable and surprising restraint, "gradually caused disdain for this prince." Many verses were written about the episode, including some to the effect that Antraguet and his companions would have done a good thing if they had eliminated a few more dandies. And the Duc de Guise said that Antraguet had acted like a gentleman and would have his full protection.[16]

Some strange combats were recorded during the century. Androuet Du Cerceau made a large engraving of a man fighting a dog, in a big circle, with ladies and gentlemen in courtly costume grouped around as spectators. The story, which concerned a formalized combat between a dog and the slayer of his master, came from the fifteenth century. In something like a judiciary duel, the dog was so successful that his human opponent was eventually hanged. It must be admitted that, in spite of the many lofty preliminaries that might precede a duel, things were not always carried on in the complete spirit of sportsmanship. Brantôme records at least two instances in which a competitor threw sand in an opponent's eyes. When the baron des Guerres was fighting the seigneur de Fandilles, over a question that was "rather foul, since it concerned sodomy," the baron was wounded. At that moment, the stands holding up the spectators broke down, and in the ensuing hubbub, the baron managed to blind his adversary with a well-tossed handful of sand — and got no worse than a draw in the fight. In a rather low-class duel with clubs and shields, a certain Mahuot threw dirt in the eyes of one Jacotin, who won the combat anyway. Very impudent persons — they usually are found in Italy — have been known to give a one-eyed opponent in an armored duel a helmet with the slit for the good eye blocked. There was also the tale of the young gentleman who gained a victory over a taller man by specifying as weapons swords, daggers, and steel collars with sharp spikes. The taller fighter could not bend over without cutting his throat, and thus was not able to keep his eyes on his shorter enemy. On the other hand, there have been many courtesies in dueling, especially in the time of "the great King Francis." The seigneur de Sourdeval, for example, put an injured adversary on a horse and took him "to the barber's" to have his wound dressed. Also, the more genteel of gentlemen would not continue a duel when an opponent had lost too much blood, nor would they make a thrust without first shouting "on guard." In demanding, too, that a conquered opponent surrender, a gentleman would use language that was courteous and not full of boasting.[17]

The Church's condemnation of duels, in the opinion of Brantôme, was not well founded, for did not David fight Goliath? This was one of the most notable duels in history, "and God approved of it." As for the modern duel, most of the theories and practices of it were considered by the French to have evolved from the Italians. Since the Italians as a people were "cold" and "cruel," any barbarisms or ungenteel operations in a duel were likely to be attributed to them. In the fifty-first story of the *Heptaméron* all the company present agree — and this is one of the few times they do agree — that Italians are vicious in their cruelties. Tavannes maintains that in dueling the Italians are more clever, but that the French are more courageous. Therefore, if a French gentleman has the choice of weapons in a duel against an Italian, he should choose to use a sword, "on foot and in a chemise." In this denuded condition, raw courage will have a better chance to be effective.[18]

During the second half of the century, the sober minds of France spoke out strongly against the exaggerated number of duels a young gentleman might have to fight, and the futile causes that brought them about. The Clergy, in its notebook to the King at the meeting of the Estates-General in 1560, asked that it be forbidden to the nobility "to put their hands on their weapons for a simple giving of the lie or other light causes, in order to prevent quarrels." The Clergy felt also that duels should be outlawed because they are not "in keeping with the spirit of Christianity." Montaigne, though he has respect for a single combat between two brave men who have disagreed, condemns most heartily the free-for-alls of his age wherein the seconds and "thirds" and "fourths" all have to fight. What was once a duel thus becomes a "battle" and a gentleman is forced involuntarily to defend the honor of another. Tavannes thinks that duels, in general, are bad, and that a court of six captains should be set up to rule on their validity. "The duel," says Tavannes, "badly understood in France, prevents [by its destruction] fathers from sending their youngsters either to war or to the Court — to the Court where, indeed, being without direction they often in dueling may lose their honor before they are able to acquire any." The youthful nobility, therefore, has to be ready with the sword, since the "intemperate desire to obtain honor through the medium of arms" makes a rash young gentleman seek a quarrel with one who is more calm. The result of such intemperance is the destruction of the flower of the nobility.[19]

That doughty warrier and man of honor, François de La

Noue, treats the question of *Duels* in the twelfth of his *Discours*, published in 1587. He has previously lamented the decline of "valor, virtue, and justice" in the nobility of his age, and the prevalence of present-day corruption. In his discussion of the frequency of duels, La Noue suggests that they are caused by too much "rashness" and "pride." "For, less than forty years ago," says La Noue, "quarrels were rare among gentlemen, and when some one was reputed to be querulous, everybody left him alone, just as they would a horse that bites or kicks: and the reason was that manners were purer then, and the true point of honor better understood than at the present time." Actions of today are dictated rather by a "false honor," which is deplored by La Noue. This "false honor" demands first that a gentleman be a good swordsman — which would be a fine thing if such skill were employed against "the enemy in war"; and then it expresses itself in "boasting, bragging, slandering, outraging, fighting, and murdering," all directed at one's neighbors, companions, and friends. Opposed to this "false honor" there is such a thing as "true honor," a laudable trait: "And what then is "true honor"? It is the fine approval and reputation that is given by the best people to some one because of his virtue, which he demonstrates in several excellent ways. These consist in the using of prudence, justice, bravery, temperance, truth, and courtesy — and other similar virtues." [20]

The critics and the logicians in most admirable fashion could settle affairs that came under the code of honor. Ordonnances were passed, councils were decreed, and a king was able to call off a duel because it was contrary to the good of the state. But nevertheless, a Bayard would still get out of his bed of fever to keep an appointment with a Spaniard on the field of honor, with no thought of asking for a postponement. A lady's misplaced smile or a misunderstood word might cause a young gentleman to unsheath his sword; and, ironically, he might die for something that really did not matter at all.[21]

XI

The Question of Women

THE GENTLEMAN OF THE RENAISSANCE WAS, by his own choice and in keeping with the example set by his King, very much in the society of women. They complicated his existence, they decorated the Court, they listened to his stories, they were his inspiration and destruction — and all this to a greater degree than in any previous era of French history. The poets dedicated their verses to them, to Méline, to Francine, to Hélène, to Cassandre, or to the mysterious Délie; the warriors wore the favorite colors of their feminine sponsors or their tokens in jousts and battles; and an influential lady at Court could begin or end a career for a young gentleman, and in the process gain for him honors or, maybe, cost him his life. Fashions in riding a horse might be set by Catherine de' Medici, or Diane de Poitiers and Queen Claude might cause little carriages to be popular on the streets of Paris. The hostility of the Duchesse d'Étampes could drive Benvenuto Cellini away from the benevolence of Francis I, and Pierre de Ronsard dedicated poem after poem to Diane de Poitiers in a vain effort to win her favor. Many of the old noblemen of France resented the power of woman at the Court during the Renaissance, and particularly the decades of influence of Catherine de' Medici, who was not only a clever woman, but a clever Italian woman, which more than doubled her potentialities. In any case, the gentleman of the period was pretty well surrounded by women, some of them great ladies who talked to kings and others from more modest social levels. There is some evidence from varied sources — the men of letters, chroniclers, and artists — on what women were like at that time, and on their position in the social plan.[1]

Women of the upper classes had their careers marked out

for them rather definitely: they got married or, if no suitable matrimonial alliance presented itself, they took religious vows and devoted their lives to the Church. The choice in either case was made early, in family conclave, and almost before the young demoiselle had finished lulling her first doll to sleep. The normal age for a young girl of good breeding to get married was twelve; theoretically, she had some choice in picking a mate but in practice it was a marriage of arrangement between two families. Louise de Savoie was married to Charles d'Orléans, Comte d'Angoulême, at the age of eleven and was a widow when she was eighteen — and the proud mother of the future Francis I. The daughter of Francis I, Marguerite — who was very gifted in languages and, some said, brighter even than her aunt, Marguerite de Navarre — was still unmarried at twenty-two, and this caused a great deal of comment. There was even more comment when Marguerite was still unmarried at the age of thirty-four, and a very doddering old maid. An "elderly" spinster in the Renaissance, in fact, had no real social niche, since the most favorable positions in society were occupied by married women and widows. Other young women of the upper social stratum, either through deep feelings of piety or through being overlooked in the matrimonial market, chose life in a convent. As a generality, marriage for the gentle maiden was little more than a lottery. She was linked at too early an age to a young gentleman for whom she might have later neither love nor compatibility, and it was for life. Divorce was almost non-existent, although there was the possibility for the annulment of a marriage if it could be demonstrated, after three amatory sessions in the presence of midwives as examiners, that the wife was still undeflowered and the husband, therefore, impotent. Adultery on the part of a wife might lead to her perpetual sequestration in a convent, or possibly a divorce. Adultery on the part of the husband, though a serious crime on the lawbooks, seldom entailed actual punishments.[2]

The legal status of a married woman in the sixteenth century, though not entirely enviable, was not such as to make her merely a chattel. She had rights of inheritance and disposition of property, and she could not easily be cast aside by a husband. Both the Protestants and Catholics spoke out strongly concerning the sacred as well as the social implications of marriage, and the undercover concubinage of the clergy was attacked on all sides. Also, clandestine marriages which were established merely on the exchange of words by the two contracting parties, were discouraged by both Church and state. All of which made the institution of marriage, founded upon an agreement between honorable families and with temporal and churchly sanction, the strong mechanism for continuing the race that it is today in France. Though the individual preferences of a child bride or a youthful gentleman might be ignored, the system was a solid one for society. It had no consideration, on the other hand, for the emotional maturing or changing in taste on the part of the wife. Therefore, in the sixteenth century, a widow was in a most enviable position: she had inherited from a husband whom she probably did not love, she had control of any children that had resulted from her marriage, and she had the privilege finally while she was still young of focusing her charms on a gentleman of her own choosing. She was in the almost impossible and satisfying position of having eaten her cake and of still having most of it left. It is no wonder that, by and large, French writers have through the years portrayed widows as being most attractive and delightful objects.

But the marriage of arrangement as practiced by the best families of the Renaissance had many flaws. According to plan, a young girl went immediately from the dominion of her parents to that of her husband, and thus she had no opportunity for making any decisions or for getting lost on any amorous side roads. This was the way her gentleman-father wanted it, and it is still the attitude of most French fathers of the present day, despite the considerable emancipation of young ladies in France that has come from two World Wars. However, the little girl of twelve was scarcely nubile, and she was married to a young gentleman usually some years her senior. It would have been difficult to plan a worse situation. The young husband, with little mental or physical companionship to be found with his child wife, sought it elsewhere. When she had reached an age of greater maturity, outside feminine relationships had most likely already been formed to interfere with the possible happiness of her ménage. And, as the child bride bloomed into womanhood, married to a man who was now an older and somewhat distant stranger, she might well find a discreet interest in a younger and more sympathetic gentleman. The Court facilitated conversations between ladies and gentlemen of kindred inclinations, and French history is full of older husbands who were deceived by their younger wives. One of the reasons, too, for the early marriages of members of the nobility was to join together two great names and fortunes, and thus add quickly to the prestige of both. The commoners, with no problems of falling off the social ladder, were more logical and gave nature a little more time to take her course. In the higher social strata, it was recognized that a greater risk was to be taken in allowing a young lady any freedom of choice, especially in view of the broadly held opinion that woman was a weak and variable creature.

The writers of the Renaissance — critical, fictional, and poetical — were rather well divided into two camps in their estimate of women. Since the greater part of the writing of the period was influenced by the Court, or under the patronage of or composed by some noble, the picture of woman portrayed will normally be a creature of the upper level of society. In general, the tellers of stories and some of the critics vilify women; the poets and others of the critics praise them and put them on a lofty pedestal. There was, certainly, in the sixteenth century a literary quarrel over women, a *Querelle des Femmes*. It was more serious than the somewhat jocular attacks on femininity in the medieval farces and the allegorical *Romance of the Rose*, though these led to the serious defense of her sex by the good fifteenth-century woman poet, Christine de Pisan. With the progressive influence of woman over the Renaissance gentleman, she was subjected to a more complete analysis in the sixteenth century. Even then, there was a lack of consistency in appraisal: those who attack her on one occasion may defend her on the next. The printed page is simply an inadequate medium in any age for the depiction of woman.[3]

The vilifiers of woman could draw on a long tradition of derogatory opinions toward femininity. Aristotle thought that woman was unequal to man, and the inferior in any relations of friendship that might exist between the sexes. Plato, though admitting that woman has the same natural gifts as man, maintained that man has them to a much higher degree. Ovid, the lawgiver for the making of love and one of the most popular pagans during the Renaissance, said that a woman's chastity lasted only until she had an opportunity to lose it. And, in later Latin, Erasmus volunteered a view on feminine intelligence: "So, woman is always a woman, that is to say, something stupid." Therefore, says Erasmus, even as it is for children, "silence is an ornamentation for women." That favored manual of courtly politeness, Castiglione's *Courtier*, while it presents both sides of the question, sums up along the way most of the arguments against women. One of the discoursers in the *Courtier*, Lord Gaspar, is most vehement in his attacks upon women. He feels that they have no judgment and are essentially less perfect than men by any standard of measurement. They are weak creatures and must be protected from temptation since they have limited powers of resistance. On the other hand, they are full of wiles and trickery and never let a lover know how he stands with them until he has worried himself almost to death. Another objection to women comes from the Spaniard, Antonio de Guevara, whose work opposing life at the Court, *Menosprecio de Corte*, was translated into French in 1542 and had great popularity. Guevara lists among the evils of the Court the presence there of women. They, in their constant and continued desire for gold, corrupt the gentlemen and bring about their dissolution. And the observing Italian, Lippomano, states that French women are very devout in appearance, but very sprightly and free underneath. They all want to be treated like genteel ladies, even the courtesans — though Lippomano makes it clear that he is not talking about the lower classes. They go around wherever they please, gossiping at will, and stay away from their homes three or four hours at a time without their husbands' being informed as to their whereabouts. French women are more avaricious than others; in all countries women are susceptible to the gleam of gold, but in France the shine of silver is sufficient.[4]

Among French men of letters, the tellers of tales and writers of satirical fiction were the most vigorous in their attacks on women; and of this group the prime vilifier was probably Rabelais. The greater portion of Rabelais's *Five Books* is given over to the over-all problem of marriage, and, though the Oracle of the Holy Bottle finally advises Panurge to "drink" at the matrimonial fount, many arguments have previously been advanced on the other side of the question, most of them uncomplimentary to woman. The most notable of Rabelais's anti-feminine outbursts comes when Panurge, in seeking advice from all the world authorities on marriage, consults the doctor Rondibilis. Rondibilis points out to him that it is the inevitable fate of all husbands to be cuckolds because of the nature and internal structure of woman: "When I speak of woman, I am talking about a sex so variable, so changeable, so inconstant and imperfect, that nature seems to me (with all due honor and respect for her) to have wandered away from that good sense through which she had created and formed everything, when she constructed woman. And, having thought about it five or six hundred times, I do not know what to conclude, except that in making woman, nature has had much more regard for the social delectation of man and for the perpetuation of the human species than for the perfection of woman as an individual. Plato, certainly, did not know in what category to put them, whether among rational beings or the brutish beasts." Rondibilis continues, in an imperfect lesson on feminine anatomy, to explain cuckoldry through the presence inside a woman's body of a small animal that demands continual appeasement. Therefore, a wife's modest demureness of demeanor in front of her husband is only a cover for the fires that rage underneath. It must be remembered, in passing, that in the breadth and gaiety of Rabelais's satire, his anti-feminism is purposefully enlarged to fit the general pattern of his story.[5]

Montaigne, who had provocative opinions on almost everything, expressed himself quite freely, and often quite derogatorily, on woman. In his very first essay, Montaigne lists as "the most feeble natures" in the world those of "women, children, and the vulgar crowd." Woman pretends a modesty that she does not have, a "virginal shame," in order to increase man's desire. Since she knows she is more attractive in her feigned inaccessibility, woman makes "this profession of ignorance of matters that she knows a thousand times better than do we men who instruct her." Woman is, in essence, more concupiscent than man, and "more capable and ardent" to the effects of love. Though marriage is an honorable, just, and useful estate, it is likely to end up by being "an insipid pleasure." Therefore, in view of woman's natural inclinations, a husband is destined for the life of a cuckold. Montaigne says that he himself has known one hundred "gentlemen" who were deceived by their wives; the men were pitied but they were not made ridiculous, since everybody around understood how a thing like that could happen. Even Ronsard, who spent most of his career dedicating verses to ladies (and to some gentlemen) of high estate, resents in a letter written in 1577 that he has served a mistress "who has no reason or judgment on our poetry" — this is apropos of his beloved Hélène de Surgères. The decisions of women, for Ronsard, "last only a day," and "they are so avaricious by nature that they would not be willing to spend a crown on any good deed."[6]

On the other side of the ledger, much was written in defense of woman during the century. The development of the neo-Platonistic doctrine before 1550 made woman more mysterious and ethereal, and symbolic of a beyond-the-earth perfection. The Italians had begun it in the Platonic Academies in Florence at the end of the fifteenth century, out of which came Marsilio Ficino's commentary on Plato's dialogue, the *Symposium*, in which Plato discusses the soul's yearning for perfection and non-earthly love — Plato, incidentally, felt as did Montaigne that the most perfect friendships exist between men. Cardinal Bembo's *Gli Asolani* and the *Courtier* added to the thesis derived from Plato that the soul yearns for an ideal of beauty and love beyond the ties of this earth, and woman became involved in the concept as a preliminary to the idealization. There is a strong defense for women in the third book of the *Courtier* by one of the discoursers, Lord Caesar. He argues that woman has a depth of virtue that makes her chaste, and that it is not fear that restrains her from misdeeds. Also, a woman will retain her purity much more as a result of her own desires to do so than from beatings given her by her father or husband! In the fourth book of the *Courtier* a strong equation is made by Bembo, who is one of the interlocutors, for beauty and goodness: beauty is good and therefore a love of it is good and holy. Woman is the earthly symbol of beauty, though Bembo admits that a woman may be beautiful and also unchaste through the provocations and machinations of unprincipled lovers. However, beauty and goodness have affinities, and the baser impulses of the senses are eventually transmuted on to more lofty ground. In the process of transfer, it is safe for an older lover to kiss his lady with no resultant firing of the senses, but with just the thought of the union of souls. A younger gentleman may be disturbed at first by mere bodily beauty, but he will eventually be lifted above these earthly vexations and carry the image of his lady purified in his heart. Then, cleansed of all things carnal, he approaches universal beauty, and hears the heavenly harmony of the angels, with all passion burned away. Bembo ends his remarks almost in a prayer and one of the ladies present catches his garment lest his soul leave his body.

These Platonistic doctrines, although they made their way very quickly into France, fell on somewhat infertile ground. They did have a literary, philosophical, and social effect for a limited time, it is true, and were important in the *Querelle des Femmes*. The peak of their influence was between 1540 and 1550, when a great deal of Platonistic poetry, with its conscious cult of obscurity and idealization of far-away femininity, was written. The great problem for the French was to bridge the gap between the carnal and the ethereal. It might be done with fair facility in rhymed couplets, but it was a more complicated operation for the young gentleman just back from the wars in Northern Italy. Even such feminists and Platonistic poets as Louise Labé and Marguerite de Navarre had trouble in detaching themselves from the coils of this sphere: Louise wrote some of the most burning sonnets in the French language and Marguerite's *Heptaméron* is full of earthiness. On the other hand, a poet like Joachim du Bellay may seek the release for his winged soul to fly away to the realms of eternal beauty, and Maurice Scève in his verses so etherealizes his lady that it is hard to tell what he is talking about. Several poets in the 1540's, drawing on the varied Platonistic sources, sought to picture the idealized lady, or perfect *amie*. It was definitely a literature of the Court, and the first of these poems, La Borderie's *Amie de Cour*, depicts an aristocratic lady of the Court who cleverly maintains a constant guard over her honor that is under continual threat from the gentlemen around her. She denies the ascendancy of man over woman, and his privilege of sensual enjoyment at her expense; but she realizes the advantages of a wealthy husband, and by coquettish dissimulation will manage to get one. The most lofty and unearthly of these poems is Antoine Héroët's *La Parfaite Amie*, which portrays woman (and woman's love) as something beyond this world, totally forgetful of self, and desirous of a union of two hearts as the mark of perfect bliss. She is not jealous, not even of another woman who might momentarily have the bodily interest of her beloved, since she knows that it is to her that his heart belongs. Nor does she care particularly what the rabble may say about the manifestations of her feelings, because the vulgar crowd has no knowledge or judgment of delicate sentiments. Eventually she will be joined with her beloved, who is most likely not her husband, in the perfect aftermath of beauty when their souls are reunited in the oneness from which they came. There were many other Platonistic writings which lifted woman high above the earth in a vague sort of way, but Platonism as a purifying agent for the relations between the sexes lost ground after the middle of the century. It was recognized in the cold light of French logic that it led simply to adultery, and was directly opposed to the ancient institution of marriage. Several other defenses of women from varying points of view were brought out during the century. Among them, Guillaume Postel said in 1553 that women ought to be sovereigns of the world, and that the regenerating spirit of a new Eve had appeared in Jeanne d'Arc. If given the opportunity, women would be able to direct mundane matters by their intuition, a quality lacking in man. François de Billon in 1555 brought out two hundred fifty-eight folios of material in woman's defense, including an answer to Rabelais's allegations of her inferiority. Billon's work is in the form of an allegory modeled after the *Romance of the Rose*, and is full of terms of military defense — woman's honor, for example, is so well established in an impregnable fort that it can resist all attacks.[7]

The most complete philosophical examination of woman's position in the sixteenth century is that made by Marguerite de Navarre in her *Heptaméron*. The Queen of Navarre, herself a person of infinite complexity and a wife not particularly compatible with her husband, gives here an excellent analysis of man's relation to woman during the golden era of the Renaissance. Marguerite is not trying primarily to build up a defense of her sex, but neither does she make a brief for man as an instrument for good or consider him the monarch of all he surveys. Since Marguerite was the greatly esteemed sister of Francis I, she was familiar with the Court and her social studies are concerned with the upper circles of society. Many of the stories in the *Heptaméron* are not lofty, but the ladies and gentlemen therein come from the best classes. The question of man-woman relationships is taken up both in the stories themselves and in the discussion of them that follows by the assembled group.

The fifteenth tale of the *Heptaméron* is a summation of many of the problems that might arise between a gentleman and his young wife. A "simple gentleman" at the court of Francis I was married to a young demoiselle who, though very wealthy, was much his junior. He spent his time with other ladies at the Court, although "after two or three years his wife became one of the most beautiful women in France." She gradually began to accept the attentions of other gentlemen, though very discreetly. The husband became suspicious of one particular young gentleman and questioned his wife about her relations with him. The wife, in the key passage of the story, defends herself most admirably, saying that she had loved her husband completely until his neglect had driven her astray, but that still she had done nothing dishonorable with the young gentleman — who was, admittedly, much younger and more attractive than her husband. But, says the wife, what about the husband's position in regard to right and honor, since he has been carrying on an affair with the wife of one of his best friends? With deep feeling, she says: "And although the law of man gives great dishonor to women who love other men than their husbands, the truth is that the law of God does not excuse husbands who love other women than their wives." The husband is so astonished at the clarity of his wife's story that he does not even beat her, and can think of no reply, "except that a man's honor and a woman's honor are not the same." The wife continues to see the young gentleman quietly, but eventually in very genteel fashion he leaves the Court to avoid a possible duel with the husband. Before his departure, the wife gives him a ring worth three thousand crowns, which he pawns for fifteen hundred crowns. The husband later redeems it, "in order to save the honor of his wife." The wife then sends the friend a diamond — more valuable than the ring — which he gladly accepts. At the death of the husband, the young gentleman sought out the wife in the hope of marrying her. She, in a change of attitude, had during his absence "found a companion that she liked better"; so the young gentleman spent the rest of his life in "hazardous occupations." None of the participants in this little drama is, obviously, completely admirable. In the discussion that follows the story, one of the men present blames the wife for being vindictive and fickle. Her actions are defended by a lady of the audience, who says that nobody knows "what a heartbreak it is to be in love and not to be loved in return."

Throughout the stories there is much evidence that man's honor and woman's honor are judged by different measurements, and that, rightly or wrongly, a double standard is in operation. Parlamente, one of the ladies of the group, in the forty-third tale attacks men and society's lax judgment of them: "Women are not the ones who are motivated by pleasure, but men, whose honor is increased by wildness and concupiscence; for a man who takes vengeance on an enemy and kills him because of the giving of the lie is esteemed as a result a more genteel companion; the same is true when he loves a dozen women other than his wife. But the honor of women has a different foundation: it is gentleness, patience, and chastity." Parlamente has said earlier, in the discussion following the twenty-first tale, that there is a difference in man's love and woman's love: man's love is founded on pleasure and woman's on God and honor. One of the few stories of the *Heptaméron* that portrays the possibility of man's faithfulness is the eighteenth: a gentleman in love with a charming lady finds in his bed a luscious demoiselle who had been put there by the lady as a test case. Because of his love for the lady the gentleman refuses the charms of the demoiselle. The lady, who had been watching the situation through an open door, is convinced of the gentleman's fidelity. The forty-second tale, which is concerned with the question of the possibility of love between a man and woman of different social strata, is full of references to masculine and feminine honor. Again, it is concluded that "honor as it applies to women" means purity and chastity.

As for marriage, there is much discussion of it in the *Heptaméron*, as well as of the legitimate control a husband can exercise over a wife. In the fortieth tale a young lady marries a young gentleman secretly. The brother of the lady, although he has much friendship for the young gentleman, has him slain by the servants when he finds the young man in the bedroom of his sister. The grief-stricken wife spends the rest of her life in a "hermitage." In the analysis of this tale by the company, it is concluded that children should never marry without the knowledge and consent of their families, "for marriage is an affair of such long duration that it should never be entered into lightly or without the advice of our best friends and relatives." Some excuse is offered for the brother's having the young gentleman destroyed since the latter was of lower social position than the sister. One of the group doubts that this class distinction is justifiable, since "the wise philosophers maintain that the least man in the world is worth more than the grandest and most virtuous lady that there might be." In the thirty-fifth tale a husband gives a wife a thrashing for becoming infatuated with a monk; afterward, there was never any doubt of her uxorial devotion. The company agrees for the most part that the husband did right, since women are rather stupid and easily deceived in matters of love. Further consideration of woman's stupidity is given at the end of the sixty-fifth tale, but the fifty-ninth tale shows a lady more clever than her husband in amorous deceptions. At the end of this tale one of the group says it shows that neither a husband nor a wife should inquire too closely into the other's activities, and they will both be happier.

A Platonistic touch is found in the twenty-sixth tale, where the young seigneur d'Avannes is enamoured of the genteel wife of his patron, a wealthy gentleman of the town of Pampelune in Navarre. The situation began when the young seigneur was still in his teens, the lady some twenty-three years of age, and the husband near fifty. The husband liked the youngster so much that he well-nigh adopted him, became his godfather, and enjoyed watching him dance with his wife. The boy as yet experienced only gratitude for his patron and respect for his wife, but the lady was conscious of "the grace and beauty of the said seigneur d'Avannes." As a few years passed, he fell most deeply in love with her; she also loved him but only in an ethereal manner, and talked to him about virtue and continence. He has now many frustrated earthly demands, and goes away to wear them down in the company of other women. On his return he is nursed back to health by the lady, who still resists bodily claims and says that she has only God and honor before her eyes. She will accept nothing but the "sight" and the "words" of the young man, "wherein lie the satisfactions of honor and good love." The lady, in Platonistic parlance, was the husband's *femme*, and the young gentleman's *dame*. She finally dies from the torments of her dual role, and the young man covered her body with kisses—

he is now just eighteen. When the husband observed the osculatory grief of the young man, he said: "Monsieur, this is too much." The seigneur d'Avannes, to reflect his sorrow over the death of the lady, wore black for two years.[8]

Marguerite de Navarre, along with other intelligent men and women of the century, was conscious of the falsity of the triangle depicted in this twenty-sixth story from the *Heptaméron.* Though she was cognizant of the fact that marriage for a number of ladies at the Court was no more than a screen to protect their reputations, she would have taken sides with those who believed in the necessity of marriage as an institution. She would have admitted many of man's prejudices against woman — against her fickleness, weakness, and variability. However, she would have maintained, with good logic, that man was more prone to evil than woman, and that many of woman's problems were caused by the dangerous and amiable gentlemen who always seemed to be hanging around.

Until the reign of Henry III, before the intrusion of the royal dandies, woman played in the Renaissance a more prominent part than she had done hitherto in French courtly circles. Anne de Bretagne began it by surrounding herself with a large feminine court of honor; Francis I basked in the radiance of a court of decorative ladies who were considered by the King to be a civilizing influence on the gentlemen, since the ladies were of good families and of good reputation; and Catherine de' Medici had at the Court an even larger collection of ladies, whom she insisted that the gentlemen in the environs treat with proper respect. Some have contended that Catherine de' Medici's group was a far cry from that "decent court of honored damsels" patronized by Anne de Bretagne — which is probably true. But the ladies attached to the Court were in no sense of the word *filles de joie*,* although a few women of this category were there under the general control of the "lady in charge of the *filles de joie* attached to the Court." In any event, the importance of ladies at the Court, where the

* Cotgrave gives several definitions of *fille de joie*, among them "strumpet," "prostitute," and "pleasant sinner."

wife of every gentleman wanted to be along with her husband, increased the influence of woman everywhere in France.[9]

Deeply learned women were not admired during the period, but neither were the beautiful and completely dumb. The normal accomplishments of a non-intellectual lady of the century would be singing, dancing, the playing of the lute, and, on the domestic side, sewing, embroidery, and a little tapestry weaving. This was not enough, in the opinion of Erasmus, to keep an intelligent young lady* occupied, and should be supplemented by the reading of good literature, which would fill in the idle time and lead the way to virtue. On the other hand, for Montaigne, the most useful and honorable occupation for a woman was the "science of housekeeping." If she does this well, there will be no dull moments — and there is nothing more discouraging than for a husband to come home at noon from the "worries of business" and find his wife still primping and doing her hair. As early as the fifteenth century, it had been claimed that women had just as much right to formal instruction as men, and that they could learn "all the subtleties of the arts and sciences" as well as men if they only had the opportunity. Women continued to ask for the privilege of using their intellects, and a woman who was both intelligent and beautiful was in a preferred position during the Renaissance. Madame de Châteaubriant, the first of the favorites of Francis I, could easily qualify in both capacities: she was beautiful, and knew both Latin and Italian. The linguistic and philosophical capacities of Marguerite de Navarre and of Francis I's daughter, Marguerite, were catalogued, as has been indicated, by all commentators of the sixteenth century. Diane de Poitiers, though not formally erudite, must have been pretty clever to hold up her side of the Henry II triangle against such a shrewd brain as that of Catherine de' Medici. The mental capacities of the great ladies at the Court were frequently demonstrated, in fact, by their clever competitions with one another — or maybe such interchanges were matters of instinct rather than intelligence.

* Erasmus contradicts himself, obviously, since he has catalogued all women as being stupid.

Nevertheless, it was not likely that a lady would stay very long at Court unless she possessed both wit and beauty.[10]

Away from the Court, in private houses in Paris, Lyon, or Poitiers, women were important in the social and literary activities of the early salons, institutions which were to be even more popular in later centuries. The circle of Jean de Morel in Paris met in a house on the present rue Séguier on the Left Bank, and not far from the Seine. All the poets of the middle of the century went there, and their verses were read aloud to music. One of the chief attractions of the salon was the brilliant wife of Jean de Morel, Antoinette; also, he had three bright and charming daughters, Camille, Lucrèce, and Diane. Camille was much admired by the fine poet, Joachim du Bellay. The town house of the Maréchale de Retz, located on a spot at the intersection today of the rue Castiglione and the rue Saint-Honoré, was the seat of a salon under the leadership of its talented hostess. It was visited by both poets and scholars, and was noted for its elegance and courtesy. In the old town of Poitiers, the salon of Madeleine des Roches and of her daughter, Catherine, was very popular in the second part of the century. Both men and women were present at its reunions, and, in the manner of the discussions in the *Courtier*, the company would discourse on a topic chosen for general analysis. On one occasion, a flea observed on the bosom of Madame des Roches inspired Etienne Pasquier to write his poem, *La Puce*, an excellent bit of salon poetry. Madame des Roches, incidentally, had the reputation of being a good housekeeper as well as being a clever conversationalist. Marguerite de Navarre had around her at Nérac in Navarre an intellectual coterie to which she gave some protection against persecution, particularly to those who were accused of leaning toward the new doctrine of Protestantism. One of the objections, in fact, to intellectual freedom for women was that they might be peculiarly susceptible to the new-fangled ideas opposing the established Church. Man, with his greater powers of rational resistance, would not be so easily led astray.[11]

A fashion of some understandable popularity in the Renaissance was that of a lady's receiving a gentleman in her bedroom. It could be on a most philosophical level of salon conversation, as was the case in the seventeenth century when the famous hostess, Madame de Rambouillet, often received in her "Blue Room." The customs of society, indeed, permitted a lady as late as the eighteenth century to welcome her visitors in her own bedroom, at times when she was in the most informal of attire. During the Renaissance, if a lady received a gentleman while in bed, it might be a purposeful Platonistic testing of his purity and loyalty, and result in nothing more than "a kiss and a kind word." Many realists of the century, in their scepticism, thought that such practices could lead to no good end, and Brantôme described them as "walking on the edge of a scaffold." A more courteous social relationship of the period was that of friendship "by alliance." It might exist between men, or between men and women, of equivalent positions in society. A person might be a father, or a son, or a daughter "by alliance"—there were few mothers "by alliance," though there were brothers and sisters related by such ties. The relation meant an assurance of mutual interest and consideration between the persons involved, somewhat like that of godparents and godchildren. Marie de Gournay, for example, was the daughter "by alliance" of Montaigne. The custom was a mark of developing politeness, and one of the civilizing influences of the century. On the other side of the record, in the examination of these masculine and feminine associations, the existence of woman's most ancient of professions might be mentioned. Montaigne states that the most beautiful women of Rome are, like the most beautiful women of Paris, those "who have beauty for sale." That there were established channels for the sale of beauty is indicated by the fact that, during the year of 1517, in Paris a brothel was torn down because it was too near the Church of Saint Denis de la Chartre.[12]

The judgment and opinion of the gentleman as to what constituted feminine beauty must have been, luckily, quite varied in the Renaissance even as now. During the Middle Ages, certainly in literature, there was a preference for blondes. The heroines of that period were, like Isolde, usually fair-haired and blue-eyed. However, in the courtly writings of the Renaissance, there is a shift in taste; Melin de Saint-Gelais, for illustration, in a little poem of ten lines says that he is just not sure whether he prefers a blonde or a brunette. Ronsard in one of his earliest odes, first published in 1547, gives in full detail the pulchritudinous specifications for his lady: she is to be young, black as to the eyes (though some in France like green eyes), of a dark complexion, and with small rounding breasts. He wants her to be erect of figure, not too lean as to legs and torso, pink of cheek, with white teeth and a sweet breath, and of small feet and long slender hands, suitable for the playing of the lute or for a caress — "and for all the wealth of the Orient I should not be willing to change my brunette." [13]

Many of the gossipers and chroniclers, with exact names and places, argued against women. Cellini, with his usual aspersions cast on all things French, says that there is not a husband in France that does not wear the horns of a cuckold. Brantôme, who in his *Des Dames* tells many stories, supposedly well-authenticated, of a scandalous nature against many ladies at the Court, states piously that one should never speak disparagingly of the fairer sex — for "King Francis, although he was of the opinion that they were inconstant and variable, would not allow the ladies to be slandered at his court." Brantôme then relates an episode involving Francis I, Madame de Châteaubriant, and Admiral Bonnivet. Bonnivet was visiting Madame de Châteaubriant's apartment when the King appeared unexpectedly, which forced Bonnivet to hide in a large fireplace that had been decorated with leaves for the summer. The King, after having had his pleasure with Madame de Châteaubriant, felt the need of relieving himself, used the fireplace therefor, and Bonnivet was the recipient. Madame de Châteaubriant thought the whole thing very funny, though she did not laugh until the King had departed and the bedraggled Bonnivet had been rescued from his ill-chosen haven. Then, "in the time of King Henry II," there was the hardware merchant who did a thriving business in chastity belts, and retained for himself an occasional passkey that was used to good advantage. Despite such incidents, says Brantôme, most of the gossip that is done about ladies comes from suitors who have been refused, though it is true that the older women at the Court have a corrupting influence on the younger ones.[14]

Women during the Renaissance occupied a place somewhere in between the pedestal created for them by some of the versifiers and the malodorous pit dug for them by the vilifying gossipers. Conditions of life had improved for them somewhat since the Middle Ages, certainly in matters of creature comfort and adornment. In addition to these advantages, the woman of good position around the middle of the century would have liked to be assured of several other things, among them: the respect of man and a diminution of his attitude of superiority, the fidelity of her husband, the rehabilitation of the institution of marriage, and the privilege of self-development and improvement. These were rather emancipated ideas but they were held by many rationalistic women who discussed such problems in the literary salons and elsewhere.[15]

The gentleman of the Renaissance made little effort to dissect such a complicated organism as woman. He was just pleased that God in His wisdom had sent her down to earth.

XII

Superstitions and Beliefs

THE INQUISITIVE MINDS OF THE RENAISSANCE, in the process of examining and assessing anew man's place on this earth, took a hard and clear look at the established Church. This was upsetting in many ways for the sixteenth-century gentleman of France, who was in most cases not deeply religious, but he would have preferred to have his traditional religion, which was Catholic, left undisturbed. He would have liked to dip fully in the Renaissance's new joys of earthly discovery without interfering with the formalized ritual by which his soul might eventually be saved. However, he was not destined to repose quietly in a spiritual edifice that was protected from examination. The excesses in high places in the Catholic Church were recognized early in the century by the Catholics themselves. The debauchery of the Borgia popes, the pseudo-celibacy of the clergy, the financial transactions necessary to the assurance of salvation — all these ills were observed in France as they were by Savonarola in Italy. The gentleman, if he could have had his way, would not have heard too much about them, and would have left it to the Councils of the Church to effect a reform. But the strident and powerful voice of Martin Luther came out of Germany, denouncing the polished and cultivated gentleman who loved the arts and polite entertainment, the patron of Raphael and the builder of Saint Peter's in Rome, the son of Lorenzo the Magnificent — Pope Leo X. The papal bull, threatening him with punishment and excommunication, was burned by Luther in Wittenberg on December 10, 1520 — and Protestantism and the Reformation were under way. The gentleman of Renaissance France would henceforth have the privilege of looking at the new religion and, if he embraced it too strongly, of dying as a heretic; for the Renaissance and Reformation, which seemed to start out hand in hand, soon took separate paths. At the separation, nobody died from walking along with the pagans of Greece and Rome, but many did because they followed the hard road of Protestantism.

The problem of Protestantism in France was one that affected primarily the intellectuals and the upper classes. The lower strata of society were not very much concerned with it until the second half of the century when politics and religion became mixed in open warfare between the Catholics and Protestants. And even then, the conflicts involved in the Wars of Religion were the result of high-level political and religious machinations, and not over the manner of saving the soul of a small sinner. The intellectual invasion of Protestantism, however, was already under way in France in the first part of the sixteenth century. The doctrines of Luther swept across the Rhine very quickly and some of them fell on fertile soil. It became customary to talk loudly of "Lutherian heretics" and to blame an unexplained misdeed on them. The Sorbonne doubled its watch for the seeds of the new heresy, and those who were suspected of sowing them were most likely to be punished. Any deviation from the religious norm, in fact, entailed heavy penalties. For example, in Paris in 1529, the first offense of blasphemy was said to be punished by a fine of sixty sous, the second offense by splitting the lips, the third offense by piercing the tongue, and the fourth by strangling and hanging. Marguerite de Navarre, who had something like a diplomatic immunity from the Inquisitors, was thought by many to look with favor on the Protestant dogma, though the chroniclers make assurance that Marguerite died in the Catholic faith. Francis I's own poet and valet de chambre, Clément Marot, suffered several varieties of imprisonment for heresy. Marot protested that he was a good Catholic, but his translations of the Psalms were sung by the Protestants in Geneva. Marguerite herself, at her court of Nérac in Navarre, gave Clément asylum when the Catholic defenders of the faith pursued him too intently, for she knew that the gay troubadour of the earlier Renaissance would have made a very poor martyr.

The great name in French Protestantism was that of John Calvin, though he was unable to stay in France. After a fine training with the best Classical scholars of Paris, he wrote in excellent Latin his *Institutes of the Christian Religion*, with a letter of dedication to Francis I. This great document, on which rests the Calvinistic phase of the Reformation, was first published in 1536. It was later translated by Calvin into very lucid French, and had a considerable influence on the formation of Huguenot belief. Calvin, before he left France permanently to form a theocracy in Geneva, found temporary protection as did so many others in Marguerite's haven at Nérac. In the second half of the century, the Huguenots became more and more numerous and included such writers as the Protestant poets, Agrippa d'Aubigné and Du Bartas. It should be remembered, in passing, that before the Protestants gained even limited rights in France they were catalogued as heretics, and in 1535 Francis I set up a tribunal, the *Chambre Ardente* — the "Burning Chamber," since so many of those convicted were burned — to consider accusations of heresy. Under these conditions, it is a somewhat strange phenomenon that so many of the nobles espoused the incendiary doctrines first promulgated by Martin Luther.

The Wars of Religion aligned against one another some of the noblest houses of France, and during the thirty-year period of weak kings (1559–1589), brought about the destruction of many of the nation's gentlemen. The great captains of an earlier period regretted this ironic situation, and wished that the nobility could be saved to give leadership against invasion by foreign powers. The Protestants (or Huguenots), in general, were concentrated in the South and were supported by the Bourbons, who were powerful in the region. The northern house of Guise, which had gained strength during the century, led the Catholic opposition. The Huguenots maintained their right to liberty of conscience, and sought to obtain freedom of worship. In a rash gesture toward forcing their demands, they attempted the abduction of Francis II in 1560, the unsuccessful conspiracy of Amboise. Another Francis — François, Duc de Guise — was given considerable power in this crisis, and he would have liked to extend it at the death of Francis II later in the year. In order to block the plans of the Guises, Catherine de' Medici, the regent Queen Mother during the minority of the new King, Charles IX, made closer alliances with the Huguenots, and in 1562 they were given privileges of worship on their own estates. Some months later in 1562, a group of Huguenots as they worshiped in a barn in the little town of Vassy were massacred by the followers of the Duc de Guise. Soon thereafter the first of the Wars of Religion broke out, and they continued intermittently for around thirty years. During this time, François, Duc de Guise, was assassinated in 1563; the Massacre of Saint Bartholomew in Paris saw in 1572 the death of thousands of Huguenots with one of their most notable leaders, Admiral Coligny; Henri, Duc de Guise, was slain in 1588 by the King's order at Blois; Henry III was himself assassinated in 1589. Numbers of fruitless battles had been fought in which many of France's gentlemen, who were already confused by the uncertainty of royal leadership, died futilely. The Guises, in all the misery that was more political than religious, hoped to take over the throne of France. However, the Bourbon from Navarre changed his own religion from Protestantism to Catholicism, and became Henry IV of France. In 1598, he signed the Edict of Nantes which gave the Huguenots civil and religious rights. The sad story of the destruction brought on by the Wars of Religion was told by Agrippa d'Aubigné in his long poem, *Les Tragiques*.[1]

It was, then, much easier and much more natural for a gentleman to be a Catholic than a Protestant during the Renaissance, unless he was a probing intellectual and wanted to die for a cause. Protestants were treated with suspicion as a class, and the name of Martin Luther was anathema, much more so than was that of John Calvin. In 1521, it was catalogued in France that a "heretic named Martin Luther" had risen up in Saxony, and was creating considerable disturbance. From this time on into the century, Lutherans were blamed for almost everything and were appropriately punished for it. On August 28, 1526, a Lutheran was burned in the Place de Grève in Paris, and he was unrepentant. In 1528, some "heretics" decapitated a stone image of the Virgin and Child, which upset Francis I so much that he made pilgrimages to the mutilated figure, with white wax candles and bared head, and to the sound of trumpets and oboes — but the heretics were not caught. And in 1530, "some Lutherans" put out the eyes of an image of Notre Dame and her Child, and pierced her heart, and "nobody ever knew who had done it," except that they were Lutherans. In 1535, several Lutherans were burned in the city of Paris, and their goods confiscated: they had been caught selling Luther's books. In the suburb of Paris, Saint-Germain-en-Laye, a certain Pierre Piefort (though he is not called a Lutheran) was burned alive for having stolen the *Corpus Domini* out of the Chapel. And, too, the vigorous and sometimes bitter historian, Belleforest, said before the end of the century that Martin Luther, after having infected Germany, then "poisoned" all Europe. But Luther died in 1546, which pleased Belleforest, since thereby was eliminated "the head of the Hydra." [2]

Some thought that the King was "much too easy" on the Huguenots, and that they should be treated with more rigor. One of the most spirited attacks on Protestantism is that made by Ronsard in his long and acid poem, *Remonstrance au peuple de France*, wherein he calls the people a "heavy mass of lead which neither sees nor feels," and which is like (among other things) a "debauched student" or a "simple woman," and thus easily misled by the Huguenots. The poet hates, he says, all names ending in *-ot*, and he calls on all classes in France to protect their nation against this heretical infusion. Ronsard, in his bitterness, blames the Huguenots for practically everything that has gone wrong in his native land. He even blames certain "preachers in Geneva" for prejudicing several great noblemen against him, a "gentleman of fine family" and "known and highly regarded as such throughout all France." [3]

All these attacks on the Protestants did not mean that the Catholics escaped criticism; every phase of the established Church came in for its share of rebuke during the Renaissance. In the early years of the sixteenth century, for example, Pope

Julius II was almost captured in the fighting in Northern Italy in the midst of a snow storm. When this project failed, a plot was hatched to poison him, but it was opposed by some of the more respectful gentlemen, though it was admitted by everybody, says the chronicler, that the Pope was a trickster and deserved a little powdered arsenic in his rations. A most scathing satire on the monastic orders of the Church was that of Rabelais when he presents his pleasantly unregulated Abbaye de Thélème, which is populated by genteel men and women whose lives are not divided into units of activity by the ringing of a bell. As for the friars themselves, they received denunciatory treatment by most of the century's tellers of tales. Many stories circulated concerning the untrustworthiness of the priests and the monks in their supposed religious ministrations to women. The Dominicans, in particular, were described as a prime threat to virginity. It should be remembered that most of these objections to the institutions of Catholicism stemmed from the Catholics themselves and had something of a tolerant sympathy, like the criticism a man might apply to his own family or government. Protestantism, on the other hand, was a foreign importation; so a gentleman normally followed without argument or analysis the religion of his fathers.[4]

Religion, whether in the Catholic or Protestant interpretation, was not the only approach of the Renaissance gentleman to the problem of existence. In an age that was not so certain as the Middle Ages had been of a happy afterlife as a reward for a career of good works done on the earth, the gentleman wanted to be sure that he had enjoyed to the fullest the offerings of this world. This was the approach of the humanist, who sought the cultivation of the best in humanity with the help of the Greeks and Romans as models. The genteel man of the Renaissance, therefore, in his admiration for the ancients and their culture, lent an ear to one of the most ancient beliefs of man: he gave heed to the propositions of the handmaiden of religion, astrology.

Astrology, as was the case with Protestantism, made its

most emphatic appeal during the Renaissance to the upper classes of society. An astrologer was a luxury that could be afforded only by those who were able to pay liberally for his predictions. Astrology itself was most easily connected with the lore of the ancient world: the planets took their names from the gods of classical mythology, the stories of the formation and arrangements of the constellations in the heavens went back to the ancients, and the days and months were named after the heroes and gods of antiquity. It was easy, then, for the gentleman who was well versed in his knowledge of the Greeks and Romans to have a sympathetic feeling for astrology.

A greal deal was written about astrology during the Renaissance and, as a science or pseudo-science, it had its strong attackers and defenders. In a century that saw the birth of modern astronomy and the Ptolemaic system of the universe beginning to fall before the logic of Copernicus, a clear distinction was made between astronomy and astrology: astronomy was the science that measured the size, distances, and orbits of the planets and stars; astrology was the method by which its practitioners, for monetary reward, tried to predict the future from the stars. The Italians in the fifteenth century had already given most of the arguments for and against astrology. Marsilio Ficino, the commentator on Plato, was moderately against it. The learned Pico della Mirandola attacked it strongly and said that the astrologers were in disagreement among themselves as to what they were trying to do. The signs of the zodiac were for Pico silly ideas, since there are no animals sitting up in the heavens. Also, says Pico, it is impossible to choose the right moment for the drawing of a horoscope, and thus all the computing in it is inexact. The whole theory of astrology is against the concept of man's exercise of his free will. Pontano, the poet and scholar of Umbria, defends astrology in almost mystic fashion: the perfect and incorruptible skies have an influence upon imperfect sublunary matter, and so can incline the destiny of man. The very word, "consideration," the process by which man reaches conclusions, means "with the stars." Nature made man a child of fortune, says Pontano, which is not guided by reason; the fortunate man is agitated by a divine frenzy, and that means that he is directed by the stars. Pontano, since his ideas fitted into ancient and medieval doctrines already popular in France, was probably the best received of the Italians during the Renaissance. The gentleman liked to think of himself as one on whom fortune smiled, and was more than glad to plan his operations on the basis of proper sidereal associations. Alchemy, too, was interlocked with astrology, in that the alchemist felt that the stars must be in proper conjunction for the transmutation of metals. Astrology and medicine also went along together, and a physician was frequently an astrologer.[5]

The French writers in the sixteenth century were, for the most part, against astrology. Rabelais would have his gigantic young gentleman, Pantragruel, learn all the rules of astronomy; but as for the "divining art of astrology," it is to be put aside as an "abuse" and "vanity." John Calvin opposed astrology on the ground that through it man was seeking to discover things that God never intended him to know. Calvin thought that man should trust God and his own conscience, and that the astrological interpretation of certain passages in the Bible is false. Pontus de Tyard, the poet and critic of the famous seven poets who were known as the Pléiade, condemns astrology in one of his discourses, which takes up "the verity of divination by astrology." In it the claims of Mantice, the astrologer, are beaten down by the clever arguments of his questioner, the *Curieux*. Tyard, himself a stargazer and admirer of the theories of Copernicus, objected to making the heavens prophets of good or evil. On the other hand, Ronsard wrote a *Hymn to the Stars*, in which he pays the stars the highest homage as directors of man's movements on this earth. The poet begins by telling how the stars were fixed in their constellations after having helped Jupiter win the battle with the Titans. Now, in their majesty, they are influential on all human activities, if they could only be properly interpreted. The poem ends with: "I salute you, children of the first night, heavenly stars divine, by whom everything is directed; while you carry out your well-ordered tasks in the skies, I shall complete here below the destiny that for me you were pleased to prescribe . . ." It would be hard to bow more humbly before the stars. Ronsard dedicated this poem to Melin de Saint-Gelais, the poet and humanist who had in an earlier work admitted the possibilities of there being something valid in astrology. And Montaigne, the sceptic who had no complete confidence in the century's new scientific findings, was inclined to wonder whether the celestial sphere might assist in the navigation of the tiny globe that it encompassed.[6]

It was the genteel classes that, regardless of the arguments of the writers, showed the greatest confidence in astrology. Astrologers were in steady demand at the Court, where their predictions were given careful consideration by those in authority. Cornelius Agrippa was the physician of Louise de Savoie and also her astrologer. He was dismissed from her services because Louise, who was very superstitious, became dissatisfied with his prognostications. Agrippa, who had very decided opinions on women as well as on astrology, later condemned astrologers and sent them to hell along with heretics. The Italian, Luca Guarico, after he had made several famous predictions in Italy was called to the court of Catherine de' Medici in France, where he drew up a horoscope for Henry II. In it he predicted that the King would have a long life, which scarcely fitted in with Henry's tragic death while riding at the barrier in 1559. Guarico did not lose his long astrological robe and beard, however, when it was discovered that he had foreseen the accident in a prognostication made in 1552. Catherine was constantly on the lookout for omens and signs, and had herself surrounded by astrologers and predictors like Guarico, Ruggieri, and Nostradamus. The city of Paris, in fact, during the sixteenth century contained thousands of astrologers and tellers of fortunes. Many of them operated in alleys and hovels, it is true, but, for the most part, it was from the patronage of the nobility that they derived their revenue and fame.[7]

Possibly the most noted of the prophets of the future was Nostradamus, the Provençal physician — he was a product of the famous medical school of the University of Montpellier —

who seemed to have an uncanny facility in foreseeing events decades or centuries before they took place. Most astrologers were adept at showing, after a happening had occurred, that they had predicted it. All that was needed was a revised interpretation of a somewhat ambiguous earlier prediction. Nostradamus, for his part, seemed to combine to a remarkable degree the qualities of scientific learning and the less tangible ones of astrology. Many persons before his death in 1566 thought he really had the gift of prophecy, and some have thought so since.[8]

Nostradamus began to attract the attention of ladies and gentlemen at the Court after the publication in 1555 of a collection of his quatrains called the *Centuries*. Later verses were added, some of them of doubtful authenticity. When these four-line French stanzas of cryptical and mysterious substance first appeared — Nostradamus had been scribbling them down for several years before they were published — there was mixed reaction to them. Some thought Nostradamus was nothing but a charlatan, but others felt that he was endowed with supernatural gifts. Among the latter group were some scholars, including the critic, Julius Caesar Scaliger, and some of the loftiest of France's nobility. Henry II and Catherine de' Medici looked on him with such favor that he was invited to Court, where he went in 1556 and was welcomed most heartily. He was installed in Paris in the palace of the Cardinal de Bourbon, and was the recipient of many royal favors. Their Majesties dispatched him to the château of Blois to see the royal children and find out what fate the stars had in store for them. He evidently did not make a full prophetic report of the tragic destinies overhanging the three princes, who later ruled as Francis II, Charles IX, and Henry III, though he did cast their horoscopes. Nostradamus returned in 1557 to his home of Salon in Southern France, where during his last infirm years he was visited by many of the great nobles. Among them were Philibert-Emmanuel, Duc de Savoie, and the intelligent Marguerite de France, Henry II's sister, who was to marry the Duc de Savoie in 1559. Charles IX stopped by to see the ailing Nostradamus in 1564 and made him royal physician, with a pension. At the time of his death, Nostradamus was looked upon by both the genteel and the learned as being an oracle.[9]

His prophecies must have been disturbing to the upper nobility who were around long enough to see some of them fulfilled, if a little interpretation may be allowed for the anagrams and symbols of the prophet. Many of the quatrains, when given a bit of critical exegesis, seem to fit events and personages as far down as the nineteenth century, and even the twentieth. With amazing accuracy, for the sixteenth century Nostradamus apparently foretold, among other things, the death of Henry II, the regency of Catherine de' Medici, the Massacre of Saint Bartholomew, the death of Henry III, and the extinction of the House of Valois. One of the most noted of Nostradamus' quatrains, the prediction of the death of Henry II, is also one of the earliest, since it was in the 1555 collection. It runs as follows:

The young lion will conquer the old
On the field of battle in single combat;
In a golden cage he will pierce his eyes,
This the first of two smashings, then comes a cruel death.

In the interpretation, the "young lion" is the captain of the guards, Montgommery, who rode against the "old lion," Henry II, in the jousts of 1559. It was a "single combat," as will be remembered, along the barrier. The "golden cage" was the visor — it was probably gilded — through which the broken lance of Montgommery pierced the King's eye. The "cruel death" indicates the agony in which Henry II lingered for several days after the accident. The "first of two smashings" refers to the fact that this was the first of the violent deaths among the Valois; the second was the assassination of Henry III at the hands of one Jacques Clément in 1589. It should be remembered that this quatrain was composed some five years or so before the death of Henry II. In view of the ease of its application, as well as of others like it, to later events, there is little wonder that the nobles tried to reach into the future through the eyes of seers and astrologers.[10]

The gentleman of the Renaissance, more than the man of humbler station, looked to the heavens for signs that might guide his destiny. In more recent times, superstitions, omens, and the black arts have been usually associated with the lower intellectual and social classes, but it was not the case during the sixteenth century. The most potent and startling signs came from the skies; and the most impressive of heavenly phenomena was a comet, with its mysterious auguries of good or evil. The superstitious Louise de Savoie was convinced in 1514, she says, that her son would have "trouble with the Swiss" — Francis I was at this time in Italy with the troops of Louis XII — "for, as I was in the woodland at Romorantin after supper between seven and eight o'clock, there appeared in the sky toward the west a terrible celestial impression, having the shape of a comet; and I was the first in the company who noticed it." The thing seemed ominous to Louise and scared her quite badly. In 1515, the mother of Francis I gave thanks for the victory of her son at Milan, a victory which was symbolized by a "torch of fire the length of a lance" that appeared in the skies. This same celestial phenomenon may have been seen in Paris, where a comet was visible a few days, in September 1515, before the King's triumph in Italy. According to the Paris report, "there was seen over the city of Anvers in Flanders and over the city of Mallines a great comet, having the figure of a large red flaming dragon in the skies and it was there for a day or so. And finally it broke up into several pieces and fell in the sea, and some said that that foretold the sign of Holy Cross Day." There was another startling comet, "all made of fire," over Paris in 1530, and it had the form of "a flaming fiery dragon or serpent, very large and very long, with a marvelous great tail. And it proceeded to fall in the canals of the city of Saint Denis, in France." Mézeray mentions a "big hairy comet" that was visible during the whole month of August in 1531. Some thought it caused the death of Louise de Savoie, he says, but it is much more probable that it inflicted a drought of three months by exhausting all the vapors of "this lowly world." In October 1575, there were "fires in the air" in the shapes of lances and armed men; many persons saw them and regarded them as a "sinister omen." And on November 7, 1577, a comet took its place in the southern skies over Paris and stayed there for forty days. All "these fools of astrologers" thought that it presaged death, and Catherine de' Medici was sure that it meant her last days on this earth. This must have been the same comet * that was seen over France by the Venetian ambassador, Lippomano, in November and December of 1577. In a different attitude toward it, he states that on it "several learned astrologers" made prognostications.[11]

Comets were not ignored by the poets. Saint-Gelais in a poem called *Song to the Stars* compares several famous ladies and gentlemen of Francis I's court to various stars and planets. Virgo, for example, is Marguerite, daughter of Francis I; Mars is the Connétable Anne de Montmorency; and Neptune is Philippe Chabot, Admiral of France. But the poet suggests mysteriously that there is in the skies "the great gleaming Comet which night and day brings the threat of death." Ronsard says at the age of fifty-six he has seen everything — war and peace, the disintegration of France, the people against the nobility, and, symbolic of the bad times, comets across the sky. He wishes that he were in a land where "comets with long pendant tails" were not, as signs of war, hanging over a nation that wanted peace. Ominously, in 1562 he finds that "threatening dreams" and "hideous comets" have augured ill for France, and he invites Catherine de' Medici to do something about the discord that is rampant over the realm. Ronsard has himself observed a "reddish comet" in the heavens close on the heels of the little planet, Mercury, and gives a mythological forecast as to its significance: Jupiter is angry at the peoples of the earth below. The gentlemen of the Renaissance, though few of them could express their feelings in the language of the poet, had little affection for comets.[12]

The dark and hidden arts of the Middle Ages — magic, charms, amulets, withcraft, demons, and the like — were also

* The 1577 comet was, in fact, the object of much interest on the part of contemporary scientists as well as astrologers.

attacked by the scientific and rationalistic minds of the Renaissance, but such beliefs were not dead. The black arts, indeed, retained considerable of their prestige, and not simply in dirty and squalid hovels. The mind of the gentleman, though it might be open to the new discoveries of science and geography, did not want to close itself to any possible aid that could come through the occult and supernatural. Late in the century the very good poet and dramatist, Pierre Le Loyer, wrote a volume of around one thousand pages entitled *Books of Specters or Apparitions and Demons Clearly Visible to Men.* The work was so popular that it had four editions in something like twenty years. In it Le Loyer tries to treat spirits, and such things, as realistic participants in man's existence on this earth. Le Loyer was no ignoramus: he was well grounded in Greek and Hebrew, and, in the opinion of the biographer Moréri, "one of the most learned men of his century, though also one of the most visionary." A disciple of the new science like Pontus de Tyard dismisses, in his *Discourses*, such things as chiromancy, numerology, and conversations with spirits as the practices of charlatans. However, a genteel and learned classicist like Ronsard makes a very vivid picture of demons in a long poem, *The Demons*, which he thought appropriate to dedicate to the diplomat and critic, Lancelot Carle. Ronsard pictures demons as almost weightless bodies drifting around in the air just above the earth. God had filled the seas with fishes, the earth with men, the skies with angels, and, having a divine aversion for a void, He peopled the air with demons. They, being so close, come down to the earth all the time; and since they can assume any kind of volatile shape, they can enter quite easily into the bodies of man or beast. They can sometimes operate for good but are more likely to be troublesome, and bring on bad dreams and nightmares. Then they have to be removed by beating or exorcising. They can also take up their habitat in satyrs, nymphs, fauns, dryads, mermaids, and other figures of classical, or sometimes, Germanic mythology. Such personalities as Circe and Medea, "and thousands of others whose miraculous deeds have made them renowned," were inspired by demons. Sometimes they "inhabit the mountains, the thickets, the forests, the valleys and the lowlands, the mounds and the hills, and often in a woodland or in the hollow of a rock, with a wavering voice, they tell of the future" — not that they know everything but they have been around so much longer than man that they can make a better forecast than he can of what is to come. Ronsard feels, nevertheless, that for the most part demons are a nuisance and he wishes that he could be rid of them. In this combination of classical mythology and medieval tradition, Ronsard makes a pretty good picture of the problems demons might bring into the life of a gentleman.[13] It is done in semi-seriousness, probably; but a Renaissance gentleman had to be at least halfway serious when he was dealing with demons.

Superstitions, magic, and charms entered most directly into the routine of the daily life of a gentleman. To a degree that is rather surprising, he believed in signs. Participants in a duel, as has been indicated, had to swear before the combat that they had no magic words or charms on their body that would give them an unfair advantage over an opponent. Brantôme lists as one of the abuses of dueling the hiding of syllables of magic on the scalp — a practice which could sometimes lead to a little impromptu barbering. And the surgeon of the Duc de Nemours, in an age that was deficient in wonder drugs, accomplished amazing cures of wounds with nothing but a piece of cloth, a little water, and magic words. The powers of magic were doubted, however, later in the century when a stern historian lists as one of the weaknesses of Henry III's court the propensity thereat of trying to read the future "through the detestable illusions of the art of magic." [14]

In an epoch that was strongly influenced by all things Italian, the major sport of the Italian upper classes, poisoning, was always in the minds of the Court. Any mysterious death was likely to be attributed to some deft poisoner. Cellini said that on one occasion he swallowed an arsenic pill, but managed to recover. A certain seigneur de Villequier, who was a chevalier of the Order of the Holy Ghost and a captain of a company of royal guards, killed his wife because she was not only having an affair with one Barbizi, but was planning to do away with the chevalier, since in her "coffers was found a mixture or paste with which he was to be poisoned." Luckily, there were some splendid tests for poisoning: a serpent's tongue engraved on an ornate goblet was supposed to neutralize the effects of any lethal admixture to the wine therein.* A frog's gizzard was very effective against venom; in aconite poisoning, proper antidotes were quick lime, iron rust, wine, and melted gold. That royal animal, the stag, made its contribution also when a hunter was bitten by a poisonous snake: an unborn baby stag was very efficacious when wrapped around the wound. The stag's marrow was described as a specific for the gout, and it must have been tried by a number of genteel gourmets with large appetites. And a powdered stag's horn destroyed worms either on the inside or outside of the body — evidently Benvenuto's doctor did not have any of this remedy when the artist almost died before he coughed up a long worm covered with green, red, and black spots. The stag itself, according to one theory, lost its horns in molting season because little white worms gnawed them off at the roots.[15]

Among other beliefs held by the gentleman was that around his manor house he would be able to locate, before digging, the most likely spot of subterranean water for his well: this was done with the help of a holly stick tipped with iron. As for his dogs, it was best for his prize bitch to be impregnated in the ascendancies of Gemini and Aquarius, so that the puppies would not have rabies. In the growing of dogs, the one heavenly body to be avoided was "a star named Arcturus." A mutual interest between gentlemen and ladies would be encouraged by the consumption of the genitals of a cockerel, which were reputed to act as a strong aphrodisiac. If the gentleman in the pursuit of the stag encountered a skeletal hunter on a black horse, that was a very bad sign. It was time for the gentleman to go home.[16]

The noblest of literary forms borrowed from antiquity,

* This belief may have derived from the fact that the serpent was one of the sacred symbols of Dionysus, the Greek god of wine and fertility. In medieval lore, the horns of the rhinoceros and unicorn were supposed, by contact, to purify poisoned water or wine.

tragedy in imitation of the Greeks and Romans, fell a victim to superstition. The genre was just getting established a little past the middle of the century, performances were being given in the schools and the châteaux, and the beginnings of a tragic theater of a professional nature did not seem to be too far away. Unfortunately, around 1560 Catherine de' Medici decided that tragedies brought bad luck, and in the death of Caesar or Cleopatra on the stage she saw symbolized the death of Catherine and all living dynasties. It is remarkable that she lived so long in the face of so many fateful portents and predictions of disaster. But it was strange that at the coronation of Henry III in Rheims the crown rolled off his head twice, which everybody said was a bad omen—and it certainly was.[17]

XIII

Famous Gentlemen

THE MANY THEORIES ON GENTILITY during the Renaissance, both those inherited from the past and others evolved from living in the nearer present, should have produced some fine gentlemen that walked and breathed, and who fitted fairly closely into the theoretical ideal. The records of the Renaissance show that a number of such men did exist during the period, men who deserved by any measurement to be called gentlemen. Such was not the case with a man like Charles, Duc de Bourbon, who, with an ancestry that went back at least to the tenth century and, as the Connétable, one of the most influential men in France, still defected to the Spaniards. Despite his ability as a soldier and his reputation of rigorous moral character, the French afterward described him as a traitor and deficient in the loyalty necessary to a gentleman. He was denounced by all the chroniclers, and loudly attacked at Court in 1523 by Louise de Savoie. It was rumored in many quarters that Bourbon's real trouble came from his having rejected the proffered hand of Louise de Savoie with the intimation that he considered her a poor matrimonial prospect. The mother of the King, somewhat understandably, was irked and did what she could to bring about the disgrace of the Connétable. In any event, the Duc de Bourbon did not remain as one of France's genteel heroes of the Renaissance. But the names of many others shone high. Among the "rare men" would be placed Lautrec, La Trémoïlle, and La Palice, all marshals of France in the first part of the century. Montaigne would put with these the chancellors Olivier and Michel de l'Hospital, the poets Ronsard and Joachim du Bellay (whose family gave so many distinguished men to France), and the scholar, Adrien Turnèbe. Because of his noble life there should be set in the very center of the temple of glory that "hero divine" and "demi-god through the honors of war," the Connétable Anne de Montmorency. Praise was lavished on brave and valiant captains like Gaston de Foix, Blaise de Monluc, the Duc d'Aumale, the second Duc de Guise, the Prince de Condé, the Duc de Nemours, and others. It will be noticed that most of the brave and gallant gentlemen mentioned by their contemporaries were men of the sword, which was to be expected in an age when the foremost occupation of a gentleman was that of war. However, a fine soldier had to have other qualities than military ability if he were to be completely a gentleman; conversely, it was difficult for a man of worth, despite whatever distinctions he might have gained in letters or the Church, to receive the accolade of loftiest gentility unless he was an able commander in the field. Two men, one from the earlier years of the century and one from around its middle, might legitimately be considered complete gentlemen of the Renaissance. They were so regarded by most writers of their time. One was a fairly modest soldier and the other was a marshal of France. They were the Chevalier Bayard and the Maréchal de Brissac.[1]

Pierre Terrail, destined to gain fame as the Chevalier Bayard, was born near Grenoble in the province of Dauphiné in 1476 and died fighting with his King in Italy in 1524. His fame was so great at his death that one year later in 1525 Symphorien Champier at Lyon wrote, in a rather dull assemblage of facts, the story of his career. A much more readable account of the life of Bayard appeared in 1527, from the pen of some admiring companion in arms who calls himself simply Le Loyal Serviteur. These two chronicles, particularly the second one, form the basis for the later legends concerning the Chevalier, who was known even in his own day as a knight "fearless and irreproachable," *sans peur et sans reproche*.[2]

When Bayard's father was eighty years of age — the name of Bayard, incidentally, was taken by the Chevalier, says Champier, only after he had become a captain of the King's foot soldiers — he called his four sons around him on his estates outside Grenoble and asked them what were their desires in life. The eldest replied that he wished to remain on his paternal lands for the rest of his days: the old man told him, somewhat scathingly, to stay there and "hunt bears." Two other sons indicated that they would like to go into the service of the Church; the father gave his tacit approval to these ambitions, since service to the Church offered a legitimate career to a non-combative gentleman. Old Terrail's second son, Pierre, announced to his father that he would like to pursue the profession of arms even as the old man had done, and many of his ancestors. The father thereupon beamed with pride and pleasure, and started to make plans for the future Bayard, who was then a little more than thirteen years old.[3]

With the assistance of his uncle, the Bishop of Grenoble, some good clothes and a spirited little horse, and a purse of seven crowns provided by his doting mother, Pierre made a good impression on Charles, Duc de Savoie. The Duc therefore took him into his service as a page. Some six months later the Duc de Savoie decided to go into the city of Lyon where the King, Charles VIII, was in residence, and tourneys, dancing, and other entertainments were in progress. The young Pierre was taken along, and so impressed the seigneur de Ligny, one of the King's men, with his riding that Ligny suggested that the boy be put in the service of the King. The Duc de Savoie was agreeable to this suggestion. Charles VIII, when he saw Pierre handle a mount, was pleased with his skill and demeanor, and assigned him to the seigneur de Ligny. And whenever the King wanted to see one of his pages come dashing by on a horse, he always asked that it be Pierre Terrail, whom he named Picquet. Picquet stayed under the guidance of the seigneur de Ligny for three years, until the age of seventeen.[4]

Three days after Picquet had ceased to be a page, he wanted to enter a tourney at Lyon. His uncle, though he at first thought the boy too young for such competition, finally provided funds to obtain two horses and equipment. Picquet, newly outfitted in jousting armor, challenged the doughty warrior, Claude de Vauldray, and defeated him. Afterward, with his face uncovered, Picquet received the plaudits of the ladies of Lyon and the approbation of the King, all of which was received with complete modesty. At the age of eighteen, with the King's approval and Ligny's advice that he "always keep honor before his eyes," Picquet went to Picardy for further experience in arms. In the town of Ayre in Picardy, the feminine population leaned out of the windows to look at the young chevalier. He himself announced a tourney for Ayre, which was proclaimed with great fanfare and which attracted a great number of gentlemen; in this tourney Pierre was victorious, though he gave the prizes to other competing knights.*

After the death of Charles VIII in 1498, Bayard, now a seasoned man of arms in his twenties, went to Italy in the service of Louis XII. During lulls in the fighting in the Piedmont area, he organized another tourney at the request of a certain lady admirer, Madame de Fluxas. The lady's detachable velvet sleeve, to which Bayard fastened a ruby, was offered as a prize. Bayard, as might be expected, won the competition; he kept the sleeve but gave away the ruby. The seigneur de Fluxas was in no sense suspicious of the relations between Bayard and his wife, because he had full confidence in Bayard's "complete gentility." [5]

The deeds of valor accomplished by Bayard in fighting the Spaniards in Northern Italy were phenomenal. On one occasion he held a bridge almost singlehanded against their attack. On another he charged their lines so hard that he found himself all alone in their midst, and was consequently captured. The commander of the enemy, Ludovic Sforza, was so impressed by Bayard's gallantry that in knightly appreciation he ordered the Chevalier released. Some time later Bayard was again captured by the Spaniards, though he did not give his name other than to say he was a gentleman; in a quiet moment he managed to escape. A Spaniard that Bayard did not like was one identified by the Loyal Serviteur simply as Don Alonce. He broke his word to Bayard, which the Chevalier considered to be very ungenteel. Therefore, when Don Alonce challenged

* See Chapter Eight, page 145.

Bayard to a duel, Bayard got out of a bed of fever and slew him. It was seldom that the Chevalier was so harsh.

In 1509, Bayard went to fight the Venetians around Padua, and was involved in a variety of skirmishes, including one in which his horse was shot out from under him — without injuring him, fortunately. Later at the capture of Brescia, he was wounded in the thigh by a pike, and was forced out of action for a month. The lady in whose house he recovered was given his full protection from invading soldiers; and so were her daughters since, as Bayard assured her, she was dealing with a gentleman. He refused her grateful gift of twenty-five hundred ducats, but gave them to her daughters and the poor. Bayard participated in 1512 in the furious battle of Ravenna, in which the Duc de Nemours was killed, just after courtesies and compliments had been exchanged with the Spaniards.* As a result of these campaigns, Bayard was greatly debilitated and smitten with fevers.[6]

When the Chevalier had recovered to some degree from his maladies, he called in his valet, the bastard Cordon, and said: "Bastard, I want you today to find some pretty girl to sleep with me; I think I shall feel better afterward." At this point the admiring biographer, Le Loyal Serviteur, says that all this happened because Bayard was a man and "not any saint." In any case, the valet found an attractive maiden of some fifteen years. When she came into the presence of Bayard, she weepingly confessed that she was a virgin of a good family and that she had been reduced to the position of soldier's companion by the rigors of poverty. Bayard conversed with her for some minutes, and then dismissed her, with three hundred crowns for a dowry and one hundred crowns to buy some pretty clothes in which to get married.[7]

During the ensuing few years Bayard fought for Louis XII against the English as well as the Spaniards and Italians. His reputation for bravery and loyalty continued to grow, and he became a valiant soldier for the new King, Francis I, who, when he was planning another of the royal campaigns in Italy, sent Bayard on ahead to make advance preparations. At the

* See Chapter Nine, page 164.

battle of Marignano in 1515, the Chevalier fought with extreme gallantry: a horse was shot out from under him, but he managed to extricate himself from a very difficult spot, find another horse, and provide a fine example of leadership in the victory against the Swiss mercenaries. All agreed that he had been most valiant, and, in the oft-told story, the King wished to be dubbed a knight by him. As for the two biographers of Bayard, they are very brief about the matter. Champier in his unembroidered account relates that the King called Bayard in and said: "Bayard, my friend, I wish today to be made a chevalier by your hands." When Bayard protested his unworthiness of such an honor, Francis I answered: "Bayard, hurry up" — and that was all there was to it. The King some time after this incident, in 1521, made Bayard a member of the Order of Chivalry, in the name of Saint Michael. It was at this time that Bayard became a captain of one hundred men of arms.[8]

Early in 1524, Bayard went into Italy with an army under the command of Admiral Bonnivet. In the fighting around the town of Biagraffa, Bonnivet sent Bayard and another captain forward to the village of Rebec, with two hundred armed men. Bayard felt that it was too small a force to hold out against the assault of the Spaniards, in which opinion he was correct, since the advanced group was almost overwhelmed by the Spaniards. The French were forced to retreat all along the line, with Bayard, like Roland, fighting in the rear-guard. It was in this difficult delaying action that he was struck by a harquebus shot just over the kidneys — which broke his spine. He was lifted from his horse and propped against a tree, where during the two or three hours that life lingered his companions in arms as well as the capturing Spaniards paid him respects. The Spaniards, in fact, erected a small pavilion over him for protection and privacy, and the Spanish commander, the Marquis of Pescara, paid him great homage. The Duc de Bourbon, the erstwhile Constable of France, offered the Chevalier the services of doctors and his pity for his suffering. Bayard refused them both, and said to Bourbon that *he* extended to Bourbon his pity for Bourbon's betrayal of his King, of his vows of loyalty, and of his native land. The Spaniards took the body of Bayard into Grenoble, where it stayed for a day and a night in the Church of Notre Dame. And all Dauphiné wept for the loss of the "noble knight who was faultless and without fear." [9]

Brantôme said that Bayard never commanded an army because he never so desired, but that he commanded the commanding generals who were glad to listen to his advice. Champier compared the Chevalier to Hannibal, Scipio Africanus, David, and Roland. The greatest tributes to the gentility of Bayard were paid, most probably, by the Loyal Serviteur, who said that Bayard was universally loved because he possessed every fine quality, for "God had given him all the virtues that could be in a perfect man." He was a Fabius Maximus, a Coriolanus, and a Hector all combined. He was generous: he would exchange a fine horse for a poor one, and he gave liberally of his money to everybody. He must have provided dowries for "a hundred orphan girls, of genteel families and otherwise." He was religious, and prayed with regularity. He was the most gracious person in the world, but "no flatterer or fawner," since he esteemed in his heart a man because that man was a gentleman, and it made no difference whether he had one hundred or one thousand francs income. The Chevalier was no gossip or slanderer, or repeater of idle stories. He was not a braggart — "he had done some notable deeds in his time, but never did anybody hear him boast about it." Other details were noted by the Loyal Serviteur, though he regrets that he is not a sufficiently "good orator" to describe the Chevalier Bayard. He has managed, despite his modesty, to give a pretty good picture of a gentleman.[10]

The Maréchal de Brissac, whose name was likely to be on any contemporary list of France's great men of the Renaissance, has already made many incidental appearances in this narrative. The Maréchal de Brissac, the first Charles de Cossé, Comte de Brissac and Maréchal de France, was born in 1507 and died in 1564. He took his name from the château of Brissac, a great feudal pile in the province of Anjou. René de

Brissac, the father of Charles, had obtained the seigniory in 1502 from Louis de Brézé, the future husband of Diane de Poitiers. In 1504, René married Charlotte Gouffier, who was connected through her mother to the important Montmorency family. The Brissacs very shortly, both René and Charlotte, began to occupy important positions at Court as tutors and advisers to the royal children. René was the guardian and tutor of the young François d'Angoulême before he became Francis I, and Madame de Brissac was the governess — a very important position — of the Dauphin François, who died in 1536. As a further mark of royal favor, René was made grand falcon-master in 1516, with all the falcons of France and the lesser falcon-keepers under his control. It was in this atmosphere that young Charles, along with his two brothers and three sisters, grew up.[11]

Charles was first under the general guidance of his maternal grandmother, but became attached as a small boy to the Household of the Dauphin François. He spent a great deal of his youth with the royal children in the châteaux along the Loire, where he participated in riding, jousting, hunting, and all the physical exercises appropriate to the training of a young gentleman. He was also exposed, it was said, to a few Latin declensions and irregular verbs. By 1523, he was officially a youthful gentleman in attendance to royalty at the Court, and received a salary of two hundred livres.

The parents of Charles and his brother, Arthur, went as hostages with the two young princes to effect the release of Francis I from captivity in Madrid in 1526. The King almost immediately renounced the terms of his agreement with Charles V, and sent an army into Italy under the leadership of Lautrec, whereupon the princes and their guardians in Madrid were considered prisoners of war. Charles de Brissac, now barely twenty years of age, sailed from Marseille with other young gentlemen to give reinforcement to Lautrec at Naples, where they were almost captured on debarkation. Once ashore, as was to be expected of a young gentleman, the beardless Brissac fought bravely and the French gained some victories only to be almost decimated by maladies, which took away their commander, Lautrec. The expedition, tattered and ill, returned to France. In 1529, René de Brissac was released in Spain by an exchange of prisoners of war, but not Madame de Brissac. Eventually, in 1530, René de Brissac and his son, Charles, went to Spain and procured the freedom of the royal princes, Madame de Brissac, and Arthur. It had been a hard captivity, and Charles had not seen his regal playmates or his mother or brother for four years. All these events built up in him a martial spirit and a cordial hatred for the Spaniards. The Brissac family, in recompense for hardships endured, were given further governmental charges upon their return to Court.

In 1532, Charles was attached to the Household of the Dauphin, and was a great favorite of the ill-fated François. The Dauphin admired the athletic ability of Charles, who was completely at home on a horse with a lance in his hand. There was one rather doubtful legend to the effect that François suggested that Charles fight a very wild beast which was being kept in restraint close by. Brissac said that he was quite willing to do it; so a furious lion that had been tied to a tree was let loose. Brissac charged it, according to the story, and put it to flight; as a prelude to the lion, Brissac and the seigneur de Fumel had engaged in a furious encounter on charging horses.

Brissac went to Avignon and Italy in 1536 when hostilities were renewed against Charles V. In 1537 he was sent into the Piedmont in command of some two hundred light cavalry, which he handled with exceptional skill. After peace was signed in 1538, he was part of a mission sent to visit Charles V, which gave him experience in diplomacy. He became a colonel in the infantry in 1542, with some six thousand men under him, and a colonel in command of light cavalry in the Low Countries in 1543, a post he filled so well that he was made a chevalier of the Order of Saint Michael. Peace came with both Spain and England in 1546; so Brissac returned to the Court and became the grand master of the King's pantry and the grand master of the King's falcons. He had previously been made governor of Anjou at the death of his father in 1540; he was so popular in his homeland that a great reception was given him on the occasion of one of his visits in 1545, when there was a lull in the fighting. Brissac was made the grand master of the royal artillery in 1547 and shortly thereafter was sent as ambassador to the court of Charles V.

Henry II continued to lavish on Brissac the favor and confidence that Francis I had shown. In 1550, Brissac was made a marshal of France, and given command of the military operations in Northern Italy. The next ten years, or the period up to the Peace of Cateau-Cambrésis in 1559, brought him great distinctions as a soldier and leader of men. He gained the reputation of being a stern but fair disciplinarian, and was praised in the thirteenth *Discours* of La Noue — who was a good judge on such matters — as being a commander under whom a young gentleman could very properly learn the art of war. The record of this period of Brissac's life was kept very admiringly in the *Mémoires* of Du Villars, which were first published early in the seventeenth century but were written much earlier. Throughout this whole lengthy chronicle, Brissac is portrayed as a man who is fiercely loyal to his nation and his King, respectful of religion, and cognizant at all times of the rights of the citizens whose lands the armies might occupy. He therefore, like "that great King Cyrus," warns his men against plundering and pillaging, and adjures them to conduct themselves with the "honesty" and "virtue" becoming to well-disciplined soldiers. The young gentlemen under him bore him a fine allegiance, and in 1553, when he had assembled a mixed army of some fifteen thousand, several gentlemen joined it just to serve under him.* And when he went far up into the front lines to give his men a word of exhortation before the attack at Villeneuve, he was welcomed with a rousing cheer. The Duke of Alba was defeated by Brissac in 1554, which caused Henry II to send to the marshal a very royal sword as a mark of his appreciation. And the Duke of Alba made the remark that he could have used advantageously "fifty thousand gentlemen" — and Brissac — on his side.[12]

An incident somewhat illustrative of the character of Brissac took place in 1556. Brissac's forces were grouped at the foot

* See Chapter Nine for other details.

of a certain hill held by the enemy in a well-established position. By keen observation, a slight breach had been discovered in the enemy's fortifications, and Brissac planned to concentrate a surprise attack on it. At a carefully planned signal, which Brissac was to give, his troops were to smash at this weak spot in the wall before it could be reinforced. But, "a bastard son of a bastard of the house of Boissy" jumped the gun, rushed out ahead, and clambered up to the proposed point of attack. Miraculously, he was not killed, other soldiers followed him without command, and they were in the process of a victorious smashing of the wall. At this point, Brissac gave the agreed signal, and with a full application of power, the operation became a glorious success. Those who had fought heroically were cited and given golden necklaces as rewards. Boissy, for his part, was arrested and condemned to death by a military court because he had disobeyed orders. It looked for a time as though he would die an ironic death, but Brissac commuted his sentence and eventually he was given full pardon. In addition, the marshal handed over to Boissy one of the golden necklaces, with the remark that his apparent immunity to death could be of still further service to the King.[13]

All was not easy in the Piedmont. Brissac suffered reverses and asked for replacements, money, and provisions to relieve the "miseries and calamities" of his army. These benefits were slow in arriving, despite many requests to the King. However, peace came in 1559, and Brissac shortly thereafter returned to the Court, where he was made a count in 1560. He served during the next few years as royal governor in other areas of France, including Picardy and Normandy. He died of an attack of the gout on March 31, 1564, counseling his children in a manner that sounded more like the advice of a man of religion than that of a great captain. The historian Petitot said he died exhausted by the "fatigues of war, hard work, and the abuse of pleasures." In any case, Brissac had lived a full life: he had acquitted himself admirably in positions of great military as well as civil responsibility, and with it all — which was permissible to a gentleman — he had enjoyed thoroughly the delights of this earth.

Many of the varied and versatile qualities, so much admired in a Renaissance gentleman, were found in Brissac. Du Villars says that he had a finely developed body, but that at the same time he was very graceful, "with hands as beautiful as could be desired by a pretty maiden." He was known as the "handsome Brissac" and Brantôme thought he was a very splendid seigneur. In his conversation Brissac was reputed to be most gracious, and he possessed the virtue of "true magnanimity," along with a conscience that was pure. Tavannes elaborates a bit on this point when he states that Brissac "believed that he could get along by his own merits, without depending on the favor of any man." On the lighter side of his character, he seemed to have been fond of games, especially of the game of chess. It was said that he and Bonnivet would at times play chess for a whole afternoon without exchanging twenty words of conversation — "and that is a great taciturnity." It was rare for him to get angry, but he became "moderately choleric" when he had lost at chess.

Brissac was sober of demeanor and inclined to be more "melancholy than jovial." He did not talk very much on any occasion, which was criticized by some of the more chattering persons at the King's court. Nevertheless, he was a great favorite of the ladies, and very much of an amateur of feminine charm, since "there have scarcely been any great captains who have not been of an amorous complexion." He was, therefore, in this respect following in the footsteps of David, Caesar, Pompey, and Mithridates. Brantôme, in something like a behind-the-hand whisper, suggested that Brissac was lacking in virility, although he married a "beautiful and honorable" lady, Charlotte d'Esquetot. On the other hand, the great gossip said that Brissac before he went into the Piedmont had an affair with a lady at Court the result of which was an illegitimate son; the matter could not be discussed very fully because the lady was too highly placed and "of too expensive cloth."

In his own century, Brissac was thought of by most chroniclers as being a fair and liberal man, and as one patient in the building of an army and the training of soldiers. He was described as a dreamer of dreams, and a zealous follower of his religious faith and beliefs. Even Brantôme admitted that Brissac was noble by any measurement, by his own virtues and by the blueness of the blood that ran in his veins. It has been pointed out by a later descendant of the family that the house of Brissac in its long history has contributed four men of arms who were able enough to become marshals of France, a number not surpassed by any other family in French history. The first of these marshals easily ranks among the great captains and fine gentlemen of the Renaissance.[14]

The real gentlemen of the Renaissance, men like Bayard and Brissac and some others, did not become extinct by around 1570, but they certainly were more and more difficult to find. The forces that had produced the gentleman had just about burned themselves out, and the age of Renaissance gentility was over. Symptomatic straws in the wind might be noted in two reports from visiting foreigners: in 1561, Giovanni Michel said that France had numerous fine captains, and he lists a rather large group of them; in 1569, Giovanni Correro said that, although France had nobles that were brave, she had no great captains to lead them. There was a vogue in the sixteenth century for the poets to write epitaphs in verse — some long, some short — of great men of the period who had recently died. In 1565, Ronsard wrote an epitaph of over one hundred verses for the good warrior, Monsieur d'Annebault, of whom the poet said:

He was courteous and he was loved by everybody,
He was wise and affable and gentle and gracious.
His enemies bore for him respect,
And the French esteemed his prudence,
And his speech, which was not affected.
He was not a shameless courtier,
Either in his actions, or his manners, or his gestures.
He endured the hostilities of fortune
Patiently, having honor as the aim
Of his lofty spirit, and not worldly gain,
Since he had always during the course of his life
Taken the essence of virtue for his guide.

By the time Henry III came along, there were not many gentlemen of this hallmark still around.[15]

XIV

After the Renaissance

THE GENTLEMAN LOST MOST OF HIS INDEPENDENCE in the seventeenth century as the prestige of the Court increased. And the "country gentleman," who was away from the Court and marooned on his estates, was often derided for his ruralism — which had not been the case in the Renaissance. On the other hand, the bourgeois improved his position: the cities grew larger, the merchants wealthier, and the status of the professional man was bettered. Paris, where the bourgeois made his money, in the early part of the seventeenth century had a fixed population of around half a million, to which would be added at various seasons of the year an additional twenty-five or thirty thousand foreigners. The city could be entered by six gates that represented the main roads that led to it. From whatever direction Paris was approached, it still had a bad odor. The few streets that were paved had a covering several inches deep of mud, animal droppings, refuse and debris that smelled bad whether it was wet or dry. Gentlemen went over the city on their horses, while magistrates, doctors and solid bourgeois rode mules.[1]

The word, *gentilhomme*, was displaced somewhat by *honnête homme*, "honest man," and "honorable man," and, therefore, "gentleman." In the tragedies of the first half of the seventeenth century, *honnête homme* normally meant a man of honor, who was worthy to sit with the noblest of Romans. In actuality, an *honnête homme* was more likely to be a courtier, though a bourgeois of good taste, manners, and education might qualify. The various treatises on gentility in the first part of the century regularly indicate that the primary aim in life of an *honnête homme* is to get along successfully at Court. This, it will be remembered, was only partially the purpose of the Renaissance gentleman.

Among the several manuals concerned with genteel behavior in the first part of the seventeenth century, the best known was that of Nicolas Faret, which bore the title *l'Honnête Homme ou l'art de plaire à la Court* — and it is obvious immediately that Faret thought that "pleasing the Court" was the first of the gentleman's functions. It would not have been so necessary to be well-mannered around the lusty and sometimes unwashed Henry IV, but later royal circles and salons like that of the cultured Marquise de Rambouillet insisted upon refinement in speech and actions. In his varied counsel, Faret advises a gentleman against "mixing with the canaille," since at times he will be greeted by his crude friends in public places. This will be a very embarrassing meeting if he happens to be in the company of "persons of quality." Faret toward the end of his discourse praises "that type of man" who possesses gentility, and lists many of the qualities of an "accomplished gentleman." He should have courtesy, modesty, and a pleasant manner of speech; he should also have probity and gallantry.[2]

That keen observer of humanity, the dramatist Molière, had much to say about man and his foibles. Two of Molière's finest plays, the *Misanthrope* and the *Bourgeois gentilhomme*, are concerned with gentility and the *honnête homme*. The *Misanthrope*, which dates from 1666, is a very philosophical study, with its contrast of two violently conflicting attitudes toward society. Alceste, the misanthrope, hates pretense and deception, whether it is found in the Court or in the city:

> *No, I can not endure this cowardly procedure*
> *That most people of fashion affect;*
> *And I hate nothing so much as the contortions*
> *Of all these great and facile talkers,*
> *These ready givers of light embraces,*
> *These vapid utterers of silly speeches,*
> *Who vie with one another in exchanging civilities,*
> *And treat in the same way an* honnête homme *and a fop.*

In this passage *honnête homme* seems to indicate an "honorable man" rather than merely a courtier, as it does earlier when Alceste attacks an unnamed fawner and flatterer of the proper people, who by his insinuations is able to win out over "the most honorable man." Molière has introduced in the *Misanthrope*, as he did in many of his plays, a typical court fop, here in the person of one Oronte. Oronte is too ornately dressed in plumes and satins, is effervescent in manner and speech, pretends to be on intimate terms with the King, and dabbles in writing verses. With no feeling of reserve he offers his services to Alceste: "I am entirely at your disposition; if you would like to be introduced at Court, everybody knows that I have the ear of the King; he heeds what I say; and in everything he treats me in the most genteel fashion in the world." Alceste is forced to listen to Oronte's poetry, although he tries to avoid it and advises Oronte against seeking to blossom out in print, and abandoning "the name you have at Court of gentleman" for that of a "ridiculous and miserable author." For his frankness and literary criticism, Alceste is challenged by Oronte to a duel. Philinte, the character in the *Misanthrope* presented in contrast to Alceste, thinks that certain adjustments should be made to keep the social order functioning, and that a little oil of politeness and moderation will make the wheels of society roll with fewer squeaks. Philinte's point of view was certainly more in keeping with contemporary ideas on what was genteel; it is summed up pretty well in the following lines:

Perfect reason avoids all extremes,
And prefers virtue that has restraint.
Those great and unyielding virtues of former ages
Are jarring to the normal customs of our century;
They expect too much perfection of mortals:
One should fit gracefully into the mores of the time;
And it is a folly like unto none other
To try to correct the whole of society.

Alceste's unyielding attitude, which was in opposition to the accepted fashions of his times, eventually brought him defeat — but it was an honorable defeat. One of his most remembered statements is: "I want a man to be sincere and, as a man of honor, to let no word come out of his mouth that does not come from his heart." In order that there may be no confusion, in these lines a "man of honor" is called an *homme d'honneur* and not an *honnête homme*.[3]

The King must have chuckled at the *Bourgeois gentilhomme* when it was first performed in 1670 for his amusement in the great hall of the Renaissance château of Chambord. In it Molière not only satirizes the wealthy bourgeois who wants to ape the manners of the upper classes, but also the foppish noble who would profit from the ignorance of the bourgeois and use him to his own advantage. The bourgeois Jourdain is ridiculous when he wants to learn to fence, dance, dress, and give ornate parties in the fashion of the nobility; on the other hand, in his frank and open desire for self-improvement he is more admirable than Dorante, a count with the manners and externals of a gentleman, but at heart tricky and dishonest. He is a very poor example of gentility.

Jourdain, whose intoxication with the upper classes is complete, is determined to marry his daughter to a gentleman, despite all the arguments of his family that the daughter, Lucile, would be much happier wed to a good solid fellow of her own class. Nicole, the servant, volunteers the information that in her village there was "the son of a gentleman" who was the greatest simpleton and booby that had ever been seen. Nevertheless, the first question Jourdain asks of Lucile's suitor, Cléonte, is whether or not he is gentleman. Cléonte's reply is a fine statement of integrity:

> Monsieur, most people on this question [of a gentleman] do not hesitate long. They decide the matter easily. This name is assumed without scruple, and custom today seems to authorize the theft of it. For my part, I confess it, I have rather more delicate feelings on this matter: I consider that all imposture is unworthy of an honorable man, and that there is cowardice in disguising the birth that Heaven has given us, in adorning oneself before the eyes of the world with a title that is stolen, in pretending to be something one is not. I was born of parents, without doubt, who discharged honorable duties. I have myself fulfilled six years of honorable military service, and I have sufficient property to have a quite acceptable position in society. But, with all that, I do not wish to give myself a name that some others in my place would think they could assume, and I shall tell you frankly that I am not a gentleman.

In spite of this open and honest reply of Cléonte, Jourdain rejects him as a son-in-law, since he wants to make Lucile a marquise — and, if his wife and servants argue too much about it, he will make her a duchess! [4]

Though there were still some great gentlemen in the seventeenth century who served the state in major capacities, the nobles became for the most part courtiers and bored sophisticates. The Duc de La Rochefoucauld, the disillusioned seventeenth-century descendant of an ancient family, said "the real gentleman is the man who does not get excited about anything." The eighteenth century saw the nobility progress in its dissolution, and with the French Revolution become, officially, extinct. The nineteenth century in the land of France experimented with empires, restored monarchies, and a few republics — and the ancient nobility got mixed up with newly gained riches. A bourgeois society completed its evolution, and the nobility, now entirely impotent politically, clung to its empty titles like a child to a broken toy. François de Curel, the great dramatist and philosopher and himself of noble descent, said at the end of the nineteenth century that his class was now one of fossils and as obsolete as the mastodons. The twentieth century has seen further upheavals in the social and political structure of France, and the deep tragedy of wars and rumors of wars.[5]

When a moment of quiet can be found in the clash of contemporary tensions, it is well to wander back for a look at the valley of the Loire. Many visible evidences still show that the gentleman of the Renaissance once lived there, and, though he was not limited to this region in the sixteenth century, somehow it seems quite likely that in it his spirit would have taken up its later abode. The lands are still fertile and slope gracefully down to the river, the wines are still good and food abundant, and the people talk with a genteel and cultured air. The crash of the bombs of World War II erased many of the bridges over the Loire, but they could not destroy the gentle bends of the river or the terrain the gentleman once wandered over with his horses and his dogs. Recently, after looking out over the considerable number of manor houses and châteaux of earlier centuries that still remain along the rivers Indre and Loire, one of France's contemporary novelists was moved to say:

> In a century where all values are confused, where the most ancient truths have no more authority than the most recent error, it is natural that there may have been lost the notion of what is a house. . . When a gentleman nowadays has a bathtub, running water, electricity, central heat, and a radio, he talks of a happy abode.
>
> Our grandfathers would have had nothing of that, but rather their large rooms with decorated woodwork, their wide and comfortable stairways, their hospitable entrance gates, their pleasant pigeon houses, their elegant turrets, high roofs, deep cellars, their barns, dependencies, and courtyards. They possessed domains where reason and good taste in living presided over everything. . .
>
> I concede that it matters little to me if some stupid optimist reproaches me for being severe on my own age. Of my own age I love the clouds, the color of the seasons, certain women, and the sweet air to breathe. But the conditions of living are of the silliest and certainly the most vile.
>
> In order to be all together and all just alike, to be amused without effort and to be warm without any bother, men are living now without nobility and independence, like ants, like termites. . .
>
> One day, our children in their disgust will insist on returning to a life that has the appearance, at least, of civilization. And, as the very first move, they will try to build again houses that are spiritual, wherein along with the body man may lodge his soul.[6]

The spirit of the gentleman of the Renaissance has not yet died, although it has undergone many transformations and changes in exterior. It is no longer necessary for that essence of gentility to be clothed in velvet and lace, or to bear a noble's title. The gentleman's legacy to his modern descendants is discernible today in their courtesy of gesture, their sense of personal honor and integrity, of modesty and reserve, and in their feeling of responsibility for strength and leadership in times of strife.

The gentleman of sixteenth-century France, despite his imperfections, made a contribution to civilizing the world.

Notes

Bibliography

Index

NOTES

Chapter One — Defining the Gentleman

1. This whole question is discussed by Jean-Richard Bloch, *L'anoblissement en France au temps de François Ier* (Paris, 1934), p. 27 ff.

2. For the demolition of the *grosse tour* of the Louvre, see Eugène Emmanuel Viollet-le-Duc, *Dictionnaire raisonné de l'architecture française du XIe au XVIe siècle* (10 vols., Paris, 1854–68), III, 183; and Ludovic Lalanne, *Journal d'un Bourgeois de Paris sous le règne de François Premier (1515–1536)* . . . (Paris, 1854), p. 329.

3. See Pierre de Bourdeille, seigneur de Brantôme, *Oeuvres complètes*, éd. Ludovic Lalanne (11 vols., Paris, 1864–82), III, 118, where it is stated that Francis I "sçavoit et connoissoit la pluspart des gentilshommes de bonne maison de son royaume, et en disait très bien leurs races et généalogies." For a discussion of the *cavaliere*, see Frederick R. Bryson, *The Point of Honor in Sixteenth Century Italy* (New York: Institute of French Studies, 1935), chapter II.

4. For Bayard, Francis I, and the general question of chivalry, see Le Loyal Serviteur, *Chronique de Bayard*, éd. Jean-Alexandre C. Buchon in his *Choix de chroniques et mémoires sur l'histoire de France* (Orléans, 1875), p. 112; Martin et Guillaume du Bellay, *Mémoires*, éd. l'abbé Lambert (7 vols., Paris, 1753), I, 88; Brantôme, *Oeuvres*, II, 311–313 and VI, 477–478; François de Scepeaux, sire de Vieilleville, *Mémoires*, éd. Claude-Bernard Petitot in his *Collection complète des mémoires relatifs à l'histoire de France* (52 vols., Paris, 1819–26), XXVI, 58; and Pierre de L'Estoile, *Mémoires-Journaux*, éd. Gustave Brunet *et al.* (12 vols., Paris, 1875–96), I, 296–297. All the short quotations are from these sources.

5. For a consideration of these royal offices, see Roger Doucet, *Les Institutions de la France au XVIe siècle* (2 vols., Paris, 1948). Vol. I, p. 94 ff. contains interesting material.

6. "Au regard de noblesse, qui est commencement de gentillesse, elle est acquise: Premierement par posséder grands offices du Prince, et par ce moyen sont anoblis eux et leurs postérités;– et par entretenance de franc mariage et de mener vie de nobles gens, se peuvent les hoirs venant d'eux se nommer gentils-hommes;– Tiercement, quand un serviteur de Prince a honorablement vécu et est fait chevalier il anoblit lui et sa postérité; et n'y a point tant a faire a créer un chevalier qu'un gentilhomme" (from J. Trévédy, *Sur le titre de noble homme* [Vannes, 1902], p. 7).

7. See Etienne Pasquier, *Recherches de la France* (2 vols., Amsterdam, 1725), I, 135 ff., for gradations of the nobility; see Bloch, *L'anoblissement*, p. 200 ff. for other details and for the Sémainville quotation.

8. All these excerpts from the notebooks of reports will be found in Louis-Nicolas-Henri Chérin, *La Noblesse considérée sous ses divers rapports* (Paris, 1788), pp. (138), (83), (130), (148), (158–159). The parentheses are Chérin's, since his book has two series of numbers.

9. *Ibid.*, p. (35).

10. *Ibid.*, p. (52).

Chapter Two — The Legacy from the Past

1. Gaston Paris in the *Histoire littéraire de la France* (38 vols., Paris, 1865–1941), XXIX, 525, speaks of "le retour direct à l'antiquité"; Ovid was called "that dangerously alluring pagan" by E. K. Rand in "The Classics in the Thirteenth Century," *Speculum*, IV (1929), 259.

2. Some of Plato's *Dialogues* came into French as follows: the *Symposium* was adapted by Antoine Héroët and presented to the King in 1536, the *Ion* was done by Richard Le Blanc in 1546, and the *Timaeus* by Louis Le Roy in 1552. The *Republic* was rendered into Latin by Manuel Chrysoloras in the early fifteenth century, and Marsilio Ficino's Latin version of the *Dialogues* was published in France in 1518. The *Republic* was variously adapted: the *République* of Jean Bodin came out in 1576, and Louis Le Roy's version toward the end of the century.

For the Platonic ideas suggested here, see the *Republic*, Benjamin Jowett translation (Oxford, 1888), pp. 30, 104 ff.

3. All the points from Plato in these two paragraphs are in the *Republic*, Jowett translation, pp. 120, 164 ff., 173, 291, 247.

4. Leonardo Bruni brought out a Latin version of the *Ethics* in 1414. The full Greek text of Aristotle, marking the beginning of his modern influence, came out in Venice in 1508.

5. For these details, see *The Nicomachean Ethics*, translated by J. Rackham (Loeb Classical Library), pp. xxii, 15 ff., 43; for the question of the soul, see page 63. Aristotle employs in this passage ἔθος, "habit," and ἦθος, "character," as well as ἀρετή, which meant in Greek, "valor," "manly dignity," and "moral excellence." It is rather difficult to sum up all these implications in a single English word.

6. The Aristotelian details in these paragraphs come from *The Nicomachean Ethics* (Rackham edition), pp. 71, 73, 77 ff., 105, 215, 158–159, 163.

7. All these points concerning the Great-Souled Man, the μεγαλόψυχος, are in Aristotle's *Ethics* (Rackham edition), pp. 221 ff., 217, 255. Justice, friendship, pleasure, etc., are taken up on page 451 and page 633.

8. Fifteen of the *Characters* were published in Nuremberg in 1527, twenty-three in Venice in 1552, and twenty-eight in Leyden in 1559.

9. For the ideas from Theophrastus, see his *Characters*, XI, XIX, XXI, VI, in the J. M. Edmonds translation (Loeb Classical Library).

10. The phrase, "a mosaic of Greek and Latin borrowings," comes from J. E. Spingarn in his introduction to the English translation of the *Galateo* by Robert Peterson (Boston, 1914). The *Galateo* was written between 1551 and 1555, and published in Venice in 1558. It was translated into French by Jean du Peyrat in 1562 and again anonymously in 1573. In 1598, it was published in Lyon in four languages — Italian, French, Latin, and Spanish.

Castiglione's *Il Cortegiano*, or the *Courtier*, was first published in Venice in 1528. There were succeeding Italian editions in 1529, 1531, 1533, 1538, 1541, and on through the century. It was translated into French by Jacques Colin and published in Paris in 1537, and also in Lyon in 1537. A revised version by Melin de Saint-Gelais of Colin's translation appeared in Lyon in 1538. A translation by Gabriel Chapuis had three editions between 1585 and 1592.

11. The opinions in the *Cortegiano* are given by specific persons, but no effort will be made to name them all.

12. This is a recurrent theme throughout the *Cortegiano*, and one of its most influential concepts, especially in England. In the second book the theory is repeated that the courtier should do everything easily and well, without appearing to have spent much time on it. If he makes a speech it should appear to be extemporaneous.

13. See the *Galateo* (Peterson edition), p. 102.

14. The *Cortegiano* was popular in England in the translation of Sir Thomas Hoby. Of the position of the *Cortegiano*, Sir Ernest Barker says: "It was the good fortune of Castiglione's *Cortegiano* that his conception of culture became the general European ideal (coloured, it is true, in each country by something of a national tincture) for that mixture of the clerk and knight, the scholar and the gentleman, which was the general aim of the sixteenth century." — *Traditions of Civility* (Cambridge University Press, 1948), p. 143.

Chapter Three — French Concepts of Gentility

1. See *Le Roman de la Rose*, verses 2083–2094; and, for the last quotation, verses 2114–2115.

2. From ms. fr. 7218, folio 223, at the Bibliothèque Nationale:

> *Nus qui bien face, n'est vilains;*
> *Mais de vilonie est toz plains*
> *Hauz hom qui laide vie maine:*
> *Nus n'est vilain, s'il ne vilaine.*

These lines are quoted in the *Histoire littéraire de la France*, XXIV, 236.

3. In the beginning of the fourth *trattato* of the *Convivio*, Dante devotes more than one hundred verses to this idea, with Aristotle and

his *Ethics* as support for the power of habit and the seeking for the golden mean. Salient points are in verses 81–88 and verses 101–104. Dante states again his concepts of nobility in the opening lines of the sixteenth *canto* of the *Paradiso*. It would be hard to locate a finer statement on the responsibilities of being a gentleman.

4. From *Renard le contrefait*:

> *Si gentis hom mais n'engendroit,*
> *Ne jamais louve ne portoit,*
> *Et grant cheval ne fust jamais,*
> *Tout le monde vivroit en paix.*

5. For the details on the casual use of *gentilhomme*, see the *Journal d'un Bourgeois de Paris* (Lalanne edition), pp. 167 ff., 401–402 — henceforth to be called the Bourgeois de Paris; Pierre de L'Estoile, *Mémoires-Journaux* (Brunet edition), I, 14 — henceforth to be called L'Estoile; and Montaigne, *Essais*, Book III, chap. XII.

6. The casual use of *gentilhomme* in military circles is to be noted in Blaise de Monluc, *Commentaires et lettres*, éd. Alphonse de Ruble (5 vols., Paris, 1864–72), III, 362 — henceforth to be called Monluc; and in Le Loyal Serviteur, *Chronique de Bayard* (Buchon edition), p. 119 — henceforth to be called Le Loyal Serviteur. For the uprising around Bourdeaux, see Vieilleville, *Mémoires* (Petitot edition), XXVI, 265–272 — henceforth to be called Vieilleville.

7. This quotation comes from Machiavelli, *Discorsi sopra la prima deca di T. Livio*, Book I, chap. LV.

8. See Le Loyal Serviteur, pp. 15–17, 108; the Bourgeois de Paris, pp. 88, 452.

9. For these points, see Robert de La Marche, seigneur de Fleurange, *Mémoires*, éd. Jean-Alexandre C. Buchon in his *Choix de chroniques et mémoires sur l'histoire de France*, pp. 217, 259 — henceforth to be called Fleurange; Brantôme, *Oeuvres*, VII, 370 — henceforth to be called Brantôme; Monluc, I, 29.

10. The originals of these two quoted excerpts are in Marguerite de Navarre, *Heptaméron*, éd. Paul Lacroix (2 vols., Paris, 1879–80), I, 245 ff.; and Pierre de Ronsard, *Abrégé de l'art poétique*, éd. Gustave Cohen in his *Oeuvres complètes* of Ronsard (2 vols., Paris, 1938), II, 1000 — henceforth to be called Ronsard.

11. Brantôme, IX, 471; Montaigne, *Journal de voyage*, éd. Pierre d'Espezel (Paris, 1931), p. 169, and *Essais*, Book I, chap. I.

12. The story of the girl who preferred *honnête pauvreté* to tarnished riches is in the *Heptaméron*, the forty-second *nouvelle*; the incidents at the court of Catherine de' Medici are in Brantôme, III, 280, and IX, 471.

13. All these are small excerpts taken from various sixteenth century chroniclers.

14. Montaigne, *Essais*, Book I, chap. XXVI.

15. The work of Symphorien Champier from which this commentary is drawn is *Le Fondement et origine des tiltres de Noblesse et excellents estatz de tous Nobles et Illustres quant a la difference des Empires, Royaumes, Duschez, Contez et aultres seigneuries*........(Paris, 1535). Champier, in addition to this study and various scientific treatises, also wrote a life of Bayard.

16. For these quoted details, see Brantôme, VI, 475; and Le Loyal Serviteur, pp. 25–30.

17. The originals of these quoted excerpts come from Monluc, III, 421, 435, 450.

18. The quoted verses are from Ronsard, *La Harangue de Duc de Guise*, II, 309; and *Les Parques*, II, 393. The remarks on the brave exploits of a gentleman and the pompous display of a coward are from Montaigne, *Essais*, Book II, chap. XVI.

19. Rabelais made his famous statement on *honneur* in *Gargantua*, chapter LVII. Ronsard, in his *Discours a M. de Cheverny*, I, 911, speaks of *honneur* and royalty:

> *Mais j'aime un homme droit, non serviteur du vice,*
> *Qui presse sous les pieds la Court et l'avarice,*
> *Qui mieux voudroit mourir que corrompre la Loy,*
> *Qui aime plus l'honneur qu'un mandement de Roy* . . .

See François de La Noue, *Discours politiques et militaires* (Basle, 1587), p. 302, for his ideas on true and false honor.

20. Montaigne, *Essais*, Book III, chap. V. Montaigne feels that *vertu* and *noblesse* have "quelque cousinage," but that *noblesse* is inferior.

21. This passage comes from Ronsard, *Des Vertus intellectuelles et moralles*, II, 1035.

Chapter Four — Brilliance of the Court

1. These short quotations all come from Louise de Savoie's *Journal*, which is a very short document filling less than ten pages in J.-A.-C. Buchon's *Choix de chroniques et mémoires*. The *Journal* is a very spotty memorandum, with little form or development.

2. Philippe de Commynes, *Commentaires*, VIII, XXV, and Brantôme, *Grands capitaines françois*.

3. Le Loyal Serviteur, p. 108.

4. Fleurange, pp. 255–256.

5. Benvenuto Cellini, *Oeuvres complètes*, tr. by Léopold Leclanché (2 vols., Paris, 1847), I, 346 — hereafter called Cellini.

6. The brief quotations on Francis I's ceremonies of coronation all come from Le Loyal Serviteur and the Bourgeois de Paris.

7. Brantôme, *Le grand Roy François Premier.*

8. Jacques Androuet Du Cerceau, *Le Premier Volume des plus excellents Bastiments de France* (Paris, 1576), p. 6.

9. François de Mézeray's *Abrégé chronologique de l'histoire de France* (3 vols., Paris, 1717), was first published between 1642 and 1651. It is not very kind to the sixteenth-century Valois monarchs. For the story of Francis I's malady, which Mézeray says he caught from the iron dealer's wife, called *La Belle Ferronière* (who had been purposely infected by her husband), see the 1717 edition of the *Abrégé*, III, 79–80. Brantôme's insinuations are scattered throughout his long chronicle.

10. For this quotation, see Gaspard de Tavannes, *Mémoires*, éd. Claude-Bernard Petitot in his *Collection*, XXIII, 217—hereafter called Tavannes: ". . . blessé des dames au corps et en l'esprit; la petite bande de madame d'Estamps gouverne. Alexandre voit les femmes quand il n'a point d'affaires, François voit les affaires quand il n'a plus de femmes."

11. François de Belleforest, *Les grandes Annales et Histoire générale de France* (Paris, 1579), p. 1534, verso, and p. 1537, verso—hereafter called Belleforest.

12. Mézeray, *Abrégé*, III, 3: "Lorsque ce Prince parut sur le Thône (sic) à la fleur de sa jeunesse, avec la mine et la taille d'un héros, avec une merveilleuse adresse dans tous les nobles exercices d'un cavalier, brave, libéral, magnifique, civil, debonnaire, et bien disant, il attira l'adoration du peuple et l'amour de la noblesse."

13. See N. Tommaseo, *Relations des ambassadeurs vénitiens sur les affaires de France au XVIe siècle* (2 vols., Paris, 1838), I, 279–283, *passim*—hereafter called Tommaseo. Tommaseo gives the Italian text and also his translation of it into French.

14. Martin et Guillaume du Bellay, *Mémoires*, éd. J.-A.-C. Buchon in his *Choix de chroniques*, p. 801.

15. Tavannes, XXIII, 407.

16. See Tommaseo, I, 287.

17. Mézeray, *Abrégé*, III, 103.

18. See Tommaseo, I, 373. Other details not quoted are on this same page.

19. Jean Porcher in his little study, *Les Livres de Diane de Poitiers* (Paris, n.d.), says that Diane looked on a book as a "beau meuble."

20. Such is the opinion of Edouard Bourciez, *Les Moeurs polies et la littérature de Cour sous Henri II* (Paris, 1886), pp. 12–13 ff.

21. Tavannes, XXIII, 410; Mézeray, *Abrégé*, III, 148; Belleforest, p. 1604; Monluc, II, 334.

22. Ernest Lavisse et Alfred Rambaud, *Histoire générale du IVe siècle à nos jours* (12 vols., Paris, 1892–1901), IV, 169: "La personne royale attire les seigneurs, comme la lumière les papillons."

23. François de La Noue, *Discours politiques et militaires* (Basle, 1587), p. 140 ff: ". . . plusieurs belles choses, comme Triomphes, Festins, Combats; apprennent à s'habiller proprement, à parler selon la qualité des personnes, et à composer leurs gestes." ". . . dissolus en paroles . . . surtout moqueurs . . . expers à mentir . . ." La Noue offers a whole program for improving the quality of young gentlemen of his time. Tavannes, XXIII, 175, thinks a gentleman should train his own son.

24. Fleurange, pp. 217–218.

25. Most of these details come from the relations of Navagero, Giustiniano, Cavalli, and Giovanni Cappello in Tommaseo, I.

26. Cellini, I, 341.

27. According to the Bourgeois de Paris, pp. 329–330, 1528 was a big building year for Francis I. He began reparations on the Louvre, after demolishing its great tower. He also started the Château Madrid, in the Bois de Boulogne, and had a "'beau chasteau" constructed at Fontainebleau, "pour soy aller esbattre."

28. This story of Nicole Sala is in ms. 191 of the *Supplément français* at the Bibliothèque Nationale in Paris. The episode related here appeared in *Bibliothèque de l'Ecole des Chartes*, Ière série (5 vols., Paris 1840–44), II, 281–5, with the title of *Combat de François Premier contre un sanglier*.

29. The story is told by the Bourgeois de Paris, by Louise de Savoie, by Martin and Guillaume du Bellay, and by Mézeray. The longest version is given in the Du Bellay *Mémoires*, which have been used as the chief source for the recapitulation here.

30. Bourgeois de Paris, pp. 13–14. The Bourgeois tells a little further on (p. 44) of the three *farceurs* who were arrested for staging a little play showing *La Mère sotte* (Louise de Savoie) throwing away the funds of the royal exchequer. These comedians were bound in irons, in 1516. There is considerable comment made (p. 55) on the King's carousing in the year 1517, which was a busy year: "Mais néantmoins le Roy et aucuns jeunes gentilz hommes de ses mygnons et privez ne faisoient quasi tous les pours que d'estre en habits dissimulez et bigarrez, ayans masques devans leurs visaiges, allant à cheval parmi la ville et alloient en aucuns maisons jouer et gaudir; ce que le populaire prenoit mal à gré."

31. See the Du Bellay *Mémoires*, éd. J.-A.-C. Buchon, p. 800.

32. This description is given by Guillaume de Marillac, *Vie du Connétable de Bourbon*, éd. J.-A.-C. Buchon, in his *Choix de chroniques*, pp. 153–154. Marillac's prosaic account of the Connétable's career embraces the years 1490 to 1521. Antoine de Laval continued the story through 1527, the year of the Connétable's death. Bourbon was disgraced at Court because he had joined the forces of Charles V and fought against the King.

33. For these and other details, see the Bourgeois de Paris, pp. 59–74 ff.

34. Bourgeois de Paris, pp. 411 ff., 436–437.

35. For the quotations on these decorations see Vieilleville, XXVI, 302 ff. Josèphe Chartrou, in her *Les Entrées solennelles et triomphales à la Renaissance* (Paris, 1928), also describes the elaborate preparations for these *entrées*.

36. Ronsard, II, 684 foresees a brilliant tourney in which Henry II is victorious. Saint-Gelais's poem is to be found in his *Oeuvres complètes*, éd. Prosper Blanchemain (2 vols., Paris, 1873), I, 162 ff.—hereafter called Saint-Gelais. Henry Estienne, in his *Apologie pour Heredote*, chapter XII, decries the daring exhibitionism of the royal *entrées*.

37. Mézeray, *Abrégé*, III, 110–11.

38. The statement about the roses and the springtime was made by La Noue. The second comes from Brantôme, III, 130. An excellent study on Francis I and Madame de Châteaubriant is that of Georges G. Toudouze, *Françoise de Châteaubriant et François Ier* (Paris, 1948).

39. From Cavalli's relation in Tommaseo, I, 279.

40. In Henri Sauval, *Histoire et Antiquités de Paris* (3 vols., Paris, 1724), II, 686.

41. See Saint-Gelais, I, 232 for the poem to the *gentilshommes*; I, 136 for the poem on the *violettes*; and I, 237 for the poem, *A une Princesse* (to Diane de Poitiers's daughter). Brantôme thought this Diane was born to Henry II by a lady of the Piedmont. Ronsard's poem, *A Elle-Mesme*, is in Cohen's edition, I, 872 ff.

42. For the royal party given the Germans, see Vieilleville, XXVI, 397–398.

43, Brantôme, VII, 346.

44. Michel de Castelnau, *Mémoires*, éd. Claude-Bernard Petitot in his *Collection*, XXXIII, 322–324. The excerpt quoted is from page 322: ". . . excellens festins, accompagnez d'une parfaite musique, par des syrènes fort bien representées ès canaux du jardin, avec plusieurs autres gentilles et agréables inventions pour amour et pour les armes."

45. Pierre de L'Estoile, I, pp. 180, 188–189. From page 180, on Henry III: ". . . ordinairement habillé en femme, ouvroit son pourpoint et descouvroit sa gorge, y portant un collier de perles et trois collets de toile, deux à fraize et un renversé, ainsi que lors les portoient les dames de sa Cour."

46. Cellini, I, 151.

47. Machiavelli, *Il Principe*, chapters IV and XIX.

48. Tommaseo, I, 275; II, 541, 513.

49. For the story about the Connétable de Bourbon, see the Du Bellay *Mémoires* (Lambert edition), I, 362: "Mais l'expérience lui apprit à mieux connoitre le caractère du François, toujours fidèle à

son Prince, et toujours prêt à lui sacrifier tout ce qu'il a de plus cher, son repos, sa fortune et sa vie." See Monluc, I, 417–418, 283, and III, 399, for the indicated passages.

50. Brantôme, III, 61 ff. and VI, 470–472.

51. Saint-Gelais, I, 198, in the epistle, *A Diane nièce*:

> *Tant plus un Prince est sage et de grand prix,*
> *Plus a de gens nobles et bien appris,*
> *Et a plus cher qu'on voye en son palais*
> *Hommes d'honneur que troupe de valets.*

Ronsard, I, 851, in a poem to the *Tresillustre Prince Charles*, Cardinal de Lorraine, says Saint-Gelais

> *. . nous enseigna l'usage*
> *De savoir chatouiller les oreilles des Rois.*

In a poem *A Jehan du Thier*, II, 394, Ronsard praises kings:

> *Qui fait honneur aux Rois, il fait honneur à Dieu:*
> *Les Princes et les Rois tiennent le plus grand lieu*
> *Après la Déité*; . . .

In his *Institution pour l'adolescence du Roy* (*Charles IX*), II, 563, Ronsard gives advice to kings. Pasquier's comment on the game of chess comes from his *Recherches de la France*, livre IV, chapter XXXI.

52. In *Ode XII*, I, 412, Ronsard makes the quoted remark on hunting and fishing. Montaigne's comment on a horse's attitude toward a king is in his *Essais*, Book III, chapter VII. And from Book I, chapter XIV: "Combien d'honnestes hommes ont rejetté tout leur certain à l'abandon, et le font tous les jours, pour chercher le vent de la faveur des roys et de la fortune!"

See Tavannes, XXIII, 305, for his remark on the futility of following the Court, since it is "good-by to pleasures," etc. Brantôme, VI, 270, says it is useless to be valiant unless the Court knows about it. Montaigne's idea that kings are not so different from "hommes de moyenne fortune" comes from Book I, chapter XVII of his *Essais*.

53. This story on the Connétable de Bourbon is in Marillac, *Vie . . . de Bourbon*, p. 154. The argument over Montmorency's banners is told by Vieilleville, XXVI, 233. For feminine gossip at Court, see Monluc, III, 138: "Le roi devroit clorre la bouche aux dames qui se meslent de parler en sa cour . . ."

54. See Montaigne, *Essais*, Book I, chapter XVII and, for the matter of dissimulation, Book I, chapter XVIII. See Ronsard, II, 856, for the "monstres de court;" and II, 1053 for Ronsard's fleeing the Court.

55. Monluc, III, 139: ". . . se faisoient bonne mine, s'embrassant and caressant comme s'ilz estoient les meilleurs amis du monde. Je n'ay sceu jamais faire ce mestier: j'ay porté au front ce que j'ay dedans le coeur."

56. An opinion expressed by R. Doucet, *Les Institutions de la France au XVIe siècle*, II, 861.

CHAPTER FIVE — MANNERS AND DRESS

1. This idea is in the second book of the *Courtier*, along with admonitions against gluttony and drunkenness.

2. For the limitation on the number of dresses a woman might have each year, see the *Ordonnances des Rois de France de la Troisième Race* (21 vols., Paris, 1723–1849), I, 324, 541. Charles VIII issued one of the earlier edicts in 1485 against luxury of dress and made the income bracket of two thousand livres a line of demarcation — see the *Ordonnances des Rois de France*, XIV, 615. Other information in this paragraph comes from the royal *Ordonnances*. Further details on the subject are to be found in Henri Baudrillart, *Histoire du luxe* (4 vols., Paris, 1878–80), vol. III; see also the Bourgeois de Paris, p. 50.
The excerpt is from Claude Haton, *Mémoires contenant le récit des événements accomplis de 1553 à 1582* (2 vols., Paris, 1857), I, 93.

3. See Tommaseo, I, 259, and Chérin, *La Noblesse*, p. 174.

4. Montaigne, *Journal de voyage* (Espezel edition), p. 62.

5. For a general treatment of the matter of costume in the Renaissance, see Jacques Ruppert, *Le Costume* (5 vols., Paris, 1930–32), vol. II, and Henri-René d'Allemagne, *Récréations et passe-temps* (Paris, circa 1900).

6. See Montaigne, *Essais*, Book II, chapter XVII, for his objections to masks. As for the device of keeping the *loups* on the face, Jacques Ruppert, *Le Costume*, II, 6, says: "Ce masque ou loup de velours noir doublé de satin blanc se ployait en deux et n'était pas attaché; une simple tige de fil d'archal terminée par un bouton de verre s'introduisait dans la bouche et procurait l'advantage de changer le son de la voix." On the question of *loups*, Larousse's *Grand Dictionnaire Universal*, X, 1302, states: "Sous François Ier, la mode du masque vénitienne, c'est-à-dire, du loup de velours ou de satin noir était en plein faveur. . . Il se fixait dans la bouche au moyen d'un fil d'archal terminé par un bouton de verre." In order for this technique to work, the mask would need to be small and fit closely to the face.

7. See Pierre de L'Estoile, I, 142 ff. for this denunciation of Henry III's favorites.

8. For these points, see Montaigne, *Essais*, Book I, chapter XLIX, and *Journal de voyage* (Espezel edition), p. 339 (for the question of a shave and a haircut). Brantôme, IV, 76, mentions the Italian plumes and Montaigne talks about feathered hats in his *Journal de voyage*, p. 274. Ronsard describes the sick republic in his *Discours de l'altération et change des choses humaines*, II, 379.

9. See Book I, chapter XLIII, *Des Lois somptuaires*, of Montaigne's

Essais for these quoted excerpts and a general discussion of excesses in manners and dress.

10. At the conclusion of the *Civilitas puerilis*, Erasmus says that it was composed in Fribourg in March 1530. There were many editions of it after this date. Another popular treatise on civility was the *Disticha de moribus, ad filium*, probably composed by Dionysius Cato, and translated into French by the poet François Habert, with the title, *Les Quatre Livres de Caton, pour la doctrine de la jeunesse* (Paris, 1559). The *Civilitas puerilis* and the *Disticha* inspired such commentaries on juvenile training as Mathurin Cordier's *Civile honnesté pour les enfants*, which came out in Paris in 1559. The book was published the same year in Poitiers with the title of *Miroir de la jeunesse.*

11. See Montaigne, *Essais*, Book II, chapter VIII, and Book III, chapter X.

12. For Castiglione's ideas on the courtier's speech, jests, etc., see the second book of the *Courtier*. For the question of a gentleman's choice of words as treated in the *Galateo*, see page 66 ff. (Peterson edition). Erasmus considers the matter of a young gentleman's language in the fifth chapter of *Civilitas puerilis.*

13. Brantôme, III, 280 ff., treats of the question of courtly conversation around Henry II. The ease of conversational exchange around Francis I has been discussed by Abel Lefranc in his *Histoire du Collège de France* (Paris, 1893), and in his *Vie quotidienne de la Renaissance* (Paris, 1938). Bourciez, *Les moeurs polies*, p. 388 ff. takes up conversational details at the court of Henry II.

14. Montaigne, *Essais*, Book I, chapter XXVI.

15. Brantôme, VII, 199.

16. See Abel Lefranc's *Vie quotidienne*, pp. 89–95; another example of lusty conversation is that found in chapter XXIX of Rabelais's *Gargantua* — see W. L. Wiley, "Concepts of Genteel Conversation in the French Renaissance," *South Atlantic Studies for Sturgis E. Leavitt* (Washington: The Scarecrow Press, 1953).

17. The original versions of these excerpts from the fifty-second and the sixty-second tales of the *Heptaméron* may be found in any standard edition of the work.

18. Brantôme, II, 404–405.

19. Montaigne, *Essais*, Book III, chapter V, *Sur des vers de Virgile.* This is a very meaty *Essai*, and full of provocative ideas on a number of subjects.

20. See Guillaume Bouchet, *Les Serées*, III, for opinions on wine, garlic, and women — and Pierre de Vaissière, *Gentilshommes campagnards de l'ancienne France* (Paris, 1903), p. 121. For the effects of wine and women on a *capitaine* in the field, see Monluc, I, 30–31, 39. The short quotations come from these pages.

21. These suggestions are all to be found in Erasmus' *Civilitas puerilis*, the fifth chapter. Other manuals repeated them, especially such a work as Mathurin Cordier's *Civile honnesté pour les enfants.*

22. See Montaigne, *Essais*, Book I, chapter XXVI.

23. This excerpt comes from the *Description de l'île des hermaphrodites*, quoted in Baudrillart, *Histoire du luxe*, III, 498.

24. The Maréchal de Saint-André was for Brantôme (V, 30), a true Lucullus who loved "ses aises, ses plaisirs, et grands luxes de table." For a description of the marshal's luxury of table, see Vieilleville, XXVI, 336.

25. All these details come from the *Mémoire pour faire un écriteau pour un banquet.* Baudrillart, III, 500, has given a quite complete listing of its contents. Tastes in food from around the beginning of the fifteenth century can be deduced from the *Menagier de Paris*, a work of a Paris bourgeois in 1393, edited by M. J. Pichon in 1846.

26. For the list of foods that Grandgousier liked, see Rabelais's *Oeuvres*, Book I, chapter III; for the way Gargantua started the day, see Book I, chapter XXI; for the great feast prepared for Gargantua, see Book I, chapter XXXVII; for the gluttonous Gastrolastres, see Book IV, chapter XL; for the dinner in the land of the Papimanes, see Book IV, chapter LI.

Guillot's place in Amiens was famous — see Georges Beaurain, "Le Cabaret Guillot," *Revue des études Rabelaisiennes*, X (1912), 75.

27. See Montaigne's *Journal de voyage* (Espezel edition), p. 22 ff. (for eating habits in Switzerland), and pp. 155, 260 ff., 267 ff., 293, 351 (for details on Italy). For Lippomano's description, see Tommaseo, II, 569.

28. Jehan de Rely, doctor in theology and *chanoine* of Paris, objected in 1484 to the excessive expenditures on the part of the nobles (see Chérin, *La Noblesse*, p. 29). Jean Bodin, the keen and caustic observer of his age, said in 1578 in a pamphlet, *La Response de M. Malestroit*: ". . . un festin n'est pas bien fait s'il n'y a une infinité de viandes sophistiquées pour aiguiser l'appétit et irriter la nature." For the reception of Giovanni Michel, see Tommaseo, II, 211 ff. The edict of Michel de l'Hospital is in the *Ordonnances des Rois de France*. Pierre de L'Estoile, I, 64, tells the story of Catherine de' Medici's illness.

29. Le Loyal Serviteur, p. 7, speaks of the discussion between Charles VIII and the Duc de Savoie at dinner. For the vineyard around the Oracle of the Holy Bottle, see Rabelais, Book V, chapter XXXIV. In the Prologue to Book III, Rabelais mentions a number of the ancients who would drink and then write. Cellini, II, 24 ff., tells how Primaticcio offered him a drink before starting their argument. For the gift of wine, see Tommaseo, II, 208–209.

30. For Rabelais's epitaph, see Ronsard, II, 784–785; for the little

Odelette—"je perds, amy, mes soucis quand je boy"—see Ronsard, II, 910.

31. Saint-Gelais mentions both the tooth powder and the earrings, II, 38, 150. Erasmus discusses methods of cleaning the teeth in the first chapter of the *Civilitas puerilis*. For other details of this paragraph, see Marguerite de Navarre's fifty-fourth tale, the Bourgeois de Paris, pp. 407–408, and Brantôme, VI, 156–157. Cellini in his autobiography refers frequently to Francis I's laughter.

32. See Tommaseo, II, 567, for this estimate of the French by Lippomano. Some of the same ideas had previously been expressed by Machiavelli.

Chapter Six — The Gentleman's Education

1. Plato takes up the question of education throughout the *Republic*. Books II and III are concerned with the correct training for a warrior. The questions of the scholar-philosopher and the proper rulers of the state are considered in Books VI, VII, and VIII. Aristotle makes the statement that the life of the intellect is the happiest in Book X of the *Nicomachean Ethics*.

2. The phrase, "talented poor," is used by Sir Ernest Barker in his *Traditions of Civility*, p. 85. Thomas Cranmer, *Works*, edited by John Edmund Cox (2 vols., Cambridge, 1844–46), I, 399, makes this point about the gentleman's son and the plowman's son in a discussion of what type of child is to be admitted to the English grammar schools: "Wherefore if the gentleman's son be apt in learning, let him be admitted: if not apt, let the poor man's child apt enter his room." This sentiment was not very strongly enunciated in France during the Renaissance, though echoes of it appear at the end of the century in Montaigne and later in Nicolas Faret.

3. Most of these details from the *Courtier* are to be found in Book I of that work. The point about a courtier's knowing music without having studied it comes from Book II. Many matters concerning ladies and gentlemen, including virtues of the mind, are discussed in Book III.

4. These quotations come from Erasmus' *Civilitas puerilis*, éd. Alcide Bonneau (Paris, 1877). The first one—"ut liberales disciplinas et amet, et perdiscat"—is on page 6. Erasmus' definition of real nobility is on page 8: "Pro nobilibus autem habendi sunt omnes, qui studiis liberalibus excolunt animum. Pingant alii in clypeis suis leones, aquilas, tauros, et leopardos; plus habent verae nobilitatis, qui pro insignibus suis tot possunt imagines depingere, quot perdidicerunt artes liberales."

5. Mézeray, *Abrégé*, III, 148, says that Henry II would have been praised for his love of belles-lettres, "si la dissolution de sa Cour, authorisée par son exemple, n'eût tourné les blus (sic) beaux esprits

à composer des romans pleins de visions extravagantes, et à faire des poésies lascives." Giovanni Michel in Tommaseo, I, 415 ff. says that Charles IX is a frail lad, that he does not like to study, and that most princely exercises are too violent for him.

6. A full treatment of Francis I's plans for various educational foundations is given by Abel Lefranc in his *Histoire du Collège du France.* I have made free use of this study for this chapter. This work was done before Lefranc became himself a professor at the Collège de France.

7. See Abel Lefranc, *Histoire*, pp. 77–80, for French translations of the Budé letters.

8. The "esparviers de Montagu" are defined as "lice" by Randle Cotgrave in his *Dictionarie of the French and English Tongues* (London, 1611); so the Collège de Montagu must have been a famous spot. The original of the quoted passage comes from Rabelais, *Gargantua*, chapter XXXVII.

The reference to Saint Innocent evidently means the cemetery and church of the Innocents in Paris, near Les Halles, which became a great loitering place in the Middle Ages and the Renaissance. At the corner of the rue Saint-Denis and the rue au Fer was the celebrated Fontaine des Innocents, erected in 1550. It was designed by Pierre Lescot and sculpted by Jean Goujon. Today, badly worn by the years and the weather, it stands in a square marking the former site of the cemetery and church.

9. These lines on the "gymnastics of nothingness" I have taken from Abel Lefranc, *Histoire*, p. 141. Ronsard, I, 414, says of Daurat, in a poem dedicated to the master:

Emmoncelle par milliers
Un grand peuple d'escoliers
Que tu tires par l'oreille.

10. In his *Epître au Roy, du temps de son exil à Ferrare*, Marot speaks of the "ignorante Sorbonne":

Bien ignorante elle est d'estre ennemie
De la trilingue, et noble Academie
Qu'as erigée.

Marot goes on further in this poem to attack the "Sorbonniqueurs" who are resentful of the fact that Francis I has made arts and letters more resplendent now than they were in the time of the Caesars. Martin du Bellay in his *Mémoires* (Buchon edition), p. 801, says of Francis I: "Il aima toutes gens d'esprit, et fonda à Paris des collèges pour les lettres latines, grecques et hébraïques, et feit venir de toutes les parties du monde gens instruits en toutes sciences et arts libéraux, pour édifier la jeunesse en bonnes moeurs et sciences . . ."

11. This famous passage comes from *Pantagruel*, Book II, chapter VIII.

12. All this material is in Rabelais's *Gargantua*, chapter XXI through chapter XXIV.

13. Much of this information on the size of the University of Paris, condition of students, etc., comes from the relations of the Venetian ambassadors in Tommaseo. Lippomano (Tommaseo, II, 605) puts the number of students at the University of Paris at thirty thousand. The statement concerning the poor students trying to improve their minds is made by Giovanni Cappello, in his report of 1554 (Tommaseo, I, 367). Cavalli's remarks are in Tommaseo, I, 263.

Rabelais speaks of "Latin verbosination" in *Pantagruel*, Book I, chapter VI. In chapter VII following we find in the Librairie de Sainct Victor the title: "*Quaestio subtilissima, utrum Chimera, in vacuo bombinans, possit comedere secundas intentiones*?" Further satire on the Sorbonne is found in Rabelais's *Fifth Book*, chapters XX and XXII, where, in the domain of Queen Quinte Essence, the monarch dines on categories, second intentions, metempsychoses, antitheses, etc., Pantagruel and others of the party are retained by the Queen as *abstracteurs*.

The Bourgeois de Paris, p. 453, says: ". . . fut cryé de par le Roy en la Cour de Parlement, que tous pauvres escoliers et indigens, non aians de quoy vivre et soy entretenir aux escolles, vuydassent la ville de Paris . . ."

Vieilleville, XXVI, 198–199, speaks of the vagabond students at the famous La Châtaigneraie-Jarnac duel, and how they wrecked the dinner that had been prepared.

Charles Estienne, in the seventh chapter of his *L'Agriculture et maison rustique* (Paris, 1564), says that a farmer does not need to know how to read and write.

14. Abel Lefranc, *Histoire*, p. 154 ff., discusses this proposed super-*collège*. Belleforest, II, 1534 verso, mentions the proposition, while Mézeray, *Abrégé*, III, 58, gives a number of details on the plans of Francis I for this *collège*.

15. Rabelais's listing of the accomplishments of the inhabitants of the Abbaye de Thélème is in the fifty-seventh chapter of *Gargantua*.

Brantôme had an unexpected interest in languages—see W. L. Wiley, "Brantôme's Interest in Languages and Literature," *Modern Language Notes*, LXV (1950), 331–336. Brantôme, VII, 373, says that Catherine spoke "fort bien françois," and (VI, 239) Lucrezia Borgia spoke "force langues." In Brantôme, VII, 73, are mentioned high officials and their "langue de veau." For the other details and persons mentioned in the text, see Brantôme, V, 239, and VII, 75–76.

16. Though the greater part of Montaigne's opinions on the education of a young *gentilhomme* are in his *De l'Institution des Enfants*,

some details are in his other *Essais* and in his *Journal de voyage*. His remarks about Greek and Roman authorities come from *Du Pédantisme* (Book I, chapter XV). The remarks on the number of young Frenchmen in Padua come from the *Journal de voyage* (Espezel edition), pp. 111–112. The statement that most of the world is made up of the *vulgaire* is in the *Apologie de Raimond Sebond*.

The passage concerning the ineptitude of instruction in France comes from *De la Praesumption* (Book II, chapter XVII): "Je retombe volontiers sur ce discours de l'ineptie de notre institution. Elle a eu pour sa fin de nous faire non bons et sages, mais sçavans: elle y est arrivée. Elle ne nous pas apris de suyvre et embrasser la vertu et la prudence, mais elle nous en a imprimé la derivation et l'etymologie. Nous sçavons decliner Vertu, si nous ne sçavons l'aymer; . . .

The question of well-born souls not being attached "à la rhetorique, à la judiciaire, à la logique, et semblables drogueries," is taken up in *De Trois Commerces*, Book III, chapter III. Montaigne's approval of the *bonnes maisons* becoming schools for the nobility is in *Sur des Vers de Virgile*, Book III, chapter V. As for the students, Ronsard in his long and bitter *Remonstrance au peuple de France* lists among those who are easily misled by the Huguenots the "escolier debauché."

17. Tavannes, XXIII, 155–209, gives his ideas on a young gentleman's education.

18. La Noue's provocative theories on education are found in his fifth *Discours*, pp. 140–157, of the 1587 edition.

19. In the seventeenth of his second book of *Odes*, Ronsard asks:

Que nous sert d'estudier,
Sinon de nous ennuyer?

In a long poem, *A Jehan du Thier*, Ronsard tells the story of the purchase of the Pindar and Simonides volumes, and how Du Thier put them in the library of his château of Beauregard.

Montaigne mentions the books he avoided reading, in his *De l'Institution des Enfants*. Tavannes, XXIII, 159, opposes the *Amadís*.

20. La Noue spends the whole of his sixth *Discours* in an attack on the *Amadís*. The *Discours*, in fact, is entitled: *Que la Lectures* (*sic*) *des livres d'Amadis n'est moins pernicieuse aux ieunes gens, que celles des livres de Machiavel aux vieux*.

21. Symphorien Champier in his *Le Fondement et origine des tiltres de Noblesse. . .* (Paris, 1535), chapter II, thinks that a *héraut d'armes* might well be able to read and write. Charles Estienne, *L'Agriculture*, chapter V, indicates that a master of an estate should stay at home and philosophize rather than run around carousing. Ronsard, in his *Abrégé d'un art poétique*, minimizes the value of the language of the Court. Brantôme, III, 93–94, favors a man of the sword as an ambassador.

Chapter Seven — Life in the Country

1. Doucet in his admirable work, *Les Institutions de la France au XVIe siècle*, I, 35, points out that at this period the relations between the monarch and the noble had a "caractère contractuel." Pierre de Vaissière, *Gentilshommes campagnards de l'ancienne France* (Paris, 1903), p. 2, calls the period from the beginning of the Renaissance to the Wars of Religion "l'âge d'or de la noblesse."

2. From Montaigne's *Des Senteurs*, Book I, chapter LV, of his *Essais*, comes: "Ces belles villes, Venise et Paris, alterent la faveur que je leur porte, par l'aigre senteur, l'une de son marets, l'autre de sa boue." Later in *De la Vanité*, Book III, chapter IX, Montaigne calls Paris "la gloire de la France et l'un des plus notables ornamens du monde." Ronsard, in his poem, *A son retour de Gascongne, voiant de loin Paris*, calls the city "la gloire des Muses."

The incident of the boat's sinking in the Seine is described in the Bourgeois de Paris, pp. 80–81.

3. The quoted excerpt concerning the château of Madrid comes from Jacques Androuet Du Cerceau's *Le Premier Volume des plus excellents Bastiments de France* (Paris, 1576), p. 7 ff. The title-page of the 1564 edition at Paris of *L'Agriculture et maison rustique* of Charles Estienne, "docteur en Medecine," indicates the great variety of subjects that will be treated in the book. The materials I have used from Estienne's work come primarily from chapters three through seven.

Details from the royal châteaux are based on my own observations of them in 1948.

4. The *Théâtre d'agriculture et mesnage des champs* of Oliver de Serres was first published in Paris in 1600. I have used the 1605 edition, which contains around one thousand pages. Most of the details I have cited, including the quoted excerpts, come from pp. 3–26. The raising of pigeons is discussed on page 395 ff. The designs for gardens begin on page 597.

There has been a good deal of critical interest in Serres' work during the last ten years.

5. See Baron Karl Reille, *Deux Cents Châteaux et Gentilhommières d'Indre-et-Loire* (Tours, 1934).

6. For Lippomano's remarks on the building stone of France, see Tommaseo, II, 489.

7. See Montaigne's *Journal de voyage* (Espezel edition), p. 38.

8. The *Journal* of Gilles de Gouberville has been published complete in the *Memoires de la Société des Antiquaires de Normandie* between 1892 and 1895. Hector de la Ferrière-Percy published in 1855 at Paris and Caen the *Journal de la Comtesse de Sanzay. Intérieur d'un château normand au XVIe siècle*. The countess' *Journal* is only a little more than fifty pages long.

9. Du Bellay's sonnet which begins, "Heureux qui, comme Ulysse, a fait un beau voyage . . .," is one of his most famous. It is here that the poet longs for "la douceur angevine." In *Gayeté* III Ronsard tells of the pleasures of fishing and the new wine. In *Ode* XVII of the second book, he describes the many succulent fruits, and relaxation by the side of a stream. From Ronsard's *Chant pastoral*, dedicated to Madame Marguerite de France, come the quoted lines on the beautiful meadow, etc.

10. Nicolas Rapin's poem, *Les Plaisirs du gentilhomme champestre*, was published in Paris in 1583. An illustrative stanza from it is:

Heureux celuy qui loin d'affaires,
Comme les gens du temps passé
Avecques ses boeufs ordinaires
Laboure les champs, que ses peres
En propre luy ont delaissé.

Included with Rapin's poem in the volume are some verses of Guy de Pybrac, Claude Binet, and the *Voyage d'Hercueil* of Ronsard.

11. Much of this information on Jacques du Fouilloux comes from Guillaume Le Riche's *Journal* (Sainte-Maixent, 1846). Other details come from Du Fouilloux's book on the chase, *La Vénerie* (Niort, 1864 and 1888), with an introduction by Jean-Francois Pressac. See also the third, *Des Femmes, et des filles*, of Guillaume Bouchet's *Les Serées* and Béroalde de Verville's *Le Moyen de parvenir*, CV, for two versions of the cradle-rocking incident.

12. In *La Chasse royale* of Charles IX, edited by Henri Chevreul (Paris, 1858), pp. 45–46, is a discussion of dogs and kennels. Etienne Pasquier, *Recherches*, p. 135 ff., speaks derogatorily of the "gentilhomme de ville."

13. For details on the château of Brissac, see the Comte de Cossé-Brissac, *Le Château de Brissac* (Paris, 1937) and l'Abbé Charles Marchand, *Charles Ier de Cossé, Comte de Brissac et Maréchal de France* (Paris, 1889). For the *Mémoires* of Guillaume de Rochechouart, which are very brief, see Petitot, *Collection*, XXXII, 512 ff. Chérin, *La Noblesse*, pp. 103–4, 157, speaks of complaints by the Third Estate against the nobles' hunting on vineyards and planted ground.

14. For Navagero's comment on Blois, see Tommaseo, I, 28–29. The story of the considerate wife is in Marguerite de Navarre's thirty-eighth *nouvelle* of the *Heptaméron*.

Chapter Eight — Sports and Diversions

1. Aristotle, in the fifth book of the *Ethics*, discusses bodily condition. Montaigne, in *De l'Institution des enfants*, quotes the Platonic admonition in the *Symposium* that the body and soul should function together "comme une couple de chevaux attelez à un mesme timon."

2. Batiffol, *Le Siècle de la Renaissance*, p. 118, says that Henry II was "tout muscles." Brantôme, III, 277 ff., describes Henry II's proficiency in all games—"et falloit toujours convier les dames pour voir tous ses esbats." The story about Bonnivet and the broad jump is in this same volume, p. 289. There was general agreement among the chroniclers about Catherine de' Medici's athletic interests and also on her appetite. Her heaviness of face and figure later in life pay tribute to the latter.

3. Erasmus, in his *Praise of Folly*, ridicules the elaborate ritual connected with the slaying of an animal. For the story of the stag hunt, I have drawn on the three manuals of Budé, Du Fouilloux, and Charles IX. Du Fouilloux has been the primary source, and the quotations included are from his *La Vénerie* (Pressac edition). Pressac considers Du Fouilloux's work "le plus célèbre" of all writings on hunting. It had twenty-five editions in French, and was translated into German in 1590, and into Italian in 1615. For Francis I's expenditures on hunting, see Tommaseo, I, 101 and 283–5.

4. See Du Fouilloux, *La Vénerie*, chapters XLVI, LV, and LX.

5. In Charles IX's *La Chasse royale* (Chevreul edition), p. 65, there is mention of what a *valet de chien* must know "pour estre digne de demeurer auprès des chiens." Most of this material comes from Du Fouilloux. I have used Henri Chevreul's edition of Jean Passerat's *Le Chien courant* (Paris, 1864). Louise de Savoie in her *Journal* speaks of the little dog, Hapeguai. In his *Epitaphe de Courte, chienne du Roy Charles IX*, Ronsard tells of the King's method of immortalizing Courte.

6. See Fleurange, pp. 217–218. Budé, in his *Traité de la Vénerie*, éd. Henri Chevreul (Paris, 1861), pp. 2–7, pays homage to Francis I's bravery as a hunter, and admits his own fear. On Henry II's love for hunting, see Tommaseo, I, 379.

7. See Fleurange, p. 220, for the grand falcon-master and his expenses.

8. For many of these details, see Paul Lacroix's *Moeurs, usages, et costumes au moyen âge et à l'époque de la Renaissance* (Paris, 1872), p. 214 ff. For the letters of Louis de Brézé, see Hector de la Ferrière, *Les Chasses de François Premier* (Paris, 1869).

9. For these remarkable shooting exploits, see Cellini, I, 220–221.

10. Symphorien Champier in *Le Fondement et origine des tiltres de Noblesse . . .*, chapters XV and XVI, discusses tourneys, etc. The short quotations come from these chapters. Le Loyal Serviteur, pp. 2, 15–17, discusses the Chevalier's success in tourneys. From these pages short quotations have been taken.

11. See Champier, *Le Fondement*, chapter XV, for the number of lances that could be shattered in one day. For jousting areas in Paris, see Henri Sauval's *Histoire et recherches des antiquités de la ville de*

Paris (3 vols., Paris, 1724), I, 621. See J.-J. Jusserand, *Les Sports et jeux d'exercice dans l'ancienne France* (Paris, 1901), pp. 1–157, for many details on jousting, etc. See Fleurange, *Mémoires*, in Petitot's *Collection*, XVI, chapter XLIV, for his and Francis I's exploits in the *pas d'armes.* Brantôme, IV, 162–165, speaks of the prowess of François de Lorraine, Duc de Guise, and the Duc de Nemours, who was "la fleur de toute chevalerie" and "aymé de tout le monde, et principalement des dames."

12. Pasquier, *Recherches*, livre IV, chapter XV, p. 395, mentions these quoted details on the development of the *jeu de paume.*

13. See Jusserand, *Les Sports*, p. 240 ff., for further information. The short quotation comes from Jusserand, p. 251.

14. Henry de Sainct Didier's *Traicté contenant les secrets du premier livre sur l'espee seule, mere de toutes armes* (Paris, 1573) is followed by his brief *Traicté sur l'exercice, et certains points requis de sçavoir au jeu de la paulme.* Neither is well written, and some of the terminology is difficult, but the treatise on the sword is profusely illustrated.

15. Many of the chroniclers spoke of the death of the young Dauphin. Brantôme intimated that he might have been poisoned.

16. In the twenty-second chapter of Rabelais's *Gargantua*, his hero plays two hundred seventeen games. Michel Psichari in a long article, "Les Jeux de Gargantua," *Revue des études Rabelaisiennes*, VI (1908), 1–37, 124–181, 317–361, and VII (1909), 48–64, has identified most of them. The quoted excerpts from Montaigne come from the essay, *De l'Institution des enfants.* The correct attitude toward games is discussed by Erasmus in the sixth chapter of his *Civilitas puerilis.*

17. See Pierre de L'Estoile, I, 189 ff., for his bitter attack on I Gelosi, who began to perform in May 1577, at the Hôtel de Bourbon in Paris, says the chronicler.

18. L'Estoile, I, 308, tells of the King's losing his money to the Italians, and suggests that dice would be forbidden in a "royaume bien policé."

19. For the details on robbers, see Cellini, I, 245–246, 344–345, from which come the quoted excerpts. Tommaseo, II, 208–209, 279, relates the difficulties the Italian ambassadors experienced with highwaymen in France.

20. See Montaigne, *Journal de voyage* (Espezel edition), p. 92, for the excerpt concerning the "usage of one's own village"; and p. 132 ff., for the quotation about the tiger.

Chapter Nine — The Gentleman at War

1. In *Il Principe*, chapter VI, Machiavelli says he favors an armed prophet as governor of a land. The solidarity of France is discussed

in chapters IV and XIX. Mercenaries are opposed in chapter XII, and the advantages of hunting, for a soldier, are taken up in chapter XIV.

2. At the end of book III of the *Republic*, Plato says warriors should have education to "civilize and humanize" them. Book V shows how the cowardly soldier is degraded; in book VIII the "bravest warriors" along with the philosophers are rewarded by being made rulers of the state. In book III of the *Ethics*, Aristotle states a preference for citizen soldiers. Castiglione takes up the points indicated here in the first book of the *Courtier*.

3. Montaigne says in his essay, *Des Récompenses d'honneur*: "La forme propre, et seule, et essentielle, de la noblesse en France, c'est la vocation militaire." In *De l'Institution des enfants*, he prefers a "parler soldatesque" to a "parler pédantesque."

Fleurange, p. 259, says that war is "le plus noble exercice que peult avoir un prince ou un gentilhomme, quand c'est bonne querelle." Ronsard, in his *Exhortation au camp du Roy Henri II*, says that fighting for one's prince is better than being poisoned or dying on a bed of fever. Monluc tells the soldier to avoid avarice, women, etc., in the first book of his *Commentaires*; II, 335, he mentions the brave captains. Tavannes, XXIII, 155, says: "Les gentilshommes riches ayans trois enfans en devroient mettre deux aux armes."

4. Pasquier, *Recherches*, II, 135 ff., discusses the nobility of the sword and its pre-eminence. Giovanni Michel (Tommaseo, II, 237 ff.) says that a French noble who does not fight is little esteemed. For Lippomano's statement, see Tommaseo, II, 645.

5. This material on weapons and equipment has been taken from Du Bellay, Cotgrave, and other commentators of the period. Cotgrave in his *Dictionarie* defines a *gendarme* as "one that serves in compleat armor, and on a great horse." The excerpts from the nobles' report are in Chérin, *La Noblesse*, p. (167). I have also used such modern historians as Lavisse and Doucet.

6. See Doucet, *Les Institutions*, II, 632 ff.

7. For the entry of Francis I into Milan, see the Du Bellay *Mémoires* (Lambert edition), I, 87; for the defection of the Swiss, and the argument over back pay, see the same *Mémoires*, I, 175 ff.

8. See the Bourgeois de Paris, p. 140 ff., for the King's departure for Milan in 1523. For the size of the army of Philippe Chabot, see the Du Bellay *Mémoires* (Lambert edition), II, 326.

9. Rabelais compares printing and artillery in *Pantagruel*, II, chapter VIII, the famous letter from Gargantua to Pantagruel. Montaigne talks about artillery and printing in his essay, *Des Coches*. For Giustiniano's comment, see Tommaseo, I, 95. For one version of the battle of Pavia, see the Du Bellay *Mémoires* (Lambert edition), I, 402 ff. For the story of the fine artillery work, see Monluc, III, 415–416.

10. François de Rabutin in his *Commentaires*, Petitot *Collection*,

XXXI, 64 ff., said that Henry II's army outside Metz in 1552 had a new type of artillery that made the noise of thunder. In chapter XII of *Il Principe*, Machiavelli comments on the reasons for Italy's military weakness. The stories of Bayard's early morning encounter with the Spaniards and of the Spanish attitude toward the death of the hero are told by Le Loyal Serviteur, pp. 91–92, 117–121.

11. Brissac's courtesies with the Spaniards are described by Du Villars in his *Mémoires*, Petitot *Collection*, XXIX, 201 ff. Monluc, II, 15 ff., describes his relations with the Spanish commander.

12. For the major decisions of war, see Rabutin, *Commentaires*, XXXI, 14. Bertrand de Salignac, in *Le Siège de Metz*, Petitot *Collection*, XXXII, 277, describes the Duc de Guise's order. The quotation is from Salignac. La Chastre in his *Mémoires*, Petitot *Collection*, XXXII, 475, describes the army of 1556 and its affection for the Duc de Guise. The quotation is from La Chastre.

13. See Du Villars, *Mémoires*, XXIX, 3 ff.

14. See La Chastre, *Mémoires*, XXXII, 493 ff.

15. For the maladies that struck Lautrec and his army, see the Du Bellay *Mémoires* (Lambert edition), II, 134, 139. Pasquier, *Recherches*, IV, chapter XXVIII, discusses the malady that struck Charles VIII's soldiers around Naples.

16. Tavannes, XXIII, 303, states that "le rasoir ami estoit plus dangereux que la balle ennemie." Mézeray, *Abrégé*, III, 58, recounts the story of the seigneur de Laval; and on page 95, Mézeray talks about the wound of the Duc d'Aumalle. The quotation is from Mézeray.

17. Montaigne makes all of these points concerning the proper size of the gentleman in his essay, *De la Praesumption*.

18. See Commynes's *Commentaires*, VIII, XXV, for the death of Charles VIII. Brantôme, I, 380–386, discusses the size of Vandernesse and Bayard; and VI, 273 ff., he speaks of the "moyenne taille" of La Châtaigneraie.

19. See Symphorien Champier, *Les Gestes, ensemble la vie du preulx Chevalier Bayard* (Lyon, 1525), chapter V, for his comment on Saint Michel. For a discussion of chivalry and its abuses, see Brantôme, I, 311–313; V, 93 ff.; VI, 477–478. See Vieilleville, XXVI, 58, for his comments on chevaliers. Castelnau, *Mémoires*, XXXIII, 38 ff., tells how Guise made too many chevaliers for his own good. Lippomano derogates the Order of Saint Michael in Tommaseo, II, 545.

20. The story of the founding of the Order of the Holy Ghost is told by Lippomano in Tommaseo, II, 403 ff. Pierre de L'Estoile, I, 296–297, also mentions the establishment of the Order. Tavannes, XXV, 155, says that the Order has lost caste.

21. For the list of men, with the military leaders at the head, see Montaigne's *De la Praesumption*. Giovanni Michel lists several of

France's fine captains in Tommaseo, I, 393. Monluc, II, 334–335, recalls a number of brave commanders who have died for France. Bayard's loftiness toward the Connétable de Bourbon was catalogued by several chroniclers — by Du Bellay, among others.

22. See Du Villars, *Mémoires*, XXVIII, 356, and XXIX, 9 ff.

23. Monluc has a great deal to say about the question of leadership. He thinks very strongly that the gentleman in command must set an example for the soldiers under him, and get out in front to spur them on when they waver. He should smear his face with *vin grec* to hide any pallor, and avoid becoming dull and slow from eating and drinking too much. A very practical reason for aggressive leadership is that the soldiers may shoot down a discredited commander from the rear. This happened to "quatre capitaines." (Monluc, I, 31–32, and II, 45 ff.)

And Ronsard gives suggestions both to soldiers and their officers in some verses from *La Harangue de tres-illustre Prince François, Duc de Guise, aux soldats de Metz*, a poem published in 1553, wherein there is much technical advice for the soldier. But it is assumed that the nobility will automatically have courage and carry out its destiny.

Chapter Ten — The Code of Honor

1. Aristotle discusses honor and honors in the fourth book of the *Ethics*. Machiavelli speaks of *virtù* and *onore* all through *Il Principe*. The "valorous ways" of a prince are taken up in chapter VI. The famous comparison of a ruler to a lion and a fox is in chapter XVIII, and in chapter XIX Machiavelli says that the people will remain content if their property and *onore* are not disturbed.

In Lavisse-Rambaud, *Histoire générale*, IV, 38, is found a discussion of the Italian concept of honor, from which the quoted excerpt is taken. See Cellini, I, 140, for his "honorable reputation."

2. Some of this material is treated more fully in Gabriel Letainturier-Fradin's *Le Duel à travers les âges* (Paris, *circa* 1892). I have borrowed the "near beating of the heart" phrase from this work. Montaigne, in his essay, *Couardise mère de la cruauté*, says the nobles do not wish to be known as good fencers.

3. The edict of Philippe le Bel may be found in the *Ordonnances des Rois de France*, I, 435 ff. Champier's treatment of the duel is in the fourteenth chapter of his *Le Fondement et origine des tiltres de Noblesse* . . . The commoner's hair was cut to see if he were hiding any magic words or sorceries on his scalp; the noble was permitted to swear that he had no such devices on his person.

4. In the Du Bellay *Mémoires* (Lambert edition), II, 73 ff., Francis I's challenge of Charles V is mentioned, and the interchange of heralds in 1527. Brantôme, I, 17, says Charles was pretty old and never took

up Francis I's challenge; later Brantôme says, VI, 455 ff., that the two monarchs could not agree on weapons. Lavisse-Rambaud, *Histoire générale . . .*, IV, 115, says that Charles V challenged Francis I in 1528 and in 1536, but was ignored both times.

For the Council of Trent's edict, see Letainturier-Fradin, *Le Duel*, p. 28 ff.

5. See Brantôme, VI, 399, for the statement concerning a noble's losing caste if he suffered *paroles injurieuses* or *desmentis*.

The original language of the first quoted cartel is as follows: "Seigneur, toutes et quantes fois que vous avez dict, faict dire, escript ou faict escripre allencontre et au préjudice de mon honneur, aultant de foys avez par la gueule menty, et le nyant avez semblablement menty. Par escript je ne veulx user d'injurieuses vilanies, comme chose plus convenable à vile et envieuse personne qu'à chevalier, me réservant si ce n'est par votre deffault, parler à vous les armes au poing." — from ms. 2259 of the *fonds français* at the Bibliothèque Nationale. The Brantôme cartel, as well as this one, is in Letainturier-Fradin, *Le Duel*, p. 22 ff.

Ronsard and Saint-Gelais wrote several amorous *cartels*. One of Ronsard's called *Autre cartel* (I, 1032) is full of dueling terms.

6. The five manuscript versions of the duel are in Paris — three at the Bibliothèque Nationale, one at the Bibliothèque Mazarine, and one in the hands of Alfred Franklin. On the basis of them all, Franklin published in 1909 *Le Duel de Jarnac et de La Châtaigneraie*. I have myself a photostatic copy of the folios of ms. 12,795, *fonds français* of the Bibliothèque Nationale, which is considered the clearest version of the heralds' story. It was preferred by Franklin.

7. See Franklin, *Le Duel de Jarnac*, pp. 63–65.

8. See Franklin, *Le Duel de Jarnac*, pp. 68–78, for the original wording of the cartels.

9. The cartel sent by La Châtaigneraie to Jarnac read as follows: "Guichot Chabot, Je vous envoie la patente de camp qu'il a plu au Roi de m'octroyer; dedans lequel je vous veux prouver avec les armes offensives que vous me baillerez, mais qu'elles soient en gentilhomme d'honneur, que vous m'avez dit que vous avez couché avec votre belle-mère et l'avoir chevauchée . . ." See Franklin, pp. 79–87.

10. See Franklin, pp. 88–98.

11. The exact phrasing of the mortal wound to La Châtaigneraie is: ". . . se seroient ruez plusieurs grands coups tant d'estoc que de taille, l'un desquels, de la part dudit de Jarnac, auroit attaint le jarret de la jambe gauche dudit de La Châtaigneraie en jetant un estoc audit de Jarnac, et derechef donné encore un autre coup sur le mesme jarret . . ." For further details, see Franklin, pp. 99–103.

12. See Franklin, pp. 103–105. The duel attracted the attention of a number of chroniclers. Brantôme, who was the nephew of La

Châtaigneraie, has scattered references to it throughout his *Discours sur les duels*. Monluc, Vieilleville, De Thou, Castelnau, and Guillaume Marcel also treat it in varying degrees of fullness.

13. Monluc, III, 138, expressed his theory on the duel very vigorously.

14. Ronsard, in his best pindaric style, wrote this ode in praise of Jarnac. Ronsard mentions Jarnac again in Ode VI, of his second book of odes.

15. The story of Bussy d'Amboise and the *X* or *Y* sleeve is taken from Letainturier-Fradin, *Le Duel*, pp. 147–148. Bussy's double duel *en chemise* and also the legend of his death come from Pierre de L'Estoile, I, 309, 321–322. The Givry-Soissons affair is described by Brantôme, VI, 473.

16. All this material, and the quotation, come from L'Estoile, I, 243 ff.

17. The legend of the duel between the man and a dog, with its sources, is described by Letainturier-Fradin, *Le Duel*, p. 127 ff. Other details here come from Brantôme's *Discours sur les duels*, VI, 235 ff.

18. Brantôme, VI, 384 ff., talks about David and Goliath; VI, 377, he calls the Italians "cold" and "cruel" in dueling. See Tavannes, XXIV, 199, for further remarks on the Italians.

19. For the Clergy's opinion on dueling, see Chérin, *La Noblesse*, p. (42). It should be noted that the Clergy does not think it a very serious thing to call a man a "simple liar." Montaigne condemns mass dueling in his essay, *Couardise, mère de la crauté*. Tavannes, XXIII, 220 and XXIV, 28–29, remarks on the futile destruction of dueling.

20. La Noue's original phrasing on quarreling and fighting is strong: "Car il n'y a pas quarante ans que les querelles estoyent rares entre les gentilshommes, et quand quelqu'un estoit noté d'estre querelleux, on le fuyoit comme on fait un cheval qui mord ou qui ruë: et la cause estoit que les moeurs estoient alors plus pures, et le vray poinct d'honneur mieux entendu qu'à ceste heure."

21. In his essay, *Couardise, mère de la cruauté*, Montaigne says: ". . . je voudrois qu'on me fist raison de ces loix d'honneur qui vont si souvent choquant et troublant celles de la raison."

Chapter Eleven — The Question of Women

1. In imitation of the ancients, the poets of the Renaissance began to dedicate collections of poetry to ladies that they admired. Even as Horace had his Lalage or Ovid his Corinna, so did Jean-Antoine de Baïf have Méline and Francine, or Ronsard his Hélène and Cassandre. Maurice Scève addressed his collection of *dizains* to Délie, "object of the highest virtue." Some of the ladies are identifiable.

Délie, for example, was supposed to be the poetess of Lyon, Pernette du Guillet.

2. The Italian ambassadors commented recurrently on the fact that Marguerite, the daughter of Francis I, was not married — see Tommaseo, I, 283 and 373 ff.

Much of this information on the legal rights of a married woman in the sixteenth century is based on Etienne Pasquier's *L'Interprétation des Instituts de Justinien . . .* (Paris, 1847). It was written by Pasquier in 1609 for his two grandchildren who were destined for a career in law. A digest of some of Pasquier's material is in Emile V. Telle's *L'Oeuvre de Marguerite d'Angoulême, reine de Navarre, et la Querelle des Femmes* (Toulouse, 1937), chapter III. I have drawn freely on Telle's excellent work for this chapter of mine.

3. Christine de Pisan thought that such writers as Ovid, Jean de Meung, and Eustache Deschamps had done a great injustice to her sex. She sought to answer them in her *Epistre au Dieu d'Amours* — see her *Oeuvres poétiques*, éd. Maurice Roy (3 vols., Paris, 1886–1896), vol. II.

4. In the eighth book of the *Ethics*, Aristotle lists friendships that may exist between unequals; such unequals are a father and a son, and a husband and a wife. Plato, in the fifth book of the *Republic*, says that man is more highly endowed than woman. In the *Amores*, I, viii, 43, Ovid says: *Casta est, quam nemo rogavit.*

Erasmus, *Opera omnia* (10 vols., Leyden, 1703–1706), makes the statement: *Ita mulier semper mulier est, hoc est, stulta* — IV, 418. In the *Civilitas puerilis* (Bonneau edition), p. 84, Erasmus says: *Mulieres ornat silentium.* The details against women cited from the *Courtier* are in the second and third books. Antonio de Guevara's *Menosprecio de corte y alabança de aldea* was translated into French by A. Alaigre and printed at Lyon by Etienne Dolet in 1542, with the title, *Le Mespris de la Court, avec la vie rustique.* It was reprinted in Paris in 1544.

For Lippomano's remarks on French women, see Tommaseo, II, 561 ff.

5. Rabelais's commentary on women is in the *Third Book*, chapter XXXII. Abel Lefranc has examined Rabelais's comments on women in "Le Tiers Livre de *Pantagruel* et la Querelle des Femmes" — *Grands Ecrivains Français de la Renaissance* (Paris, 1914), pp. 252–260. This is a basic study on the question.

6. In the fifteenth *Essai* of his second book, *Que nostre desir s'accroit par malaisance*, Montaigne speaks of woman's pretended virginal shame. In the *Essai*, *Sur des vers de Virgile*, Montaigne has much to say about women. It is here that he speaks of "concupiscence feminine," of marriage being a "plaisir plat," and of women being "plus capables et ardentes aux effects de l'amour que nous." Toward the end of this essay, he says: "Je sçay cent honnestes hommes coqus,

honnestement et peu indecemment: un galant homme en est plaint, non pas desestimé."

Ronsard, II, 1053, in a letter to M. de Sainte-Marthe berates his mistress for her lack of judgment and her avariciousness.

7. Du Bellay's soul goes off seeking "the perfect Idea" in the famous sonnet which begins:

Si notre vie est moins qu'une journée
En l'éternel, si l'an qui fait le tour
Chasse nos jours sans espoir de retour,
Si périssable est toute chose née, . . .
—*from* l'Olive

Scève's *dizains* to Délie in many cases are very Platonistic; Délie herself is probably an anagram for *l'idée.*

La Borderie's *Amie de Cour* and Héroët's *La parfaite Amie,* two narrative poems strongly influenced by Castiglione and Ficino, appeared in 1541 and 1542 respectively. They were later published in 1568 in a single volume, along with Guevara's *Menosprecio de corte* . . . (in Alaigre's translation) and several other Platonistic compositions. A study of these documents is made by Telle, *L'Oeuvre de Marguerite* . . . , chapter V.

Guillaume Postel defends women in his *Les très merveilleuses victoires des Femmes du Nouveau Monde et comment elles doivent à tout le monde par raison commander et même à ceulx qui auront la Monarchie du Monde Vieil* (Paris, 1553). François de Billon's work, *Le Fort inexpugnable de l'honneur du sexe féminin,* came out in Paris in 1555. There was another Parisian edition of it in 1564.

8. It is not necessary to give the French equivalents for all the excerpts, long and short, from the *Heptaméron.* They can be found in any standard edition of the work.

9. Baudrillart, *Histoire du luxe,* III, 425, says that Catherine de' Medici's *cour des dames* was "loin de cette cour décente de filles d'honneur créée par Anne de Bretagne." For the *filles de joie* attached to the Court, see Terrasse, *François I*[er] . . . , II, p. 318.

10. Erasmus makes this comment on intelligent women in his *Christiani matrimonii institutio.* It will be noted that this is a different approach to women from that assumed by Erasmus when he says that woman is "always stupid." Telle, p. 370 ff., discusses the question of woman's education.

Montaigne in his essay, *De la Vanité,* says: "La plus utile et honnorable science et occupation à une femme, c'est la science du mesnage. . . Je vois avec despit, en plusieurs mesnages, monsieur revenir maussade et tout vilain du tracas des affaires, environ midy, que madame est encore après à se coiffer et atiffer en son cabinet. . ."

This statement of Christine de Pisan's on feminine education comes from her *La Cité des Dames*—see Telle, p. 35.

11. For the salons of the sixteenth century, see Abel Lefranc's *La Vie quotidienne au temps de la Renaissance*, page 53 ff.; also L. Clark Keating, *Studies on the Literary Salon in France, 1550–1615* (Harvard University Press, 1941), and George E. Diller, *Les Dames des Roches* (Paris, 1936).

12. The "kiss and kind word"—*la parolle et le baiser*—comes from Marguerite de Navarre's eighteenth *nouvelle*. Brantôme, II, 178, calls Platonistic intimacies "se pourmener à l'entour de l'eschafaut." The "beauty for sale" comment of Montaigne comes from his *Journal* (Espezel edition), p. 151. The Bourgeois de Paris, p. 73, mentions the destruction of the brothel in Paris.

13. See Saint-Gelais's *Oeuvres* (Blanchemain edition), I, 99, for this *dizain*. The editor thinks the poet might have had two specific *filles d'honneur* in mind when he wrote the verses.

Ronsard in *Ode* XL (II, 680–681), describes the physical qualities he wants in his lady.

14. Cellini, II, 32, talks of the deceptions played on French husbands. Brantôme, IX, 711 ff., tells the story involving Bonnivet. Brantôme, IX, 474, speaks of Francis I and his refusal to allow gossip about women at his court. In Brantôme, IX, 133, the hardware merchant is mentioned; and in IX, 141, the corrupting influence of the *vieilles* is claimed.

15. Telle treats in his work these and other aspirations of woman around the middle of the sixteenth century.

Chapter Twelve — Superstitions and Beliefs

1. All this discussion of the rise of Protestantism and the Wars of Religion in France during the sixteenth century is based on standard historical material. I have tried simply to fit the gentleman into it. The comments on penalties for blasphemy in 1529 come from the Bourgeois de Paris, pp. 402–403. An interesting book on the last part of the whole struggle is Jacques Vivent's *La Tragédie de Blois, le Roi de France et le Duc de Guise, 1585–1588* (Paris, 1946).

As for the word, *Huguenot*, there is no absolute agreement as to its origin. Some authorities think it comes from the German, *eidgenoss*, "confederate." However, Cotgrave, who was very close to the period, says in his *Dictionarie* that the word came from a gate in the city of Tours called Hugon, where the Reformists first assembled—and from a Latin motto they had at "the beginning of their first Protestation," *Huc nos venimus*.

2. For these details, see the Bourgeois de Paris, pp. 94, 291, 347 ff., 410, 444 ff.; Louise de Savoie's *Journal*, p. 302; Belleforest, pp. 1408, 1534.

3. Monluc, III, 213, thinks the King is not hard enough on the Huguenots. See Ronsard, II, 573–592, for his *Remonstrance au peuple*

de France; and II, 982–984, for his *Response* to the "Prédicants et Ministres de Genève."

4. For the poisoning of the Pope, see Le Loyal Serviteur, p. 66 ff. Rabelais spends several chapters of his *First Book* on the Abbaye de Thélème, beginning with chapter LII. *Conteurs* like Bonaventure des Périers and Marguerite de Navarre mention the carnal desires of the Catholic clergy — see, in particular, the *Heptaméron*, XXXIII, XLI, LVI.

5. The monumental work on all these matters is Lynn Thorndike's *History of Magic and Experimental Science* (6 vols., New York, 1929–1941). Ficino's opinions on astrology are in his *Theologia Platonica* and *De vita*, in the first volume of his *Opera* (Basle, 1561). Pico della Mirandola's arguments are found primarily in his *Disputationes adversus astrologiam*, which appeared in his *Opera* in Venice in 1577. Pontano's defense of astrology is in his *De rebus coelestibus*, in his *Opera omnia* (Venice, 1518–1519). A summarization of Italian conclusions on astrology is in Don Cameron Allen's *The Star-Crossed Renaissance* (Durham, 1941), which I have used freely.

6. Rabelais opposes astrology in the famous letter of Gargantua to Pantagruel, in the eighth chapter of the *Second Book*. Calvin attacked astrology formally in his *Advertissement contre l'astrologie . . .* (Genève, 1549). Pontus de Tyard's *Mantice, ou discours de la vérité de divination par astrologie* came out in Lyon in 1558. A recent analysis of Tyard's opinions on the earth and the stars was given by John C. Lapp in his *The Universe of Pontus de Tyard*, A Critical Edition of *l'Univers* (Ithaca, 1950).

Ronsard's *Hymne des Astres* was dedicated to Melin de Saint-Gelais, who had published in 1546 his *Advertissement sur les jugements d'astrologie*. The last lines of Ronsard's poem are:

Je vous saluë, Enfants de la premiere Nuit,
Heureux Astres divins, par qui tout se conduit;
Pendant que vous tournez vostre tasche ordonnée
Au Ciel, j'accompliray çà-bas la destinée
Qu'il vous pleut me verser, bonne au mauvaise, alors
Que mon âme immortelle entra dedans mon corps.

Ronsard's poem dates from 1555.

Montaigne wonders about the universe in his *Apologie de Raimond Sebond*, as well as in other essays.

7. See Eugène Defrance, *Catherine de Médicis, ses astrologues et ses magiciens-envoûteurs* (Paris, 1911); Auguste Prost, *Corneille Agrippa: sa vie et ses oeuvres* (2 vols., Paris, 1881–1882); Don Cameron Allen, *The Star-Crossed Renaissance*, p. 49 ff.

8. Nostradamus is still regarded by many with a certain mystified awe. A short motion picture was made some few years ago dramatizing his predictions.

9. Much has been written both in French and English about Nostradamus. I have used, among other sources, Charles A. Ward's *Oracles of Nostradamus* (New York, 1940), published originally in the 1890's.

Ronsard dedicated a poem to Nostradamus.

10. The original of this quatrain is:

Le lyon jeune le vieux surmontera
En champ bellique par singulier duelle:
Dans cage d'or les yeux lui crevera,
Deux classes une, puis mourir, mort cruelle.

It should be noted that *classes* apparently means "breakings" or "smashings," from the Greek, κλάσις.

11. For all these comets, see Louise de Savoie, pp. 298–299; Bourgeois de Paris, pp. 26, 403–404; Mézeray, *Abrégé*, III, 58; Pierre de L'Estoile, I, 90, 221; Tommaseo, II, 359.

Holyrood Day, or the Bourgeois de Paris's *journée Sainte Croix*, was September 14, according to Cotgrave.

12. Saint-Gelais's poem, *Chanson des Astres*, contains the verses:

La grand' Comete qui reluyct
Menace le jour et la nuict
La mort et fin de vie
De Polyphemus, qui se dict
L'avoir si bien servie.

Ronsard, in the first of his *Amours diverses*, dedicated to the seigneur de Villeroy, foresees many disasters, which are confirmed by "ces Devins qui contemplent les tours des Astres." Saturn in four years is going to devastate the land — I, 280. The "comet with long hair" is in *Les Isles fortunées*, dedicated to M.-A. Muret, the fine scholar. The *Discours des misères de ce temps* contains the "threatening dreams" and "hideous comets." In the *Hymne X, De Mercure*, a *comète rousse* pursues Mercury.

13. Pierre Le Loyer's *Livres des spectres ou apparitions et démons se monstrans sensiblement aux hommes* was first published in 1586.

14. For magic words in duels and the curing of wounds, see Brantôme, V, 45, 302 ff. For the "future read by magic art," see Mézeray, *Abrégé*, III, 148.

15. See Cellini, II, 172 ff., for the arsenic pill; and I, 212 ff., for the spotted worm. For the story of the seigneur de Villequier, see L'Estoile, I, 204 ff. For the frog's gizzard and aconite poisoning, see Ronsard, *La Grenouille*, and a *Sonnet* from his *Meslanges* — II, 798–799. For all the details on the stag, see Du Fouilloux, *La Vénerie*, chap. XV ff., and Charles IX, *La Chasse*, chapters I through VI.

16. Charles Estienne, *L'Agriculture*, chapter IV, p. 3, b, tells how to find water underground. Du Fouilloux takes up the question of

dog raising in *La Vénerie*, chapter VI ff. The matter of aphrodisiacs is treated by Brantôme, IX, 220 ff. Abel Lefranc in *La Vie quotidienne de la Renaissance*, p. 122 ff., speaks of superstitions and quotes from the 1578 text of Ronsard's *Les Daimons* the story of the black horse and its skeletal rider.

17. The episode of the crown rolling off the head of Henry III is told by L'Estoile, I, 50.

Chapter Thirteen — Famous Gentlemen

1. The Connétable de Bourbon, who died in 1527 fighting around Rome, still remains something of a mystery. Ronsard praises the three marshals of France, and other great men, in his *Hymne de France*, published in 1549. In his *Temple de Messeigneurs*, dedicated to Odet de Coligny, he praises Anne de Montmorency as a "héros divin" and as one made into a "demi-Dieu par l'honneur de la guerre."

Montaigne, in *De la Praesumption*, praises many of the great men of his time who have served France in varied capacities. Giovanni Michel in Tommaseo, I, 393, lists a number of France's brave and valiant captains.

2. Symphorien Champier's account of the life of Bayard, *Les Gestes, ensemble la vie du preulx chevalier Bayard* . . . appeared in Lyon, in Gothic type, in 1525. The much more readable story, *La très joyeuse et très plaisante Histoire composée par Le Loyal Serviteur des faits, gestes, triomphes et prouesses du bon chevalier sans paour et sans reprouche, Le Gentil Seigneur de Bayart*, came out in 1527. It is a much longer history than that of Champier.

Both spellings of the Chevalier's name, Bayard and Bayart, were used in the sixteenth century.

3. See Le Loyal Serviteur, p. 2.

4. For these details, see Le Loyal Serviteur, pp. 3–8; Champier, *Les Gestes*, Book II, feuillet XIII, verso.

5. Le Loyal Serviteur goes into great detail when he tells about these tourneys in which Bayard is always victorious. Bayard, incidentally, spent a lot more money on his first jousting equipment than he had been allowed. However, nobody seemed to mind. For these points, see Le Loyal Serviteur, pp. 8–22.

6. A longer history of these incidents will be found in Le Loyal Serviteur, pp. 22–92, and Champier, *Les Gestes*, Book II, chapters IV and V. One interesting feature of this campaign in Italy was that spies seem to have been used. Le Loyal Serviteur, p. 50, says Bayard had one that he had always considered trustworthy — "and also Bayard had enriched him with more than two hundred ducats."

7. See Le Loyal Serviteur, pp. 99–100.

8. For this material, see Le Loyal Serviteur, pp. 108–112, and Cham-

pier, *Les Gestes*, Book III, chapters III–V. Other chroniclers during the century mentioned the episode of the knighting of Francis I by Bayard. The story of Bayard's being made a *chevalier de l'ordre* by the King, and of Bayard's being given a company to command, is told in the Du Bellay *Mémoires* (Lambert edition), I, 175.

9. Both biographers give a full account of the death of Bayard — Le Loyal Serviteur, pp. 117–121, and Champier, *Les Gestes*, Book III, chapter VII. Neither emphasizes the pitying attitude of Bayard, as he was dying, toward the Duc de Bourbon — a point that most of the chroniclers stress.

Montaigne, in his essay, *Nos affections s'emportent au delà de nous*, says of the death of the chevalier: ". . . Bayard . . . se sentant blessé à mort d'une harquebusade dans le corps, conseillé de se retirer de la meslée, respondit qu'il ne commenceroit point sur sa fin à tourner le dos à l'ennemy; et, ayant combatu autant qu'il eut de force, se sentant defaillir et eschapper du cheval, commanda à son maistre d'hostel de le coucher au pied d'un arbre, mais que ce fust en façon qu'il mourust le visage tourné vers l'ennemy, comme il fit."

10. Brantôme, I, 385, says that Bayard, though only a captain, often commanded "au général." For the eulogies paid to Bayard at his death, see Champier, *Les Gestes*, Book III, chapter VII; and, in particular, Le Loyal Serviteur, pp. 121–123.

11. Almost all the chroniclers of the sixteenth century have something to say about the Maréchal de Brissac. The *Mémoires* of François de Boyvin, baron Du Villars, in volumes XXVIII, XXIX, and XXX of the Petitot *Collection*, treat in detail Brissac's operations in Italy from 1550 to 1559. The Abbé Charles Marchand's *Charles Ier de Cossé, Comte de Brissac et Maréchal de France, 1507–1564* (Paris, 1889) and the Abbé Charles Gautier's *Histoire de Brissac, de son château et des familles qui l'ont possédé* (Angers, 1920) are more recent studies of the marshal's career. All these sources have been used.

12. Many more details are told by Marchand and Gautier. For further information on Brissac's army in 1553, and the loyalty of the soldiers to him, see Du Villars, *Mémoires*, XXIX, 196 ff.

13. See Du Villars, *Mémoires*, XXX, 45 ff.

14. Du Villars begins his story of Brissac with several bits of information about his person and character — XXVIII, 356 ff. Some short quotations have been taken from this portion of Du Villars's history. Petitot makes this statement about Brissac in his introduction to the Du Villars *Mémoires*.

The excerpt from Tavannes is in his *Mémoires*, in the *Panthéon littéraire*, p. 239. Brantôme, IV, 74 ff., discusses Brissac. The fact that the Brissac family has had in it four marshals of France is pointed out by the Comte de Cossé-Brissac, *Le Château de Brissac* (Paris, 1937).

15. The opinions of the visiting Italian ambassadors, Giovanni

Michel and Giovanni Correro, can be found in Tommaseo, I, 393, and II, 149 ff. See Ronsard, II, 493–496, for the *Epitaphe de feu Monsieur d'Annebault.*

Chapter Fourteen — After the Renaissance

1. Much of the information on conditions in Paris during the early seventeenth century will be found in Emile Magne's *La Vie quotidienne au temps de Louis XIII* (Paris, 1948).

2. *L'Honneste Homme ou l'art de plaire à la Court* of Nicolas Faret was first published in Paris by T. Du Bray in 1630. Succeeding editions came out in 1631, 1636, two in 1639, two in 1640, 1658, 1664, and 1681. The treatise was translated into Spanish in 1634, while a critical edition of it was made in 1925 by Maurice Magendie. Magendie points out the many indebtednesses to the *Cortegiano*, but suggests that Faret puts *vertu* on a higher level than did Castiglione.

Other manuals for the guidance of the gentleman-courtier in the early seventeenth century were: Du Souhait, *Le Parfaict Gentilhomme* (Paris, 1600); Nervèse, *Le Guide des Courtisans* (Paris, 1606); Nicolas Pasquier, *Le Gentilhomme* (Paris, 1611); and the anonymous *Courtisan français* (Paris, 1611).

3. The passages that have been used to illustrate the conflicting philosophies of Alceste and Philinte all come from the first act of the *Misanthrope*, verses 41–48, 288–292, 151–158, 35–36.

4. Cléonte's speech comes from *Le Bourgeois gentilhomme*, Act III, scene XII. It is also in this scene that Jourdain threatens to make his daughter a duchess.

5. La Rochefoucauld, in his melancholy disillusionment over the weakened position of the nobility under Louis XIV, wrote between 1664 and 1678 his collection of clever but tart *Maximes*, the general theme of which is to the effect that all of man's actions are motivated by selfishness. One of the most famous of these *Maximes* is: "Le vrai honnête homme est celui qui ne se pique de rien."

The thoughtful François de Curel wrote a play in 1891, *Les Fossiles*, in which the fossils are the symbols of the nobility.

6. These words are taken from René Benjamin's *Préface* to Baron Karl Reille's *Deux Cents Châteaux et Gentilhommières d'Indre-et-Loire.*

BIBLIOGRAPHY

This is a selected bibliography of works actually quoted from in the text or referred to in the notes.

Allemagne, Henry-René d'. *Les Cartes à jouer du XIVe au XXe siècle.* 2 vols. Paris: Hachette, 1906.

Allen, Don Cameron. *The Star-Crossed Renaissance.* Durham: Duke University Press, 1941.

Androuet Du Cerceau, Jacques. *Les plus excellents Bastiments de France.* 2 vols. Paris, 1576–1579.

Aristotle. *The Nicomachean Ethics*, translated by H. Rackham in the Loeb Classical Library. London and New York, 1926.

Barker, Sir Ernest. *Traditions in Civility.* Cambridge: Cambridge University Press, 1948.

Barrière, Pierre. *Montaigne gentilhomme français.* Bordeaux: Delmas, 1940.

Batiffol, Louis. *Le Siècle de la Renaissance.* 10th edition. Paris: Hachette, n. d.

Baudrillart, Henry. *Histoire du luxe.* 4 vols. Paris: Hachette, 1878–1880. The third volume treats the Middle Ages and the Renaissance.

[Bayard]. *La très joyeuse et très plaisante Histoire composée par Le Loyal Serviteur des faits, gestes, triomphes et prouesses du bon chevalier sans paour et sans reprouche Le Gentil Seigneur de Bayart*, in J.-A.-C. Buchon's *Choix de chroniques . . .*, pp. 1–123. Orléans: H. Herluison, 1875.

Belleforest, François de. *Les grandes Annales et Histoire générale de France.* 2 vols. Paris: Chez Gabriel Buon, 1579.

Billon, Françoys de. *Le Fort inexpugnable de l'honneur du sexe féminin.* Paris: J. d'Allyer, 1555.

Bloch, Jean-Richard. *L'Anoblissement en France au temps de François Ier.* Paris: Alcan, 1934.

Bourciez, Edouard. *Les Moeurs polies et la littérature de Cour sous Henri II.* Paris: Hachette, 1886.

Bourgeois de Paris. *Journal d'un bourgeois de Paris sous le règne de François Premier (1515–1536)*, publié pour la Société de l'Histoire de France . . . par Ludovic Lalanne. Paris: Jules Renouard, 1854.

Brantôme, Pierre de Bourdeille, seigneur de. *Oeuvres complètes*, publiées . . . par Ludovic Lalanne. 11 vols. Paris: Librairie de la Société de l'Histoire de France, 1864–1882.

Bryson, Frederick R. *The Point of Honor in Sixteenth Century Italy: An Aspect of the Life of the Gentleman.* New York: Columbia University Press, 1935.

Buchon, Jean-Alexandre C. *Choix de chroniques et mémoires relatifs à l'Histoire de France.* Panthéon littéraire. Orléans: H. Herluison, 1875.

Budé, Guillaume. *Traitté de la Vénerie*, traduict du latin en françois par Loys Le Roy . . . publié par Henri Chevreul. Paris: Aubry, 1861.

Castelnau, Michel de. *Mémoires*, in C.-B. Petitot's *Collection* . . . , vol. XXXIII.

Castiglione, Baldassare. *Il Cortegiano.* Firenze: Sansoni, 1929.

Castiglione, Baldassare. *The Book of the Courtier*, translated by Sir Thomas Hoby. London: Dent, 1937.

Cellini, Benvenuto. *Oeuvres complètes*, traduites par Léopold Leclanché. 2 vols. Paris: Paulin, 1847.

Champier, Symphorien. *Les Gestes, ensemble la vie du preulx Chevalier Bayard* . . . Lyon, 1525.

Champier, Symphorien. *Le Fondement et origine des tiltres de Noblesse et excellens estatz de tous Nobles et Illustres quant a la difference des Empires, Royaumes, Duschez, Contez, et autres seigneuries. . .* Paris, 1535.

Charles IX. *La Chasse royale*, éditée par Henri Chevreul. Paris: Aubry, 1858.

Chartrou, Josèphe. *Les Entrées solennelles et triomphales à la Renaissance (1484–1551).* Paris: Presses universitaires, 1928.

Chérin, Louis-Nicolas-Henri. *La Noblesse considérée sous ses divers rapports, dans les assemblées générales et particulières de la nation. . .* Paris: Boyez, 1788.

Cimber, L. et F. Danjou. *Archives curieuses de l'Histoire de France depuis Louis XI jusqu'à Louis XVIII.* 30 vols. Paris: Beauvais, 1834–1841.

Cossé-Brissac, Comte de. *Le Château de Brissac.* Paris, 1937.

Dayot, Armand. *L'Image de la Femme.* Paris: Hachette, 1899.

Della Casa, Giovanni. *Galateo.* Translated into English by Robert Peterson, with an introduction by J. E. Spingarn. Boston: Merrymount Press, 1914.

Doucet, Roger. *Les Institutions de la France au XVIe siècle.* 2 vols. Paris: Picard, 1948.

Du Bellay, Martin et Guillaume. *Mémoires* . . . auxquels on a joint les *Mémoires* du Mareschal de Fleurange . . . et le *Journal* de

Louise de Savoie. Edités par M. l'abbé Lambert. 7 vols. Paris: Nyon fils, 1735.

Du Bellay, Martin et Guillaume. *Mémoires*, in J.-A.-C. Buchon's *Choix de chroniques*. . . Orléans: H. Herluison, 1875.

Du Fouilloux, Jacques. *La Vénerie* . . . precédée de la biographie de Jacques Du Fouilloux, par Jean-François Pressac. . . Niort: L. Favre, 1864 and 1888.

Du Villars, François de Boyvin, baron. *Mémoires*, in C.-B. Petitot's *Collection* . . . , vols. XXVIII–XXX.

Erasme. *La Civilité puérile*, traduction nouvelle, texte latin en regard . . . par Alcide Bonneau. Paris: I. Lisieux, 1877.

Erasmus. *Opera omnia*. 10 vols. Leyden: P. Van der Aa, 1703–1706.

Estienne, Charles. *L'Agriculture et maison rustique*. Paris: J. Du Puis, 1564.

Faret, Nicolas. *L'Honneste Homme ou l'art de plaire a la Court*. Paris: T. Du Bray, 1630.

Fleurange, Robert de la Marche, seigneur de. *Mémoires*, in J.-A.-C. Buchon's *Choix de chroniques* . . . , Orléans: H. Herluison, 1875.

Franklin, Alfred. *Les anciens Plans de Paris*. Paris: L. Willem, 1878–1880.

Franklin, Alfred. *Le Duel de Jarnac et de la Châtaigneraie*. Paris: Emile-Paul, 1909.

Gautier, l'Abbé Charles, *Histoire de Brissac, de son château et des familles qui l'ont possédé*. Angers: Gaultier, 1920.

Gébelin, François. *Les Châteaux de la Loire*. 3 ème éd. Paris: Alpina, 1947.

Guazzo, Stephano. *La Civile conversation*. . . Traduict d'italien en françoys par F. de Belleforest. Paris: Cavellat, 1579.

Guevara, Antonio de. *Menosprecio de corte y alabança de aldea*, traduict par A. Alaigre. Lyon: E. Dolet, 1542.

Haton, Claude. *Mémoires*, contenant le récit des événements accomplis de 1553 à 1582 . . . publiés par M. Félix Bourquelot. 2 vols. Paris: Imprimerie Impériale, 1857.

Jusserand, J. J. *Les Sports et jeux d'exercice dans l'ancienne France*. Paris: Plon, 1901.

La Chastre, Claude de. *Mémoires*, in vol. XXXII of C.-B. Petitot's *Collection*. . . Paris: Foucault, 1819–1826.

Lacroix, Paul. *Moeurs, usages, et costumes au moyen âge et à l'époque de la Renaissance*, 2 ème éd. Paris: Firmin Didot, 1872.

La Ferrière-Percy, Hector de. *Journal de la Comtesse de Sanzay. Intérieur d'un château normand au XVIe siècle*. Paris: Dumolin, 1855.

La Ferrière-Percy, Hector de. *Les Chasses de François Ier*, racontées par Louis de Brézé, précédées par *La Chasse sous les Valois*. Paris: Aubry, 1869.

La Noue, François de. *Discours politiques et militaires*. Basle: François Forest, 1587.

Lavisse, Ernest et Alfred Rambaud. *Histoire générale du IVe siècle à nos jours*. 12 vols. Paris: Colin, 1892–1901.

Lefranc, Abel. *Histoire du Collège de France*. Paris: Hachette, 1893.

Lefranc, Abel. *Le Vie quotidienne au temps de la Renaissance*. Paris: Hachette, 1938.

Le Loyal Serviteur. See Bayard.

Le Masson, Le Commandant Bernard. *Les Portraits de Bayard*. Grenoble: Saint Bruno, 1924.

L'Estoile, Pierre de. *Mémoires-Journaux* . . . conforme aux manuscrits originaux . . . par Gustave Brunet, *et al.* 12 vols. Paris: Librairie des Bibliophiles, 1875–1893.

Letainturier-Fradin, Gabriel. *Le Duel à travers les âges*. Paris: Flammarion, *circa* 1892.

Louise de Savoie. *Journal*, in J.-A.-C. Buchon's *Choix de chroniques*. . . . Orléans: H. Herluison, 1875.

Magne, Emile. *La Vie quotidienne au temps de Louis XIII*. Paris: Hachette, 1948.

Machiavelli, Niccolò. *Il Principe*, e *Discorsi*. . . Firenze: Le Monnier, 1857.

Machiavelli, Niccolò. *The Prince* and *The Discourses*. New York: The Modern Library, 1940.

Marchand, l'Abbé Charles. *Charles Ier de Cossé, Comte de Brissac et Maréchal de France (1507–1564.)* Paris: Champion, 1889.

Marguerite de Navarre. *L'Heptaméron*. Paris: Librairie de la Société des Gens de Lettres, 1883.

Marillac, Guillaume de. *Vie du Connétable de Bourbon*, in J.-A.-C. Buchon's *Choix de chroniques* . . . Orléans: H. Herluison, 1875.

Mézeray, François de. *Abrégé chronologique de l'histoire de France*, nouvelle édition augmentée. 3 vols. Paris: Chez Esprit Billiot, 1717.

Monluc, Blaise de. *Commentaires et lettres*, édition revue sur les manuscrits et publiée avec les variantes pour la Société de l'Histoire de France par M. Alphonse de Ruble. 5 vols. Paris: Renouard, 1864–1872.

Montaigne, Michel de. *Essais*, publiée d'après l'édition de 1588 avec les variantes de 1595 . . . par H. Motheau et D. Jouaust. 7 vols. Paris: Librairie des Bibliophiles, n. d.

Montaigne, Michel de. *Journal de voyage*, publié . . . par Pierre d'Espezel. Paris: Cité des Livres, 1931.

Ordonnances des Rois de France de la Troisième race. 21 vols. Paris: Imprimerie Royale, 1723–1849.

Pasquier, Etienne. *Oeuvres* . . . contenant ses *Recherches de la France*. . . 2 vols. Amsterdam: Libraires Associés, 1723.

Passerat, Jean. *Le Chien courant* . . . édité par Henri Chevreul. Paris: Aubry, 1864.

Petitot, Claude-Bernard. *Collection complète des mémoires relatifs à l'histoire de France.* 52 vols. Paris: Foucault, 1819–1826.

Plato. *The Republic*, translated into English by Benjamin Jowett. 3rd edition. Oxford: The Clarendon Press, 1888.

Rabelais, François. *Oeuvres*, texte établi et présenté par Jean Plattard. Les Textes français. 5 vols. Paris: Fernand Roches, 1929.

Rabutin, François de. *Commentaires* . . . , in vol. XXXI of C.-B. Petitot's *Collection*. . . Paris: Foucault, 1817–1826.

Rapin, Nicolas. *Les Plaisirs du gentilhomme champestre.* Paris: Veuve Lucas Breyer, 1583.

Reille, Baron Karl. *Deux Cents Châteaux et Gentilhommières d'Indre-et-Loire.* Préface de René Benjamin. Tours: Imprimerie Tourangelle, 1934.

Ronsard, Pierre de. *Oeuvres complètes.* Texte établi et annoté par Gustave Cohen. 2 vols. Paris: Bibliothèque de la Pléiade, 1938.

Ruppert, Jacques. *Le Costume.* Les Arts décoratifs. 5 vols., in one. Paris: R. Ducher, 1930–1932.

Sainct Didier, Henry de. *Traicté contenant les secrets du premier livre sur l'espee seule, mere de toutes armes*, . . . fort utile et profitable pour adextrer la noblesse, et suposts de Mars. . . Paris: Iean Mettayer et Matthurin Challenge, 1573. Reprinted exactly in 1907 by the Société du Livre Ancien et Moderne.

Saint-Gelais, Melin de. *Oeuvres complètes*, éditées par Prosper Blanchemain. 2 vols. Paris: Bibliothèque Elzévirienne, 1873.

Salignac, Bertrand de. *Le Siège de Metz (1552)*, in vol. XXXII of C.-B. Petitot's *Collection*. . . Paris: Foucault, 1819–1826.

Sauval, Henri. *Histoire et recherches des antiquités de la ville de Paris.* 3 vols. Paris: Moette, 1724.

Serres, Olivier de. *Le Théâtre d'agriculture et mesnage des champs.* Paris: Chez Abr. Saugrain, 1605.

Tavannes, Gaspard de. *Mémoires*, in vols. XXIII, XXIV, and XXV of C.-B. Petitot's *Collection*. . . . Paris: Foucault, 1819–1826.

Telle, Emile V. *Marguerite de Navarre et la Querelle des Femmes.* Toulouse: Lion et fils, 1937.

Terrasse, Charles. *François Ier, le Roi et le Règne.* 2 vols. — a third in preparation. Paris: Grasset, 1943.

Theophrastus. *Characters*, translated by J. M. Edmonds. Loeb Classical Library. London and New York, 1929.

Thorndike, Lynn. *A History of Magic and Experimental Science.* 6 vols. New York: MacMillan, 1929–1941.

Tommaseo, N. *Relations des ambassadeurs vénitiens sur les affaires de France au XVIe siècle*, recueillies et traduites par M. N. Tommaseo. 2 vols. Paris: Imprimerie Royale, 1838.

Toudouze, Georges G. *Françoise de Châteaubriant et François Ier.* Paris: Floury, 1948.

Vaissière, Pierre de. *Gentilshommes campagnards de l'ancienne France.* Paris: Perrin, 1903.

Vieilleville, François de Scepeaux, sire de. *Mémoires*, in vols. XXVI, XXVII, and XXVIII of C.-B. Petitot's *Collection. . .* Paris: Foucault, 1819–1826.

Vivent, Jacques. *La Tragédie de Blois, le Roi de France et le Duc de Guise, 1585–1588.* Paris: Hachette, 1946.

INDEX

AT